Margaret Robertson

Christie Redfern's Troubles

Margaret Robertson

Christie Redfern's Troubles

ISBN/EAN: 9783337024499

Printed in Europe, USA, Canada, Australia, Japan

Cover: Foto ©Andreas Hilbeck / pixelio.de

More available books at **www.hansebooks.com**

Christie Redfern's Troubles

By

MRS. ROBERTSON

Author of 'The Orphans of Glen Elder'

TWENTY SEVENTH IMPRESSION

LONDON

THE RELIGIOUS TRACT SOCIETY

4 Bouverie Street & 65 St. Paul's Churchyard

PREFACE.

THE requirement of the gospel is that, having first given ourselves to Christ, we should then devote all we have, be it little or much, to His service. The largest gifts fall infinitely below what He deserves from us; the smallest will not be rejected by Him. For it is the motive, not the gift, which our Lord regards. The poor widow's mite was more acceptable to Him than the ostentatious and lavish donations of the wealthy. Yet the smallness, the seeming worthlessness, of our means is often pleaded as an excuse for withholding them altogether. Because men can do so little, they do nothing. It was the servant who had received only one talent that wrapped his lord's money in a napkin, and buried it in useless, unprofitable obscurity. When the multitudes hungered in the wilderness, the disciples hesitated to bring the five barley loaves and two small fishes, asking, 'What are they among so many?' They were taught, however, to produce their little all, utterly inadequate as it was to the exigencies of the case, and lay it in the hands of Omnipotent Love, that He might by His blessing increase it to the feeding of the five thousand. 'God

A

hath chosen the foolish things of the world to confound
the wise ; and God hath chosen the weak things of the
world to confound the things which are mighty ; and
base things of the world and things which are despised
hath God chosen, yea, and things that are not, to bring
to nought things that are, that no flesh should glory in
His presence.'

This great truth is admirably illustrated in the
following pages. In the life of Christie Redfern we
may see how the simple desire to serve God, felt and
acted upon by a poor, suffering child, may give an
almost heroic strength of character, and may produce
results, the magnitude and grandeur of which are
altogether out of proportion to the feebleness of the
means employed.

CONTENTS.

CONTENTS.

'SHE MUST GO HOME, THEN, I AM AFRAID,' SAID MRS. SEATON.

[See page 324.

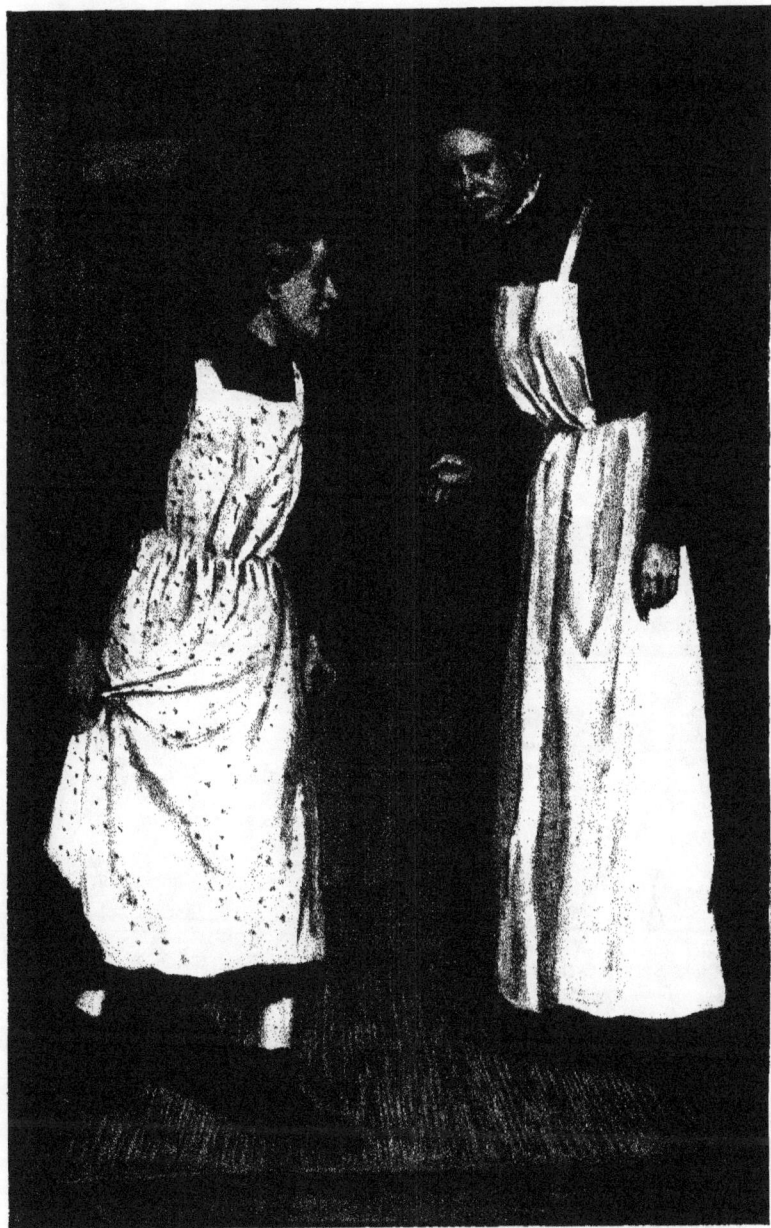

'I HATE YOU, AUNT ELSIE! I WISH I WERE DEAD!'

[*See page* 20.

CHRISTIE WATCHED HIM WITH WISTFUL EYES.

CHRISTIE REDFERN'S TROUBLES.

CHAPTER I.

CHRISTIE'S CHILDHOOD.

'I'VE heard folks say it—I've seen it in a book myself—and I heard my father read something like it, out of the Bible, last Sunday—"Ask, and ye shall receive," and in another place, " In everything by prayer and supplication let your requests be made known unto God." I might try it, anyway.'

But the voice that spoke was by no means a hopeful one, and there was anything but a hopeful look on the face of the little girl who slowly raised herself up from a mossy seat, where she had been quite hidden by the branches of a tall birch-tree, that hung so low as to dip themselves into the waters of the brook at the times when it ran fullest. It was a very pretty place, and a very strange place for any child to look anxious or discontented in. But the little girl looked as if she were both; and there was, besides, a great deal of weariness in her manner, as she leaned for a moment against a branch, and then stooped to let the water flow over a spray of crimson maple that she held in her hand.

'I might try it, anyway,' she repeated, as she left the place.

In some spring or autumn long ago, the swollen waters of the brook had quite washed away the soil from between the roots of the birch-tree; and the roots themselves, and the hollow place which the waters had made, were covered with grass and soft moss now. In this pretty natural seat, after an eager, half-frightened glance around, the little girl placed herself, kneeling. She closed her eyes, and folded her hands with a reverent gesture; but a doubtful, uneasy look passed over her face as she let her head droop, and murmured:

'Our Father who art in heaven, hallowed be Thy name, Thy kingdom come'—and so on to the end.

Then her head was raised; but the doubtful look had not passed away.

'That's no' just what I'm needing,' she continued. 'I have my daily bread. I'm no' sure about the other things; and I canna mind another prayer. I would make one, if I knew the way. I need so many things!'

There was a pause, and then she said, softly:

'O Lord, dinna let Aunt Elsie be vexed with me for biding here so long. I'm sure I need that. And, O Lord, mind Effie to bring home the book she promised me. Oh, there are so many things that I need! and I'm no' sure that I'm asking right. But the Bible says, "Whatsoever ye ask in My name, believing, ye shall receive."'

She slipped from her kneeling posture, and leaned,

with her eyes still closed, against the shining bark of
the birch-tree. She lay quiet for some time, as if she
were thinking of many things; then, kneeling again,
with her head bowed down on her clasped hands, she
said:

'O Lord, make me a good child, and take me to
heaven when I die, for Jesus' sake!'

Then she opened her eyes, and rose up with a sigh.

'Oh, how long the shadows have grown! I should
have been at home a long while ago. But now I'll see
if Aunt Elsie's no' vexed. If she doesna scold me, I'll
ken that there is some use in praying. And if Effie
brings me a book, such a book as I like, I shall be sure,
sure. Then I shall know that God hears people when
they pray; and that will be something.'

And, really, the tired, pale little creature looked as
though she needed something to make her look more
cheerfully on a world which generally seems so happy
a place to the young something to banish the look of
discontent which seemed to have settled on her face.

This was little Christie Redfern—just such a plain,
common-looking child as one might see anywhere without turning to look again. Her eyes were neither
black nor blue, but gray, and dark only when the long
lashes shaded them. Her mouth was too wide to be
pretty, and her lips were pale and thin. She might
naturally have had a fair, soft skin; but it was tanned
and freckled by exposure to the air and sun, and looked
neither fair nor soft now. Her brow was high and
broad, and would have been pretty but that she gathered
it together in wrinkles when she looked at anything
closely with her short-sighted eyes. She wore a dark
cotton frock and checked pinafore, and her feet, without

stockings, were slipped into shoes that seemed a world too big for them. She would not have been pretty in any circumstances; but shuffling along in her big shoes and odd dress, she was a very queer-looking little creature indeed.

But there was something about the child more to be deplored than the wide mouth, or the dim eyes, or the drooping figure. There was a look of unhappiness upon her face which, as any one might see, was in conse-quence of no momentary trouble. It seemed to be habitual. As she plodded along with her eyes cast down on the rough pathway, it never changed. Once, when the sun, which she thought had set, flashed out for a moment through the clouds of purple and crimson, causing her to look up suddenly, the sad expression passed away; but when her eyes fell it was there again, and she sighed wearily, as though her thoughts were always sad. It was a long time before she looked up again.

Indeed, there was not very much in the scene around her to attract the attention of the child, even if her short-sighted eyes could have taken in the view. There were the clouds; but their crimson and purple glories had faded. There was the little grove of birch and maple by the side of the brook—the prettiest place on her father's farm, Christie thought; and that was all. A bird's-eye view of the country for many miles around showed no variety of scenery, except the alternation of long, broad fields of grass and wheat, or, rather, fields where grass and wheat had been, with wide, irregular stretches of low-lying forest. There was scarcely a hill deserving of the name to break the monotonous level. It was a very fine country indeed in the estimation of the busy groups who were here and there gathering in the last sheaves of a plentiful harvest. The farmers of Laidlaw were wont to boast, and with reason, too, of their wheat-crops, and their fine roads and fences, declaring that there was not in all Canada a district that would surpass or even equal theirs in respect of these things. But beauty of this sort a child cannot be supposed to appreciate. Christie's home for the first ten years of her life had been in a lovely Scottish village, within three miles of the sea on one side and less than three miles from the hills on the other; and the dull, unvaried level, the featureless aspect of her present home, might well seem dreary to the child.

But the contrast between the old life and the new was greater still; and here lay the secret of the shadow that seldom left the face of the little girl now. For in the old times, that seemed so long ago, Christie had been the one delicate child in a large and healthy family, and therefore her loving mother's constant and peculiar care. And her mother was dead now. I need not say more to prove how sad and changed her life had become.

I think that, meeting her on her homeward way that afternoon, one might have almost seen the motherless look in her pale face and drooping figure and in the lingering tread of her weary little feet. It was a look more painful to see than the look of sadness or neglect which motherless children sometimes wear. It was of a wayward temper grown more wayward still for want of a mother's firm and gentle rule. One could not doubt that peevish words and angry retorts fell very naturally from those pale lips. She looked like one who needed to be treated with patience and loving forbearance, and who failed to meet either. And, indeed, the rule to which Christie was forced to submit was neither firm nor gentle. Sometimes it was firm, when Christie, as she not unfrequently did, ventured to resist it; but gentle—never.

When Christie's mother died, all their friends said the little Redferns were very fortunate in having an Aunt Elsie to supply her place in the household; and in some respects they were. If a constant and conscientious determination to do her duty to her brother's motherless children would have made up to them for their loss, they would have been quite happy under Aunt Elsie's care. She made a great sacrifice of her own ease and comfort when she left her quiet home to devote herself to their interests; and if they had all been wise and good and thoughtful, they would not have needed to be reminded so frequently of her self-denial as Aunt Elsie seemed to think necessary. But few children are so wise, or good, or thoughtful as they ought to be; and there were oftentimes secret murmurings, and once or twice during the first year of her stay there had been open rebellion among them.

It could hardly have been otherwise. No middle-aged woman unaccustomed to the care of a family, whose heart had never been softened by the helpless loveliness of little children of her own, could have filled the place of a mother, wise, firm, and tender, all at once; and so for a time their household was not a happy one. Their father left his children to the care of their aunt, as he had always left them to the care of their mother; and if an appeal from any decision of hers were made to him, it very seldom availed anything.

It was not so bad for the elder ones. They were healthy, good-tempered girls, who had companions and interests out of the home-circle; and they soon learned to yield to or evade what was distasteful in their aunt's rule. With the little children she was always lenient. It was the sickly, peevish little Christie who suffered most. More than any of the rest, more than all the rest put together, she missed her mother: she missed her patient care and sympathy when she was ill, and her firm yet gentle management amid the wayward fretfulness that illness brought upon her. Night after night did her weary little head slumber on a pillow which her tears had wet. Morning after morning did she wake up to the remembrance of her loss, with a burst of bitter weeping, angry at or indifferent to all her aunt's attempts to console her or win her love. No wonder that her aunt lost patience at last, calling the child peevish and wilful, and altogether unlovable, and declaring that she had more trouble and unhappiness with her than with all her sisters put together.

And, indeed, so she had. She rather enjoyed the excitement of keeping a firm hand over the elder ones, and she soon learned to have patience with the noise and heedlessness of the little ones. But the peevishness and wayward fancies of a nervous, excitable child, whom weakness made irritable, and an over-active imagination made dreamy, she could neither understand nor endure; and so the first year after the mother's death was a year of great unhappiness to Christie.

After that, there was a great change in the family life. Losses in business, and other circumstances, induced Mr. Redfern to give up his home and to remove with his family to Canada. Though this decision was made contrary to the advice of his sister, she would not forsake him and his children : so she had come with them to the backwoods.

A new and changed life opened to them here, and all the changes that came to them were not for the better. Mr. Redfern knew nothing about practical farming; and so, though he had means to purchase a sufficient quantity of good land, it was not surprising to his neighbours that his first attempt should be unsuccessful. His children were of the wrong sort, too, his neighbours said; for only one of the eight was a lad, and he was only six when he came to his new home. No pair of hands could gather, from ever so good a farm, food enough to fill so many mouths; and more than one of the kind people who took the affairs of the new-comers into their especial consideration, shook their heads gravely over their prospects. And for a time they were badly off.

Soon after their arrival in their new home, Aunt Elsie was seized with an illness which lingered long, and left her a cripple when it went away; and her temper was not of the kind which suffering and helplessness are said sometimes to improve. It was a trying time to all.

But winter passed over. Spring came, and with it came a measure of health to Aunt Elsie. She could move about on a crutch and give directions in the house, and do many things besides, which a less energetic person would never have attempted. The elder girls, Effie, Sarah, and Annie, proved themselves of the right sort, so far as energy, and strength, and a right good-will were concerned, and worked in the fields with their father as though they had been accustomed to it all their lives. So, when two or three years had passed away, the glances which the neighbours sent into the future of the Redferns revealed by no means so dreary a prospect as formerly.

A change for the better had come over Christie, too. She would never be as hopeful or as healthy as her sisters, her aunt said; but in health and hopefulness, and in temper too, there was a great change for the better in Christie at the end of the first three years of her Canadian life. But Christie was far from being what she ought to be in respect to the latter item even then, as her aunt often told her; and she had good cause to be of her aunt's opinion many times before the summer was over.

It was, for several reasons, a time of trial to the child. Her eldest sister Effie, whom she loved best of all, was away from home as school-mistress in a neighbouring township, only returning home for the Sunday, and not always able to do that. Her absence made the constant assistance of Sarah and Annie indispensable to their father. So the work of the household, and the care of the dairy during the greater part of the summer, fell to Christie, under the super-intendence of Aunt Elsie; and a great deal more strength and patience was needed than Christie had at her disposal. She would gladly have changed with her sisters for their harder places in the fields; but the cold of the spring and autumn mornings chilled her, and the heat of summer exhausted her, and there was no alternative but the work of the house. This would have been wearisome enough under any circumstances to a child not very strong; and it was sometimes

rendered more than wearisome by the needless chidings
of her aunt.

Not that her aunt meant to be unkind, or that her
chidings were always undeserved or her complaints
causeless.   Her mother could not have been more
careful than her aunt was, that Christie should not put
her hand to work beyond her strength.   But probably
her mother would have felt that a child might become
weary, even to disgust, of a never-ending, never-changing
routine of trifling duties, that brought no pleasant
excitement in their train, that could scarcely be named
or numbered when the day was done, yet whose
performance required time and strength and patience
beyond her power to give.   But if her aunt ever
thought about this, she never told her thoughts to
Christie; and to the child the summer days often
passed wearily enough.   It is to be doubted whether
the elder sisters, after a long harvest-day, went to bed
more tired and depressed than did Christie, who, in
their opinion, had been having an easy time.   Not but
that Annie and Sarah understood in some measure the
troubles that might fall to Christie's lot under the
immediate superintendence of Aunt Elsie; and they
were sometimes ready enough to congratulate themselves on their own more free life out of doors.   But,
strong and healthy as they were, they could not understand how the work which would have seemed like
play to them could be such a burden to their little
sister; and they sometimes sadly added to her discontent by making light of her troubles, and ascribing to
indolence and peevishness the complaints which, too
often, fell from her lips.

There had not, during all the summer, been a more

uncomfortable day than the one whose close found Christie sitting so disconsolately under the birch-tree by the brook. It had begun badly, as too many of those days did. In looking for something in the garret, Christie had found a book that had been missing for a long time. It was one of her favourites. She had read it often before, but not recently; and in those days new books were rare, and old books proportionably precious.

Sitting down on the floor, amid the scattered contents of the chest she had been rummaging, she forgot, in the charm of 'The Family Tryst,' that the dough of her batch of bread was fast approaching that stage of lightness that needed her attention, and that her oven was by no means in a proper state to receive it when that point should be reached. Page after page she turned with a vague feeling that each should be the last, till even this half-consciousness of wrong-doing was lost in the intense enjoyment of the tale; and then —the charm was broken.

Aunt Elsie's sharp, quick tones, coming suddenly upon her, must have startled the nervous child with a shock of pain quite apart from any thought of the consequences of her fault; and it was with hands that trembled violently that the book was hidden and the scattered contents of the chest were gathered together again. Then she thought of her bread; and her heart failed within her.

'Oh, I'm so sorry!' she said to herself; but no such word was spoken to her aunt. Indeed, to her she said nothing; and it was not sorrow for her fault, but sullenness or indifference, or something that might easily be mistaken for these, that her aunt saw on her face as

she came down-stairs. It was very provoking. The
bread was ready for the oven, but the oven was by no
means ready for the bread. And now for the next three
days, at least, the children and the hungry harvest-people
must content themselves with sour bread, in conse-
quence of Christie's carelessness. It was Christie's wilful
disobedience, her aunt declared; and, really, the sullen,
unrepentant look on the girl's face was almost enough
to excuse her aunt's bitter words and the sudden blow
that fell on her averted cheek. A blow was a very rare
thing with Aunt Elsie. It was not repeated now.
Indeed, she would hardly have ventured to strike again
the white, indignant face that was turned towards her.
Surprise and anger kept the girl for one moment silent;
then, in a voice she could hardly make audible for the
beating of her heart, she gasped:

'I hate you, Aunt Elsie! I wish I were dead!'

'Be quiet, with your wicked words!' cried Aunt
Elsie. 'You are far from being in a fit state to die,
you disobedient, bad child.'

But Aunt Elsie was vexed with herself for the blow
she had given, and all the more vexed with Christie on
that account. Christie was really sorry for her fault;
but, quite forgetting that she had given no sign
of sorrow, she called her aunt unjust and cruel, and
bitterly resented both word and blow. Anger and
pride gave her strength to obey the command to carry
the bread to a cool place, and to keep back a rush of
tears till her task was done. But it failed her then;
and, throwing herself on the ground, out of sight, she
wept and sobbed, and uttered words as wicked and
passionate as those which her aunt had reproved.

This was the beginning; and after that nothing could

be expected to go well. Though her head ached and her hands trembled, the work of the house must be done; and more than her usual share fell to Christie to-day. For Aunt Elsie's rheumatism was bad again, and much that she usually did was left to Christie. But her aunt did not say she was ill. The added tasks were assigned with a voice and in a manner that seemed to declare them a part of the punishment for the fault of the morning; and we cannot wonder much that they were sullenly performed.

'I don't care,' repeated Christie to herself, over and over again, that day. 'There is no use in trying to please Aunt Elsie. It makes no difference. She's cross always. I never do anything right, she says; and I don't care!'

But she did care, for all that. She was very wretched. She avoided her sisters when they came home to dinner, saying she had a headache, and didn't want any— which, indeed, was true; and her sisters, thinking that she and Aunt Elsie had had a falling-out which would be made up before night, left her to herself. So Christie sat on the garret-floor, too miserable to read, her heart full of angry thoughts against her aunt, her sisters, and all the world.

But into the very midst of her vexed and angry murmurs against them there came the feeling that all the fault was not theirs—that she was herself to be blamed. And by and by the anger passed away; but the misery remained, and oftener, and with more power, came the consciousness that she was a very cross, unamiable child, that she was not like her older sisters or the little ones, that she was a comfort to no one, but a vexation to all. If she only could die! she thought.

No! she would be afraid to die! But, oh, if she had never been born! Oh, if her mother had not died!

And yet she might have been a trial to her mother, too, as she was to all the rest. But no! she thought; her mother would have loved her and had patience with her; and Aunt Elsie never had. Amid a rush of angry tears, there fell a few very bitter drops to the memory of her mother.

With a weary pain at her head and heart, she went about the household work of the afternoon. The dinner-dishes were put away, and the room was swept and dusted, in silence. The pans were prepared for the evening milk, and the table was laid for supper; and then she sat down, with a face so woe-begone and miserable, and an air so weary that, even in spite of her anger, her aunt could not but pity her. She pitied herself more, however. She said to herself that she was at her wits' end with the wilful child. She began to fear that she would never be other than a cross and a trial to her; and it did seem to Aunt Elsie that, with her bad health and her hard work among her brother's children, she had enough to vex her without Christie's untowardness. It did seem so perverse in her, when she needed her help so much, to be so heedless and sullen.

'And yet what a poor, pale, unhappy little creature she seems to be!' thought she. 'Maybe I haven't all the patience with her that I ought to have. God knows, I need not a little to bear all my own aches and pains.'

But her relenting thoughts did not take the form of words; and Christie never fancied, when she was bidden go for the cows at once, and not wait for the coming of the children from school, that her aunt sent

her because she thought the walk to the pasture would
do her good. She believed it was a part of her
punishment, still, that she should be required to do
what had all the summer been the acknowledged work
of Will and her little sisters. So, though she was too
weary and miserable to resist, or even to murmur, she
went with a lagging step and a momentary rising of
her old angry and resentful thoughts.

It was not very far to the pasture through the
wheat-field; and she was soon there. But when the
cows had passed through the gate she let them go or
not, just as they pleased, and turned aside, to think
over again, by the side of the brook, the miserable
thoughts of the afternoon; and the end of these was
the murmured prayer with which my story began.

Her thoughts were not very cheerful as she plodded
along. She had no wish to hurry. If she did, she
would very likely have to milk Brownie and Blackie
and the rest, besides Fleckie, her own peculiar care.
She said to herself, there was no reason why she should
do her sisters' work, though it was harvest-time and
they would come home tired. She was tired too—
though nobody seemed to think she ever did anything
to tire her. She could milk all the cows well enough.
She had done it many a time. But it was one thing
to do it of her own free will, and quite another to do so
because her aunt was cross and wanted to punish her
for her morning fault. So she loitered on the road,
though the sun had set and she knew there was danger
of the cows passing the gate and getting in among the
wheat, where the fence was insufficient, in the field
below.

'I don't care,' she said to herself. 'It winna be my

fault. The bairns should have been at home. It's
their work, not mine, to mind the cows. Oh, I wish
Effie was at home ! There's nothing quite so bad when
she is here. But I'll see to-night if my prayer is
heard; that will be something; and then I'll begin
again, and try to be good, in spite of Aunt Elsie.'

CHAPTER II.

THE COLPORTEUR.

THE cows had not passed the gate. Somebody had opened it for them, and they were now standing or lying in the yard, in the very perfection of animal enjoyment. The girls were not at home to milk them, however. Christie had heard her father's voice calling to them in the lower field, and she knew it would be full half an hour, and quite dark, before they could be at home. So, with a sigh, she took the stool and the milk-pails from a bench near the door, and went to the yard to her task.

If her short-sighted eyes had seen the long, low wagon [1] that stood at the end of the house, curiosity would have tempted her to go back to see who might be there. If she had known that in that wagon her sister Effie had ridden home a day sooner than she was expected, she would not have seated herself so quietly to her milking.

Christie was not lazy, though her aunt sometimes accused her of being so. When her heart was in her work, she could do it quickly and well; and her

---

[1] In America, any light four-wheeled vehicle is called a wagon.

strength failed her always before her patience was exhausted.

She knew she must finish the milking alone now, and she set to it with a will. In a surprisingly short time she was standing between two foaming milk-pails at the gate. To carry them both at once was almost, though not quite, beyond her strength; and as she stood for a moment hesitating whether she would try it, or go with one and return for the other, the matter was decided for her.

'Christie!' said a voice—not Aunt Elsie's—from the door.

Turning, Christie saw her sister Effie. Surprise kept her riveted to the spot till her sister came down the path.

'Dinna lift them, Christie: you are no more able to do it than a chicken. I'll carry them.'

But she stooped first to place her hands on her little sister's shoulders and to kiss her softly. Christie did not speak; but the touch of her sister's lips unsealed the fountain of her tears, and clinging to her and hiding her face, she cried and sobbed in a way that, at last, really frightened her sister.

'Why, Christie! Why, you foolish lassie! What ails you, child? Has anything happened?—or is it only that you are so glad to see me home again? Don't cry in that wild way, child. What is it, Christie?'

'It's nothing—I dinna ken—I canna help it!' cried Christie, after an ineffectual effort to control herself.

Her sister held the trembling little form for a moment without speaking, and then she said, cheerfully:

'See, Christie! It's growing dark! We must be quick with the milking.'

'Why didna you come last week, Effie?' said Christie, rousing herself at last.

'Oh, partly because of the rain, and partly because I thought I would put my two holidays together. This is Thursday night, and I can stay till Monday morning—three whole days.'

Christie gave a sigh, and smiled.

'Come,' said Effie; 'I'll help you. I was waiting till you came from the pasture. I didna see you come.'

'No; I didna go in.'

It seemed to Christie that a very heavy burden had been lifted from her heart. She smiled without the sigh, as soon as she met her sister's grave look.

'Did you walk home, Effie?' she asked.

'No; I got a chance to ride with the book-man. He was at the corner, and offered to bring me home, as he was coming this way. How beautiful your pans look, Christie! Will you need them all?'

They were in the milk house now. It was a large, low place, partly made by digging into the side of the hill. It was a cool, pleasant place in summer, and well suited to the purpose for which it had been built. It was dark, however, when the girls entered, and would have been very gloomy but for Christie's shining milk-pans and the rows of cream-covered dishes beyond.

They were all needed, and some new ones had just been brought from the tinman's. 'I like them,' said Christie: 'they're lighter than the earthen ones, and no' so easily broken. We've got much more milk since the cows went into the upper field. You'll see what a pailful Fleckie gives.'

'Fleckie is your favourite yet,' said Effie, smiling, as they left the dairy together.

'Oh, yes! she's the best of them all—and so gentle! and I'm sure she knows me. I don't think she likes any one to milk her half so well as me.'

'She'll let me milk her to-night, though,' said Effie, removing her cuffs and turning up her sleeves.

'You'll spoil your pretty frock,' said Christie, doubtfully.

'There's no fear. I'll take care. Give me the stool.'

Christie hesitated.

'But there's Blackie and Brownie to do yet—unless you would rather milk Fleckie.'

'I would rather milk them all,' said Effie. 'I'm sure, child, you look as though you had had enough of it for one day.'

'Oh, no; I expected to milk them all. I'm not very tired.'

Christie ran for another stool, and seated herself beside her favourite. She was quite near her sister, too; and they went on talking.

'I suppose this was churning-day?' said Effie.

'No; we churned yesterday, and we'll churn again to-morrow. It's harder, and takes longer, now that the nights have got cooler. But the butter is beautiful. We have the two tubs full, and we put the last we made in a jar. I'll show it to you when we go in.'

'I suppose Annie and Sarah have but little time to help you now? No wonder you are tired,' said Effie.

'No; they cannot help us except on a rainy day. But I never churn alone. Aunt Elsie helps me. It took us three hours last time.'

'I shouldna wonder if that is the reason that Aunt Elsie's shoulder is worse,' said Effie, with a sigh.

Is it worse? asked Christie. 'She has said nothing about it.'

'No; she says there is no use in complaining. But I do hope she is not going to be ill, as she was before. It would be terrible for us all.'

'I hope not, indeed,' said Christie; and in a moment she added, 'You would need to bide at home then, Effie.'

Effie shook her head.

'No; I should need all the more to be away if that were to happen. What should we all do for shoes, if it werena for my school-money?'

Christie's countenance fell; but in a little time she said—

'But the harvest is a great deal better this year, Effie.'

'Yes; but there winna be much to sell. If we don't have to buy, it will be a great thing for us. And the shoes we must have, and new harness, and other things. I mustna think of staying this winter, I'm sure, Christie.'

Christie gave a long sigh, as she rose with her full pail.

'I wish I was old enough and able to keep a school, or do something!'

'Do something!' echoed Effie. 'I'm sure you do a great deal. Think of the butter! And you've made bread all the summer, and swept, and ironed, and washed the dishes.'

'But all that comes to very little,' said Christie, disconsolately.

'Indeed it does—to more than my school-keeping, I dare say. And I'm sure it's far pleasanter work.'

'Pleasanter!' repeated Christie; and there was such

a protesting echo in her voice that Effie could not help laughing; but she said, again—

'Yes, pleasanter. Don't you think it must be far nicer to be at home with all the rest, than to stay among folk that don't care about you, and have to bear your trouble alone?'

Christie opened her eyes wide.

'But, Effie, folk do care about you. And what troubles can you have to bear?'

Effie laughed softly; but she looked grave immediately.

'Well, I havena so many as I might have, I suppose.'

'I'm sure if I were you I should be perfectly happy,' said Christie.

'That's only one of the mistakes you have fallen into,' said Effie, gravely. 'Do you remember the story of the burdens, and how every one was willing to take up his own at last?'

Nothing in the world would have convinced Christie that her sister's lot was not much pleasanter than her own; and she said to herself, how gladly she would change burdens with her! but aloud she only asked—

'Has anything new happened? What's troubling you, Effie?'

'Oh, nothing has happened,' said Effie, cheerfully. 'I'm getting on well. The worst of my troubles are those I find at home—Aunt Elsie's rheumatism, and your pale, tired face, and the wearing out of the children's clothes. And you have all these too: so I dare say my burden is the lightest, after all. Now let me see your butter.'

It was well worth seeing. There was one tub made when the weather had been warm, and, for that reason,

was pronounced by Christie not quite so good. Then
there was a large one, with over a hundred and twenty
pounds in it — so hard, and yellow, and fragrant!
Christie was not a little proud of it; and Effie praised
it to her heart's content. There was no better butter
in all Glengarry, she was sure.

'And a hundred and twenty pounds of it! It's worth
twenty-five cents a pound, at least. Think of that,
Christie!—thirty dollars in all! That is something of
your doing, I should think.'

'Partly,' said Christie. 'I only helped.' But she
was very much pleased. 'If we could only sell it, it
would get us shoes, and lots of things.'

'But I'm afraid we mustna sell it,' said Effie. 'We
shall have so little meat all the winter—and it is so
dear, too; and we shall need the butter. And how
many cheeses are there? Five?'

'Five uncut. One is nearly done since the harvest.
See, these two are better than the others. But it is
getting so dark you canna see them. I think the
cheese will be a great help. We had none last winter,
you know.'

'Yes, indeed!' said Effie, heartily. 'We shall have
a better winter than the last was.'

'Except that you winna be at home,' said Christie,
desponding a little again.

'Well, I would like to be at home, if it were best;
but we canna have all we would like, you know. If
you have milk to skim, you will need a candle,
Christie.'

'No: I skimmed it before I went away. See, father
and the girls have come home at last. How glad they
will be to see you, Effie!'

Yes, everybody was glad to see Effie—though no one said much about it that night. Indeed, it was rather a silent party that partook of the frugal supper. Except that the book-man (as the colporteur was called) exchanged now and then a remark with Mr. Redfern, little was said till supper was over and the Bible laid on the table for worship. The Redfern family had the custom of reading verse-about, as it is called, partly because lights were sometimes scarce, and partly because, after the work of a long summer day, both great and small were too tired to enjoy protracted reading; and it must be confessed that, at times, morning and evening devotions were both brief and formal. They were not so to-night, however; for they were led by Mr. Craig, the book-man, a cheerful and earnest Christian, to whom, it was easily seen, God's worship was no mere form, but a most blessed reality. Indeed, so lengthened was the exercise to-night that the little ones were asleep before it was done; and so earnest was he, so elevated were his ascriptions of praise, so appropriate his confessions and petitions, that the elder members of the family, notwithstanding their weariness, could not but listen and join with wonder and delight.

'*He* believes that it is worth one's while to pray, at any rate,' said Christie to herself; and all at once it flashed upon her that a part of *her* prayer had been answered. Aunt Elsie had not spoken one word of reproof for her long delay by the side of the brook. Not a little startled, Christie paused to consider the matter further.

'She could hardly have scolded me while a stranger was here. And, besides, Effie's here, too, and I wouldna have much cared if she had. And it's no' too late yet.

She'll be sending me to my bed the moment the dishes are put by.'

But she did not. Long after the little ones, and even Annie and Sarah, were asleep, Christie was allowed to sit without rebuke, listening to the pleasant talk of her father and Mr. Craig, and now and then saying a word to Effie, on whose lap her head was laid. The only words that Aunt Elsie spoke to her that night were kind enough; and some of them were spoken while Effie was not there.

' So that it couldna be to please her,' thought Christie. ' What if God should hear my prayer, after all ? '

The thought was quite as startling as it was pleasant. Then she wondered if Effie had brought the book. She did not like to ask her. She did so want to believe that she might fall back on God's help in all her troubles; but if Effie had not brought the book she could not be sure that her prayer had been heard. ' Could it be possible ? ' she said to herself. It seemed altogether too good, too wonderful, to be true. And yet there were verses in the Bible very plain, very easy to be understood—' Ask, and ye shall receive; seek, and ye shall find;' and many more besides that.

She repeated the words slowly and earnestly. That must be true, she thought. Every one believed the Bible. And yet how few live and pray and trust as though they really do believe it! She had heard discussions, many and long, between her father and some of their neighbours, on difficult passages of Scripture and difficult points of doctrine. She had heard the Scriptures quoted to support doctrines very different in their nature. She had heard passages

C

commented upon and explained away to suit the views of the speaker, until she had come to think, sometimes, that the most obvious meaning of a text could not possibly be the true one; and she said to herself, what if she had been taking comfort from these promises too soon? What if they meant something else, or meant what they seemed to mean only to those to whom they were spoken? What if, for some unknown, mysterious reason, she were among those who had no part nor lot in the matter?—among those who hearing hear not, or who fail to understand? And before she was aware, the hopefulness of the last half-hour was vanishing away before the troubled and doubtful thoughts that rushed upon her.

'I wish there was any one that I could ask about it! I wonder if Effie would know? I'll see if she has brought me the book; and that will be something. Maybe the book-man could tell me all about it. Only I don't like to ask him.'

She turned her eyes towards him, as the thought passed through her mind. His face was plain and wrinkled and brown; but, for all that, it was a very pleasant face to look at. It was a grave face, even when he smiled; but it was never other than a pleasant one. There was something in it that brought to Christie's mind her favourite verse about 'the peace that passeth all understanding.'

'He has it, I do believe,' she said, while she quietly watched him as he listened or talked.

'It must be a weary life you live,' Aunt Elsie was saying, 'going about from morning till night, in all weathers, with those books of yours; a weary life and a thankless.'

'Do you think so?' said Mr. Craig, with a smile. 'I don't think it is a harder life than most of the people that I see are living. No harder than the farmers have during this busy harvest-time. No harder than the pedlars of tin-ware and dry goods have, that go about the country in all weathers.'

'But it's different with the farmer, who tills his own land. He is working to some end. Every tree he cuts, every sheaf he reaps and gathers in, is so much gain to him; and even these pedlars must have a measure of enjoyment when their sales are good. They are gaining their living by their travels.'

'Well, so am I, for that matter,' said Mr. Craig, still smiling. 'I am on equal terms with them there; though I cannot say that the greatest part of the pleasure I have in my work arises from the gain it is to me. But why do you say it is a thankless work?'

Instead of answering directly, Aunt Elsie asked, a moment after:

'Are you always well received, — you and your books?'

'Oh, yes; in this part of the country, always,—quite as well as other pedlars are, and sometimes far better, for my work's sake. I have been in places where the reception I met with was something worse than cold. But I now and then met, even in those places, some that welcomed me so warmly for the work's sake I was doing as to make me little heed the scoffs of the others.'

'You are sent out by a society, I think?' said Aunt Elsie. 'It is mostly Bibles that you sell?'

'Yes; it's mostly Bibles that I carry with me.'

There was a pause. The colporteur sat looking into the red embers, with the smile on his face which

Christie had found so attractive. In a little while Aunt Elsie, not without some hesitation, said :

'And is all the time and trouble and money spent by this society worth their while?'

Aunt Elsie would have been shocked had any one expressed a doubt of her sincere respect for the Bible. Her respect was hereditary. Not one day in her childhood or womanhood had passed in which she had not heard or read some portion of the Holy Book. Nothing could have induced her to part with one of the several Bibles that had been in her possession for years. One had been hers when a girl at school, one had lain in her seat at the kirk for many a year, and a third had lain on her parlour-table and been used by her at family worship when she kept house for herself. It would have seemed to her like sacrilege to let them pass into other hands. That the superiority of the Scottish people over all other nations (in which superiority she firmly believed) was in some way owing to the influence of God's Word, read and understood, she did not doubt. But her ideas of the matter were by no means satisfactory even to herself. That the Bible, read and understood, should ever change the mixed multitudes of her new and adopted country into a people grave and earnest and steadfast for the right, was altogether beyond her thought. The humble labours of this man, going about from house to house, to place perhaps in careless or unwilling hands the Bible (God's Word though she acknowledged it to be), seemed a very small matter—a means very inadequate to the end desired. So it was a doubtful and hesitating assent that she yielded to the reply of Mr. Craig in the form of a question.

'Is not God's Word His appointed instrument for the salvation of men? And will He not bless it to that end? I do not doubt it,' continued Mr. Craig. 'How can I doubt it, in the face of the promise that His word shall not return unto Him void—that it *shall* prosper in that whereunto He sendeth it? I never let a Bible pass from my hands without asking from God that it may be made the means of a lasting blessing to at least one soul. And I have faith to believe that my prayer will be heard and granted.'

Aunt Elsie's motions expressed some surprise.

'And is not that presumption on your part?' she asked.

'Which? The prayer, or the expectation?' said Mr. Craig. 'Not the prayer, surely, when He says, "Ask, and ye shall receive; seek, and ye shall find." "Whatsoever ye shall ask in My name, believing, ye shall receive." "Ask, and ye shall receive, that your joy may be full." Is it presumption to ask blessings for those whom God so loved that He sent His only begotten Son into the world to die that they might live? "Will He not with Him also freely give them all things?" Truly, I think the presumption would lie in *not* asking, or in asking and not expecting to receive.'

In the pause that followed, Christie, with a strange feeling at her heart, pondered the words.

'Well,' said Aunt Elsie, in a moment, 'I dare say it is as well that you have these thoughts to encourage you. The Bible can do nobody harm, at any rate; and it may do good to the bairns at the school.'

Mr. Craig opened his lips, as though he were going to answer her; but he did not. By and by he said— quite as much as though he were speaking to himself as to her:

'Yes; it is indeed a good thing to have God's promise to fall back upon. My work would be vain and weary work without that. And so would any work to which I could put my hand. There *are* folk in the world who live with no hope or trust in God's promised blessing. How they do it I cannot tell.'

'God is good to many a one who thinks little of Him or of His care; or what would become of the world and the thousands in it?' said Aunt Elsie, with a sigh.

Mr. Craig gave her a quick look.

'Yes: He is kind to the evil and the unthankful. But I was thinking of the blessedness of those who have the daily and hourly sense of God's presence with them and His fatherly care over them. In time of trouble, and at all times, indeed, it is sweet to know that we have His word and promise for all that we possibly need.'

'Yes,' said Aunt Elsie, uneasily, and rather coldly. 'There is much truth in what you say.'

Mr. Craig continued: 'There is no fear of being forgotten. He who sees the sparrow when it falls, and does not forget to number the hairs of our heads, may well be trusted. And may we not trust in Him who is not ashamed to call His people brethren? Our Elder Brother! He who suffered being tempted—who is touched with the feeling of our infirmities! It is worth while to have His promise to fall back upon—for me in my journeys, for you amid your household cares, and for this little maiden here amid whatever life may bring to her.'

In the interest with which she listened, Christie had forgotten her shyness, and had drawn quite near;

and now she sat with her eyes fastened on the good man's face, her own quite expressive of intense eagerness.

'Christie,' said her aunt, as her eye fell upon her, 'it is high time you were in bed. There will be no getting you up in the morning. Your sisters are all asleep. Haste away.'

Christie would have given much for courage to ask one question; and perhaps a glance into the kind face that was looking down upon her might have given it to her, had her aunt not been there. Perhaps he guessed her thought; for he said, as he put out his hand and laid it softly on hers:

'Yes, my lassie; it is not beyond belief that the kind care and the loving eye of this Elder Brother should be over you, if you are one of His little ones. Are you?'

The last words were spoken after a momentary pause, and the little brown hand was gently pressed as they were uttered. If Christie could have found words with which to answer him, she could not have uttered them through the tears and sobs that had not been far from her all the evening. Slowly obeying the admonishing touch of her aunt, she withdrew her hand from the gentle pressure that detained it, and crept away in the dark to the room where all her sisters, except Effie, were already asleep.

And what a tumult of glad, wondering and doubtful thoughts was stirring her heart as she seated herself on the floor and leaned her weary head upon her hand! Could it all be true? Did God see and hear and care for people? And for her too? The Elder Brother! What a sweet name to give to Jesus! It seemed easier

to believe that He would care for her, calling Him by
that name.

And if it were really true that God heard her prayers
and would answer them, certainly things would not go
so badly with her any more. But was she one of His
little ones? Surely there was no one more helpless
and hopeless and troubled—nobody that needed help
more!

'Oh, if I could only be sure!' she whispered. 'But
I'll see to-night. Aunt Elsie wasna vexed to-night.
And if Effie has brought me the book, I'll take it for a
sign. Oh, I wish she would come!'

And yet, when Effie came in with a light in her
hand, Christie was in no haste to speak. Effie moved
about very quietly, for fear of waking her sisters; and
then she sat down, shading the light from their
faces.

'Haste you, Christie dear,' she whispered. 'I thought
you were in bed. It is more than time.'

Christie slowly undressed, and after kneeling a little
while, laid herself down on the low bed beside her little
sister. But she did not sleep. She did not even close
her eyes, but lay watching sometimes the motionless
figure of Effie and sometimes her shadow on the wall,
wondering all the while what could keep her occupied
so silently and so long. Yet when at last the book
was closed and Effie began to move about the room,
she could not find courage to speak to her at once.

'Effie,' she said, by and by, 'did you bring me the
book you promised?'

Effie started.

'Christie, I thought you were asleep! Do you know
how late it is?'

'Did you bring me the book you promised?' repeated the child, eagerly.

Effie could not resist the beseeching face; and she came and seated herself on the side of the bed.

'I wanted it so much,' continued Christie. 'I thought you would bring it! Did you forget it? Or were you not up there this week?'

'I was there, and I didna forget it; but—'

'Did you bring it?' cried Christie, rising, in her eagerness. 'Where is it?'

Effie shook her head.

'I didna bring it, Christie.'

Poor little Christie! She laid herself back on her pillow without a word. The disappointment was a very bitter one; and she turned her face away, that her sister might not see the tears that were gushing from her eyes. She had all the week been looking forward to the pleasure of having a book—'The Scottish Chiefs' —a stolen glance or two of which had excited her interest to the highest degree; and the disappointment was great. But that it should have failed to come on this particular night was harder still to bear.

'If God only hears half our prayers, and that the half we care least about, what is the use of praying at all? Oh, dear! I thought I had found something at last!'

'Christie,' said her sister, laying her hand on her shoulder, 'why are you crying in that way? Surely you have had tears enough for once? What ails you, child? Speak to me, Christie.'

'Oh, you *might* have brought it!' she exclaimed, through her sobs. 'You almost promised.'

'No, Christie, I didna promise. I didna forget it.

But I am afraid—indeed, I am sure—that the reading of the book would do you no good, but harm ; and so I didna bring it to you. You are wrong to be so vexed about it.'

'Is it a bad book ?' asked Christie.

'I am not sure that it is a *bad* book. But I think it might do you harm to read it. I am afraid your imagination is too full of such things already.'

This had been said to her in far sharper words many a time before ; and Christie made no answer.

'You know yourself, Christie, when you get a book that interests you, you are apt to neglect other things for the pleasure of reading it Almost always Aunt Elsie has to find fault with you for it.'

'Aunt Elsie always finds fault with me!' sighed Christie.

'But you give her reason to find fault with you when you neglect your duties for such reading, as you must confess you do ; even to-day, you know.'

'I believe it grieves Aunt Elsie's heart to see me taking pleasure in anything,' said Christie, turning round passionately. 'She never heeds when Annie or Sarah takes a book; but if I look the way of one, she's at me. I believe she would be glad if there was no such thing as a book in the house.'

'Hush, Christie ! You are wrong to speak in that way. It is not true what you are saying. Aunt Elsie is fond of reading ; and if she doesna object to Annie and Sarah taking a book, it is because they don't very often do so. They never neglect their work for reading, as you too often do.'

All this was true, as Christie's conscience told her ;

but she was by no means willing to confess as much; so she turned away her face, and said, pettishly:

'Oh, well, I hear all that often enough. There's no use in saying anything more about it.'

Effie rose, and went to the other side of the room. When she returned, she carried something wrapped in paper in her hand.

'Look, Christie; I brought you a book—a better book than "The Scottish Chiefs." Turn round and look at it.'

Slowly Christie raised herself up and turned round. She was ashamed of her petulance by this time. Something shone in the light of the candle which Effie held.

'What is it?' she asked; and her sister placed it in her hand.

It was a Bible, a very beautiful one, bound in purple morocco, with clasps and gilt edges. It was small, but not too small even for Christie's eyes.

'Oh, how beautiful!' exclaimed Christie, forgetting everything in her delight. 'It is the very thing I have been wishing for!'

Effie said nothing, but watched her, well pleased.

'But, Effie,' said Christie, suddenly, 'this must have been very dear. A plainer one would have done just as well. Did it cost much?'

'Not very much,' said Effie, sitting down beside her again. 'A Bible is for one's whole lifetime, and so I got a good one, and a pretty one, too; you are so fond of pretty things. If I had known that the book-man was coming here I might have waited and let you choose it for yourself. We might have changed it now, but see, I have written your name in it.'

She turned to the fly-leaf, and read 'Christina

Redfern,' with the date, in Effie's pretty handwriting. She gave a sigh of pleasure as she turned it over.

'No, I don't believe there is a nicer one there. It's far prettier than yours, Effie. Wouldna you have liked it? Your old one would have done for me.'

'Oh, no, indeed! I would far rather have my own old Bible than the prettiest new one,' said Effie, hastily.

'Yes, I suppose so,' said Christie. 'Mother gave it to you.'

'Yes; and, besides, I have got used to it. I know just where to find the places I want, almost without thinking of the chapter.'

'It is a perfect beauty of a Bible; and such clear print! But I am afraid it cost a great deal—as much as a pair of shoes, perhaps?' she continued, looking at her sister.

Effie laughed.

'But what comparison is there between a Bible and a pair of shoes? You must read it every day, dear; and then you'll be sure to think of me.'

'I do that many times every day,' said Christie, sighing.

'I'm glad you like it, dear. Mr. Craig ask me if it was for myself; and I told him no, it was for my little sister at home.'

Christie started. This, then, was one of the Bibles that the book-man had said he asked God to bless for the good of at least one soul. And he seemed so sure that his prayer would be heard. And, then, had not her prayer been heard?—not just as she had hoped, but in a better way. The thought filled her with a strange glad wonder. Could it be possible? Her eye fell on the open page, and her hand trembled as she read:

' Ask, and ye shall receive, that your joy may be full.'

'Effie,' she said, softly, 'I thank you very much. Lay it in my little box; and good-night.'

The tears that wet her pillow were very different from the drops that had fallen on it a little while before.

'Nothing will be so bad again,' she murmured. 'Nothing—nothing. Whatever happens, I can always pray !'

CHAPTER III.

THE next two days passed pleasantly enough; as the days always did, Christie thought, when Effie was at home. There was plenty to do, more than usual; but the elder sister was strong and willing, and, above all, cheerful, and work seemed play in her hands. Even Aunt Elsie forgot to scold when any little misfortune happened through neglect or carelessness, and Effie's cheerful 'Never mind. It canna be helped now. Let us do the best we can,' came between her and the culprit.

Effie was not so merry as she used sometimes to be, Christie thought; and very grave indeed she looked while discussing ways and means with Aunt Elsie. There was a good deal to be discussed, for the winter was approaching, and the little ones were in need of clothes and other things, and Aunt Elsie did Effie the honour to declare that her judgment on these matters was better worth having than that of all the rest of them put together. Certainly, never were old garments examined and considered with greater attention than was bestowed on the motley pile brought from 'the

blue chest' for her inspection. No wonder that she
looked grave over the rents and holes and threadbare
places, sure as she was that, however shabby they had
become, they must in some way or other be made to
serve for a long time yet. It looked like a hopeless
task, the attempt to transform by darning and turning,
by patching and eking, the poor remnants of last winter's
frocks and petticoats into garments suitable for home
and school wear.

'Surely no children ever grew so fast as ours!' said
Effie, after turning her little sister Ellen round and
round, in the vain hope of persuading her aunt and
herself that the little linsey-woolsey frock was not much
too short and scant for the child. 'Katie will need to
have it, after all. But what can we do for Nellie?'
And Effie looked sorely perplexed.

'It's no' often that folk look on the growing of bairns
as a misfortune,' said Aunt Elsie, echoing her sigh. 'If
it werena that we want that green tartan for a kilt for
wee Willie, we might manage to get Nellie a frock out
of that.'

Effie considered deeply.

'Oh, Effie,' whispered Christie, when her aunt's back
was turned, 'never mind that heap of trash just now.
You promised to come down to the burn-side with me;
and it will soon be time for the milking.'

'But I must mind,' said Effie, gravely. 'The bairns
will need these things before I can get two whole days
at home again, and my aunt and the girls have enough
to do without this. Duty before pleasure, Christie.
See; you can help me by picking away this skirt. We
must make the best of things.'

Christie applied herself to the task, but not without

many a sigh and many a longing look at the bright sunshine. If Effie once got fairly engaged in planning and patching, there would be no use in thinking of a walk before milking-time.

'Oh, dear!' she said, with a sigh. 'I wish there was no such a thing as old clothes in the world!'

'Well, if there were plenty of new ones in it, I wouldna object to your wish being gratified,' said Effie, laughing. 'But as there are few likely to come our way for a while, we must do the best we can with the old. We might be worse off, Christie.'

'Do you like to do it?' asked Christie.

'I like to see it when it's done, at any rate. There is a great deal of pleasure in a patch of that kind,' she said, holding up the sleeve she had been mending. 'You would hardly know there was a patch there.'

Christie bent her short-sighted eyes to the work.

'Yes; it's very nice. I wonder you have the patience. Aunt Elsie might do it, I'm sure.'

Effie looked grave again.

'I am afraid Aunt Elsie won't do much this winter. Her hands are getting bad again. I must be busy while I am here. Never mind the walk. We'll get a long walk together if we go to the kirk.'

'Yes, if it doesna rain, or if something doesna happen to hinder us.'

But she looked as though she thought there was nothing so pleasant in store for her as a long walk with Effie; and she worked away at the faded little garment with many a sigh.

Sunday came, and, in spite of Christie's forebodings, the day rose bright and beautiful. The kirk which the Redferns attended lay three long miles from the

farm. The distance and the increasing shabbiness of
little garments often kept the children at home, and
Christie, too, had to stay and share their tasks. They
had no conveyance of their own, and though the others
might be none the worse for a little exposure to rain or
wind, her aunt would never permit Christie to run the
risk of getting wet or over-tired. So it was with a face
almost as bright as Effie's own that she hailed the
bright sunshine and the cloudless sky. For Sunday
was not always a pleasant day for her at home. Indeed,
it was generally a very wearisome day. It was Aunt
Elsie's desire and intention that it should be well kept.
But, beyond giving out a certain number of questions
in the catechism, or a psalm or chapter to be learned
by the little ones, she did not help them to keep it.
It was given as a task, and it was learned and repeated
as a task. None of them ever aspired to anything more
than to get through the allotted portion 'without
missing.' There was not much pleasure in it, nor in
the readings that generally followed; for though good
and valuable books in themselves, they were too often
quite beyond the comprehension of the little listeners.
A quiet walk in the garden, or in the nearest field, was
the utmost that was permitted in the way of amusement; and though sometimes the walk might become a
run or a romp, and the childish voices rise higher than
the Sunday pitch when there was no one to reprove,
it must be confessed that Sunday was the longest day
in all the week for the little Redferns.

To none of them all was it longer than to Christie.
She did not care to share the stolen pleasures of the
rest. Reading was her only resource. Idle books were,
on Sundays, and on weekdays too, Aunt Elsie's peculiar

aversion; and, unfortunately, all the books that Christie cared about came under this class, in her estimation. All the enjoyment she could get in reading must be stolen; and between the fear of detection and the consciousness of wrong-doing, the pleasure, such as it was, was generally hardly worth seeking.

So it was with many self-congratulations that she set out with Effie to the kirk. They were alone. Their father had gone earlier to attend the Gaelic service, which he alone of all the family understood, and Annie and Sarah, after the labours of a harvest-week, declared themselves too weary to undertake the walk. It was a very lovely morning. Here and there a yellow birch, or a crimson maple bough, gave token that the dreary autumn was not far away; but the air was mild and balmy as June, and the bright sunlight made even the rough road and the low-lying stubble-fields look lovely, in Christie's eyes.

'How quiet and peaceful all things are!' she thought.

The insects were chirping merrily enough, and now and then the voice of a bird was heard, and from the woodland pastures far away the tinkle of sheep-bells fell pleasantly on the ear. But these sounds in no way jarred on the Sabbath stillness; and as Christie followed her sister along the narrow path that led them by a near way across the fields to the half-mile corner where the road took a sudden turn to the right, a strange feeling of peace stole over her. The burden of vexing and discontented thoughts, that too frequently weighed on her heart, seemed to fall away under the pleasant influence of the sunshine and the quiet, and she drew a long sigh of relief as she said, softly:

'Oh, Effie! such a bonny day!'

'Yes,' said Effie, turning round for a moment, and smiling at her sister's brightening face. 'It seems just such a day as one would choose the Sabbath to be—so bright, yet so peaceful. I am very glad.'

But they could not say much yet; for the path was narrow, and there were stones and rough places, and now and then a little water to be avoided; so they went on quietly till they reached the low stone wall that separated the field from the high-road. The boughs of the old tree that hung over it were looking bare and autumn-like already, but under the flickering shadow they sat down for a while to rest.

'Hark!' said Christie, as the sound of wheels reached them. 'That must be the Nesbitts. They never go to the Gaelic service. I dare say they will ask us to ride.' There was an echo of disappointment in her tone; and in a moment she added:

'It is such a bonny day, and the walk would be so pleasant by and by in the cool shade!'

'Yes,' said Effie. 'But if they ask us we'll ride; for six miles is a long walk for you. And it will be nice to ride, too.'

And so it was. The long wagon was drawn by two stout horses. No one was in it but John Nesbitt and his mother; and they were both delighted to offer a seat to the young girls. Christie sat on the front seat with John, who was quite silent, thinking his own thoughts or listening to the quiet talk going on between Effie and his mother; and Christie enjoyed her drive in silence too.

How very pleasant it seemed! They went slowly, for they had plenty of time; and Christie's eyes wandered over the scene—the sky, the changing trees, the brown fields and the green pastures—with an interest and enjoyment that surprised herself. There was not much to see; but any change was pleasant to the eyes that had rested for weeks on the same familiar objects. Then the unaccustomed and agreeable motion exhilarated without wearying her. And when at last they came in sight of the kirk, Christie could not help wishing that they had farther to go.

The kirk, of itself, was rather an unsightly object than otherwise. Except for the two rows of small windows on each side, it differed little in appearance from the large wooden barns so common in that part of the country. The woods were close behind it; and in the summer-time they were a pleasant sight. On one side lay the graveyard. On days when the sun did not shine, or in the autumn before the snow had come to cover up the long, rank grass, the graveyard was a very dreary place to Christie, and instead of lingering in it she usually went into the kirk, even though the Gaelic service was not over. But to-day she sat down near the door, at Effie's side, and waited till the people should come out. Mrs. Nesbitt had gone into a neighbour's house, and the two girls were quite alone.

'Effie,' said Christie, 'I think the minister must preach better in Gaelic than he does in English. Just look in. Nobody will see you. The folk are no' thinking about things outside.'

Effie raised herself a little, and bent forward to see. It was a very odd-looking place. The pulpit was placed, not at the end of the house, as is usual in places of worship, but at one side. There was no aisle. The door opened directly into the body of the house, and from the place where they stood could be seen not only the minister, but the many earnest faces that were turned towards him. The lower part of the place was crowded to the threshold, and tier above tier of earnest faces looked down from the gallery. No sound save the voice of the preacher was heard, and on him every eye was fastened. A few of the little ones had gone to sleep, leaning on the shoulders of their elders; but all the rest were listening as though life and death depended on the words he uttered. The minister was speaking rapidly, and, as Effie knew, solemnly, though she could only here and there catch the meaning of his words. Indeed, it must have been easy to speak earnestly when addressing such a multitude of eager listeners, who were hungry for the bread of life.

'I dare say the difference is in the hearers rather than in the preaching,' said Effie, turning away softly.

'But, Effie, many of them are the very same people. I wish I knew what he was saying!'

'I dare say it is easier to speak in Gaelic, for one thing. The folk, at least most of them, like it better, even when they understand English. And it must make a great difference to a minister when he sees people listening like that. I dare say he says the very same things to us in English.'

Christie still stood looking in at the open door.

'It aye minds me of the Day of Judgment,' she said, 'when I see the people sitting like that, and when they come thronging out into the kirk-yard and stand about among the graves.'

She shuddered slightly, and came and sat down beside Effie, and did not speak again till the service was over. What a crowd there was then! How the people came pouring out—with faces grave and composed, indeed, but not half so solemn, Christie thought, as they ought to have been! The voices rose to quite a loud hum as they passed from the door. Greetings were interchanged, and arrangements were made for going home. Invitations were given and accepted, and the larger part of the crowd moved slowly away.

The English congregation was comparatively small. The English sermon immediately followed; but, whatever might be the reason, Christie said many times to herself that there was a great difference in the minister's manner of preaching now. He looked tired. And no wonder. Two long services immediately succeeding each other were enough to tire him. Christie strove to listen and to understand. She did not succeed very well. She enjoyed the singing always, and especially to-day singing out of the Psalms at the end of her own new Bible. But though she tried very hard to make herself think that she enjoyed the sermon too, she failed; and she was not sorry when it was over and she found herself among the crowd in the kirk-yard again. She had still the going home before her.

To her great delight, Effie refused a ride in the Nesbitts' wagon, in order that some who had walked in the morning might enjoy it. She hoped to have her sister all to herself for a little while. She did not, however. They were joined by several who were going their way; and more than one lengthened their walk and went home the longest way, for the sake of their company. It was not until they found themselves again at the half-mile corner that they were quite alone. Christie sighed as she leaned for a moment on the wall.

'You are tired, dear,' said Effie. 'It is well we didna have to walk both ways. Sit and rest a while.'

'I am not *very* tired,' said Christie; but she sighed again as she sat down.

'Effie, I wish I liked better to go to the kirk.'

'Why, Christie?' said her sister, in surprise. 'I thought you liked it very much. You said so in the morning.'

'Yes, I know; I like the walk, and the getting away from home; and I like the singing, and to see the people. But the preaching—others seem to like it so much; but I don't. I don't understand half that is said. Do you?'

'I don't understand always,' said Effie, a little doubtfully.

'And sometimes I canna help thinking about other things—the foolishest things!—stories, and bits of songs; and sometimes I get *so* sleepy.'

'It's wrong to think about other things in the kirk,' said Effie, scarcely knowing what to say.

'But I canna help it! Now, to-day I meant to try; and I did. Some things I seemed to understand at the time; but most that he said I didna understand, and I have forgotten it all now. I don't believe I could tell even the text.'

'Oh, yes, you could,' said Effie. '"Therefore, being justified by faith, we have peace with God through our Lord Jesus Christ." Don't you mind?'

'Yes; I mind now,' said Christie, turning to the verse in her new Bible, and reading it, with several that followed. 'Do you mind what he said, Effie?'

'Some things. He said a great many very important

things.' She paused, and tried to recollect. 'He told us what justification meant. Don't you mind?'

'Yes; but I knew that before, from the catechism.' And she repeated the words.

She paused a moment, considering, as if the words had a meaning she had not thought of before.

'Yes,' said Effie; 'and he went on to explain all about it. I canna repeat much of it; but I understood the most of it, I think.'

'I was always waiting to hear something about the peace,' said Christie; 'but he didna get to that.'

'No. He told us he had kept us too long on the first part of the subject. He'll give us the rest next Sabbath.'

Christie sighed. The chances were very much against her hearing what was to be said next Sabbath. In a moment she repeated, musingly:

'"Pardoneth all our sins; accepteth us as righteous." I never thought about that before. "The righteousness of Christ imputed to us." What is "imputed," Effie?'

'It means put to our credit, as if it were our own,' said Effie. 'I have read that somewhere.'

'Do you understand all the catechism, Effie?' asked Christie, looking wonderingly into her face. Effie laughed a little, and shook her head.

'I don't understand it all, as the minister does, but I think I know something about every question. There is so much in the catechism.'

'Yes, I suppose so,' assented Christie. 'But it's a pity that all good books are so dull and so hard to understand.'

'Why, I don't suppose they *are* all dull. I am sure they are not,' said Effie, gravely.

'Well, *I* find them so,' said Christie. 'Do you mind the book that Andrew Graham brought to my father—the one, you know, that he said his mother was never weary of reading? And my father liked it too—and my aunt; though I don't really think she liked it so much. Well, I tried, on two different Sabbaths, to read it. I thought I would try and find out what was wonderful about it. But I couldna. It seemed to me just like all the rest of the books. Did *you* like it, Effie?'

'I didna read it. It was sent home too soon. But, Christie, you are but a little girl. It's no' to be supposed that you could understand all father can, or that you should like all that he likes. And besides,' she added, after a pause, 'I suppose God's people are different from other people. They have something that others have not—a power to understand and enjoy what is hidden from the rest of the world.'

Christie looked at her sister with undisguised astonishment.

'What *do* you mean, Effie?' she asked.

'I don't know that I can make it quite clear to you. But don't you mind how we smiled at wee Willie for wanting to give his bonny picture-book to Mrs. Grey's blind Allie? It was a treasure to him; but to the poor wee blind lassie it was no better than an old copy-book would have been. And don't you mind that David prays: "Open Thou mine eyes, that I may behold wondrous things out of Thy law"? That must mean something. I am afraid most of those who read God's Word fail to see "wondrous things" in it.'

Effie's eyes grew moist and wistful as they followed
the quivering shadows of the leaves overhead; and
Christie watched her silently for a while.

'But, Effie,' she said, at last, 'there are parts of the
Bible that everybody likes to read. And, besides, all
the people that go to the kirk and listen as though
they took pleasure in it are not God's people—nor all
those who read dull books, either.'

Effie shook her head.

'I suppose they take delight in listening to what the
preacher says, just as they would take pleasure in
hearing a good address on any subject. But the Word
is not food and medicine and comfort to the like of
them, as old Mrs. Grey says it is to her. And we don't
see them taking God's Word as their guide and their
law in all things, as God's people do. It is not because
they love it that they read and listen to it. There is a
great difference.'

'Yes,' said Christie; 'I suppose there is.'

But her thoughts had flown far away before Effie had
done speaking. A vague impression, that had come to
her mind many times before, was fast taking form: she
was asking herself whether Effie was not among those
whose eyes had been opened. She was different from
what she used to be. Not that she was kinder, or more
mindful of the comfort of others, than she remembered
her always to have been. But she was different, for
all that. Could it be that Effie had become a child of
God? Were her sins pardoned? Was she accepted?
Had old things passed away, and all things become new
to her? Christie could not ask her. She could hardly
look at her, in the midst of the new, shy wonder that

was rising within her. Yes, there were wonder and pleasure, but there was pain too—more of the latter than of the former. Had a barrier suddenly sprung up between her and the sister she loved best? A sense of being forsaken, left alone, came over her—something like the feeling that had nearly broken her heart when, long ago, they told her that her mother had gone to heaven. A great wave of bitterness passed over her sinking heart. She turned away, that her sister might not see her face.

'Christie,' said Effie, in a minute or two, 'I think we ought to go home. There will be some things to do; and if Annie and Sarah went to the Sabbath-class, we should be needed to help.'

It was in Christie's heart to say that she did not care to go home—she did not care to help—she did not care for anything. But she had no voice to utter such wrong and foolish words. So, still keeping her face turned away, she took her Bible and began to roll it in her handkerchief—when a thought struck her.

'Effie,' she asked, quickly, 'do you believe that God hears us when we pray?'

In the face now turned towards her, Effie saw tokens that there was something wrong with her little sister. But, accustomed to her changing moods and frequent petulance, she answered, quietly:

'Surely, Christie, I believe it. The Bible says so.'

'Yes; I ken that,' said Christie, with some impatience in her tone. 'The Bible says so, and people believe it in a general way. But is it true? Do *you* believe it?'

'Surely I believe it,' said Effie, slowly.

She was considering whether it would be best to say

anything more to her sister, vexed and unhappy as her voice and manner plainly showed her to be; and while she hesitated, Christie said again, more quietly:

'If God hears prayer, why are most people so miserable?'

'I don't think most people *are* miserable,' said Effie, gravely. 'I don't think anybody that trusts in God can be very miserable.'

Christie leaned back again on the stone, from which she had half risen.

'Those who have been pardoned and accepted,' she *thought;* but aloud she *said,* 'Well, I don't know: there are some good people that have trouble enough. There's old Mrs. Grey. Wave after wave of trouble has passed over her. I heard the minister say those very words to father about her.'

'But, Christie,' said her sister, gravely, 'you should ask Mrs. Grey, some time, if she would be willing to lose her trust in God for the sake of having all her trouble taken away. I am quite sure she would not hesitate for a moment. She would smile at the thought of even pausing to choose.'

'But, Effie, that's not what we are speaking about. I'm sure that Mrs. Grey prayed many and many a time that her son John might be spared to his family. Just think of them, so helpless—and their mother dead, and little Allie blind! And the minister prayed for him too, in the kirk, and all the folk, that so useful a life might be spared. But, for all that, he died, Effie.'

'Yes; but, Christie, Mrs. Grey never prayed for her son's life except in submission to God's will. If his death would be for the glory of God, she prayed to be made submissive to His will, and committed herself and her son's helpless little ones to God's keeping.'

Christie looked at her sister with eyes filled with astonishment.

'You don't mean to say that if Mrs. Grey had had her choice she wouldna have had her son spared to her?'

'I mean that if she could have had her choice she would have preferred to leave the matter in God's hands. She would never have chosen for herself.'

'Christie,' she added, after a pause, 'do you mind the time when our Willie wanted father's knife, and how, rather than vex him, Annie gave it to him? Do you mind all the mischief he did to himself and others? I suppose some of our prayers are as blind and foolish as Willie's wish was, and that God shows His loving kindness to us rather by denying than by granting our requests.'

'Then what was the use of praying for Mrs. Grey's son, since it was God's will that he should die? What is the use of anybody's praying about anything?'

Effie hesitated. There was something in Christie's manner indicating that it was not alone the mere petulance of the moment that dictated the question.

'I am not wise about these things, Christie,' she said. 'I only know this: God has graciously permitted us to bring our troubles to Him. He has said, "Ask, and ye shall receive; seek, and ye shall find." He has said, "He that asketh receiveth, and he that seeketh findeth." And in the Psalms, "Call upon Me in the day of trouble, and I will deliver thee, and thou shalt glorify Me." We need not vex ourselves, surely, about *how* it is all to happen. God's word is enough.'

'But then, Effie, there are prayers that God doesna hear.'

'There are many things that God does not give us when we ask Him; but, Christie, God does hear the prayers of His people. Yes, and He answers them too —though not always in the way that they wish or expect, yet *always* in the *best* way for them. Of this they may be sure. If He does not give them just what they ask for, He will give them something better, and make them willing to be without the desired good. There is nothing in the whole Bible more clearly told than that God hears the prayers of His people. We need never, *never* doubt that.'

But Christie did not look satisfied.

'"His people,"' she murmured, 'but no others.'

Effie looked perplexed.

'I am not wise in these matters, as I have just told you,' she said, gravely. 'Until lately I havena thought much about them. But I think that people sometimes vex themselves in vain. It is to the thirsty who are seeking water that God promises to open fountains. It is to the weary and heavy-laden that Christ has promised rest. I am sure that those who feel their need of God's help need not fear that they will be refused anything—I mean, anything that is good for them.'

'There is a difference, I suppose,' she added, after a pause. 'We may ask for many a temporal blessing that might be our ruin if God were to grant it to us; and in love He withholds such, often. But when we ask for spiritual blessing, for the grace of strength to do or of patience to bear His will, if we ask for guidance, for wisdom to direct us, we need not fear that we shall be denied. And, having these, other things don't matter so much, to God's people.'

"To God's people," ' repeated Christie to herself again. 'Well, I am not one of them. It's nothing that can do me any good.'

She did not answer her sister, but rose up slowly, saying it was time to go. So she climbed over the low stone wall, and walked on in silence. Effie followed quietly. Not a word was spoken till they reached the bend of the brook over which hung the birch-tree. Past this, her favourite resting-place, Christie rarely went without lingering. She would not have paused to-night, however, had not Effie, who had fallen a little behind by this time, called her.

'Oh, Christie! look at the clouds! Did you ever see anything so beautiful? How beautiful!' she repeated, as she came and stood beside her. 'It was a long time before I could become used to the sun's sinking down in that low, far-away place. I missed the hills that used to hide him from us at home. How well I remember the sunsets then, and the long, quiet gloamings!'

'Home' was over the sea, and 'then' was the time when a mother's voice and smile mingled with all other pleasant things; and no wonder that Effie sighed, as she stood watching the changing hues near the low horizon. The 'home' and 'then' were the last drops added to Christie's cup of sad memories; and the overflow could no longer be stayed. She kept her face turned away from her sister, but could not hide the struggle within, and at Effie's very first word her sobs broke forth.

'What is the matter, Christie? There must be something you have not told me about. You are weary: that is it. Sit down here again, and rest. We need not hurry home, after all.'

Christie sank down, struggling with her tears.

'It's nothing, Effie,' she said, at last. 'I'm sure I didna mean to vex you with my crying; but I canna help it. There is nothing the matter with me more than usual. Never mind me, Effie.'

'Well, sit still a little,' said Effie, soothingly. 'You are tired, I do believe.'

'Yes,' said Christie, recovering herself with a great effort. 'It's partly that, I dare say; and——' She stopped, not being further sure of her voice.

Effie said nothing, but gently stroked her hair with her hand. The gentle touch was more than Christie could bear, at the moment.

'Effie, don't!' she cried, vainly struggling to repress another gush of tears. In a little while she grew quiet, and said, 'I know I'm very foolish, Effie; but 1 canna help it.'

'Never mind,' said Effie, cheerfully; for she knew by the sound of her voice that her tears were over for this time. 'A little shower sometimes clears the sky; and now the sun will shine again.'

She stooped down, and dipping her own handkerchief in the brook, gave it to her sister to bathe her hot cheeks; and soon she asked, gravely:

'What is it, Christie?'

'It's nothing,' said Christie, eagerly. 'Nothing more than usual. I'm tired, that's all,—and you are going away,—and it will be just the same thing every day till you come back,—going to bed tired, and getting up tired, and doing the same thing over and over again to very little purpose. I'm sure I canna see the good of it all.'

Effie could not but smile at her words and manner.

'Well, I suppose that will be the way with every one, mostly. I'm sure it will be the way with me. Except the getting up tired,' she added, laughing. 'I'm glad to say I don't very often do that. I'm afraid my life is not to much purpose either, though I do wish it to be useful,' she continued, more gravely.

'Oh, well, it's very different with you!' said Christie, in a tone that her sister never liked to hear.

She did not reply for a moment. Then she said:

'It will be easier for you now that the harvest is over. Annie and Sarah will be in the house, and you will have less to do. And, besides, they will make it more cheerful.'

Christie made a movement of impatience.

'You are like Aunt Elsie. You think that I like to be idle and don't wish to do my share. At any rate, the girls being in the house will make little difference to me. I shall have to be doing something all the time —little things that don't come to anything. Well, I suppose there is no help for it. It will be all the same in the end.'

Poor Christie! She had a feeling all the time that she was very cross and unreasonable, and she was as vexed as possible with herself for spoiling this last precious half-hour with Effie by her murmurs and complaints. She had not meant it. She was sorry they had waited by the brook. She knew it was for her sake that Effie had proposed to sit down in her favourite resting-place; but before she had well uttered the last words she was wishing with all her heart that they had hurried on.

Effie looked troubled. Christie felt rather than saw it; for her face was turned quite away, and she was gathering up and casting from her broken bits of branches and withered leaves, and watching them as they were borne away by the waters of the brook. Christie would have given much to know whether she was thinking of her foolish words, or of something else.

'I suppose she thinks it's of no use to heed what I say. And now I have spoiled all the pleasure of thinking about to-day.'

Soon she asked, in a voice which had quite lost the tone of peevishness:

'When will you come home again, Effie?'

Effie turned towards her immediately.

'I don't know. I'm not quite sure, yet. But, Christie, I canna bear to hear you speak in that way—as though you saw no good in anything. Did you ever think how much worse it might be with you and with us all?'

In her heart, Christie was saying she did not think things *could* be much worse, as far as *she* was concerned; but she only looked at her sister, without speaking.

'For, after all,' continued Effie, 'we are very well off with food and shelter, and are all at home together. You are not very strong, it is true, and you have much to do and Aunt Elsie is not always considerate; or,

rather, she has not always a pleasant way of showing
her considerateness. She's a little sharp sometimes, I
know. But she suffers more than she acknowledges,
and we all ought to bear with her. You have the most
to bear, perhaps; but——'

'It's no' that, Effie,' interrupted Christie. 'I don't
mind having much to do. And I'm sure it never enters
into Aunt Elsie's head that I have anything to bear
from her. She thinks she has plenty to bear, from me
and from us all. I wouldna care if it came to anything.
I could bear great trials, I know, and do great things;
but this continual worry and vexation about nothing—
it never ends. Every day it is just to begin over again.
And what does it all amount to when the year's
over?'

'Hush, Christie,' said her sister. 'The time may
come when the remembrance of these words will be
painful to you. The only way we can prove that we
would bear great trials well is by bearing little trials
well. We don't know how soon great trials may come
upon us. Every night that I come home, I am thankful
to find things just as I left them. We need be in no
hurry to have any change.'

Christie was startled.

'What *do* you mean, Effie? Are you afraid of
anything happening?'

'Oh, no,' she said, cheerfully. 'I hope not. I dare
say we shall do very well. But we must be thankful
for the blessings we have, Christie, and hopeful for the
future.'

'Folk say father is not a very good farmer. Is that
it, Effie?' Christie spoke with hesitation, as though

she was not quite sure how her sister would receive her remark. 'But we are getting on better now.

Effie only answered the last part of what she said.

'Yes, we are getting on better. Father says we have raised enough to take us through the year, with something to spare. It's all we have to depend on—so much has been laid out on the farm; and it must come in slowly. But things *will* wear out; and the bairns—I wish I could bide at home this winter.'

'Oh, if you only could!' cried Christie, eagerly.

Effie shook her head. 'I can do more good to all by being away. And my wages have been raised. I couldna leave just now. Oh, I dare say we shall do very well. But, Christie, you must not fret and be discontented, and think what you do is not worth while. It is the motive that makes the work of any one's life great or small. It is little matter, in one sense, whether it be teaching children, or washing dishes, or ruling a kingdom, if it is done in the right way and from right principles. I have read, somewhere, that the daily life of a poor unknown child, who, striving against sin, does meekly and cheerfully what is given him to do, may be more acceptable in the sight of God than the suffering of some whom their fellow-men crown as martyrs. If we could only forget ourselves and live for others!' She sighed as she rose to go. 'But come, child: we must hurry home now.'

Christie had no words with which to answer her. She rose and followed in silence. 'If we could forget ourselves and live for others!' she murmured. That was not *her* way, surely. Every day, and every hour of the day, it was herself she thought of. Either she was

murmuring over her grievances, or pitying herself for
them, or she was dreaming vain dreams of a future that
should have nothing to vex or annoy. Her life's work
was worth little, indeed, judging it by Effie's standard.
She did all that she did, merely because she could not
help it. As to forgetting herself and thinking of
others—

But who did so? No one that she knew, unless,
perhaps, Effie herself. And Effie had a great many
things to make her life pleasant, she thought. Perhaps
her father? But then, her father did what he did for
his children. All fathers did the same, she supposed.
No; she doubted whether any one came near Effie's
idea of what life should be. It would be a very different
world indeed if all did so.

They were quite close to the house before Christie
got thus far; and a glimpse of her father's careworn
face filled her with something like self reproach.

'I wish I could do him some good! But what can I
do? He has never been the same since mother died.
Nobody has been the same since that—except Effie;
and she is better and kinder every day. Oh, I wish I
could be like her! but it's of no use wishing;—I can
never be like her. Oh, how tired I am!'

She started at the sound of Aunt Elsie's voice asking,
rather sharply, what had kept them so long. She
turned away, impatient of the question, and impatient
of the cheerful answer with which Effie sought to turn
aside her aunt's displeasure. She was impatient of
Annie's regrets that their long delay had spoiled their
supper, and of Sarah's questions as to who had been at
the kirk, and answered them both shortly. She was

impatient of the suppressed noise of the little ones, and
vexed at her own impatience more than all.

'I dinna think your going to the kirk has done you
much good. What ails you, Christie? One would
think you had the sins of a nation to answer for, by
your face.'

'Whisht, Annie,' interposed Effie. 'Christie's tired,
and her head aches, I'm sure. Dinna vex her—poor
thing!'

'Well, if she would only say that, and no' look so
glum!' said Annie, laughing, as she set aside the bowl
of milk intended for Christie's supper. In a moment
she returned with a cup of tea, and placed it where the
bowl had stood. 'There!' she said; 'that will do your
head good, and your temper too, I hope. I'm sure you
look as though you needed it.'

Christie would fain have resented both her sister's
kindness and her thoughtless words, by taking no notice
of the tea; but Effie interposed again:

'You are very kind, Annie. What a pity you should
spoil all by those needless words!'

Annie laughed.

'Nonsense!' she said. 'I didna mean to say anything unkind. Christie mustna be so testy. Don't tell
me that you like milk better than tea. Christie will
enjoy hers all the better if you take one too.' And she
placed it before her.

'Thank you. It's very nice,' said Effie. 'But the
milk would have done very well.'

The quick tap of Aunt Elsie's cane was heard
approaching.

'I doubt you are getting away from Sabbath subjects,' said Aunt Elsie. 'Haste you with your supper, bairns—your father's waiting to have worship. Christie, if you are tired, you should go to bed at once.'

For once, Christie did not wait for a second bidding. She was very tired; and long before the usual Sabbath evening's examination was over, she had forgotten her doubts and fears and vexing thoughts in sleep.

CHAPTER IV.

ORPHANHOOD.

WHEN Christie was complaining of the small vexations and unvaried sameness of her daily life, she little dreamed how near at hand was the time when Effie's words were to prove true. Before the frost came to hush the pleasant murmur of the brook, or the snow had hidden alike the turf seat and the sear leaves of the birch-tree beside it, Christie was looking back over the stolen moments passed there on summer afternoons, with feelings with which were mingled wonder and pain and self-reproach. For the shadow of a coming sorrow was over their household. Day by day they seemed to be drawing nearer to a change which all saw, but which none had courage to name. The neighbours came and went, and spoke hopefully to the awed and anxious children; but they were grave, and said to one another that the poor young Redferns would soon be fatherless.

The harvest was quite over, and the assistance of the girls was no longer necessary out-of-doors, when one day Mr. Redfern went alone to bring home the last load of turnips from a distant field; and when his children saw his face again it was like the face of the dead,

Whether he had been thrown from the cart he had been driving, or whether he had fallen in some sort of fit, they could not tell. Even the doctor, who had been sent for from the next town, could not account for the state of stupor in which he found him. Two days of painful suspense passed; and then, contrary to the expectation of all, Mr. Redfern opened his eyes and spoke. For a few days he seemed to revive so rapidly that the doctor had hopes of his entire recovery. It would be a work of time, he said. His back had been much injured by the fall. He could never expect to be so strong as he had been before; but he did not doubt that a few weeks would restore him to a good degree of health and strength again. And so they all took courage.

Effie, who had been summoned home, would fain have remained for the winter; but this did not seem best. The surplus of the harvest, over which she and Christie had so lately rejoiced, would be required to pay the wages of the man who must for the winter take their father's place; and Effie's increased salary would be of more value than ever to the family. With a face which she strove to make cheerful for the sake of those she left behind, she went away; but her heart was heavy, and when she kissed Christie a good-bye and bade her keep her courage up for the sake of all, she could hardly restrain her tears till the words were spoken.

Those who were left at home needed all the cheerfulness they could gather from each other; for it was a very dreary winter that lay before them. The passing weeks did not bring to Mr. Redfern the health and strength so confidently promised by the doctor and so earnestly hoped for by his children. In her brief visits,

Effie could see little change in him from week to week —certainly none for the better. He gradually came to suffer less, and was always cheerful and patient; but the times when he could be relieved from the weariness of his bed by changing his position to the arm-chair were briefer and at longer intervals.

And, in the meantime, another cloud was gathering over them. Aunt Elsie's rheumatism, which during the autumn had given her much trouble from time to time, was growing daily worse. Painful days and sleepless nights were no longer the exception, but the rule; and not long after the coming in of the New Year, the help which for a long time she had positively and even sternly refused, became a necessity to her. She could neither rise nor lie down without assistance, and she was fast losing the use of her limbs. She was patient, or at least she strove to be, towards her nieces; but she murmured audibly against God, who had so heavily afflicted them.

The firm health and cheerful spirits of the girls, Annie and Sarah, stood them in good stead during those long months of suffering. Sarah was the housekeeper, and she fulfilled the many and complicated duties of her office with an alacrity and success that might well surprise them all. She planned and arranged with the skill of a woman of experience, and carried out her plans with an energy and patience that seldom flagged. Indeed, she seemed to find positive pleasure in the little make-shifts which their straitened means made every day more necessary, and boasted of her wonderful powers in a way so merry and triumphant that she cheered the rest when they needed it most.

Annie's task was harder than her sister's. The

constant attendance upon the sick-beds of her father and her aunt was very trying to a girl accustomed to daily exercise in the open air; and there were days when her voice was not so cheerful nor so often heard among them as it might have been. But she was strong and patient, and grew daily more efficient as a nurse; and though she did not know it, she was getting just the discipline that she needed to check some faults and to strengthen her character at the points where it needed strengthening most.

As for Christie, she was neither nurse nor house-keeper; or rather, I ought to say, she was both by turns. It was still her duty to attend to little items here and there, which seem little when done, but the neglect of which would soon throw a household into confusion. It was 'Christie, come here,' and 'Christie, go there,' and 'Christie, do this and that,' from morning till night, till she was too weary even to sleep when night came. Her sisters did not mean to be exacting. Indeed, they meant to be very kind and forbearing, and praised and petted her till she was ready to forget her weariness, as well as their unmindfulness of it. She did try very hard to be gentle, and patient, and useful, and almost always she succeeded; and the home-coming of Effie on Saturday night was the one event to which all her thoughts turned through the week, whether she was successful or not.

And, indeed, Christie was not the only one of them whose chief pleasure was a glimpse of Effie's cheerful face. It did them all good to have her among them for a day or two every week. All looked to her for help and counsel; and she seldom failed or disappointed any one. Whatever sad thoughts of the present or misgivings for the future she might have, she kept them, during her visits at home, quite to herself. So they who needed it so much enjoyed the good of her cheerfulness, and she suffered the doubts and suspense and painful anxiety of an elder sister in silence.

The winter passed slowly and sadly away to the two invalids, in spite of the hopes that spring might do for them what those long winter months failed to do. March came and passed, and April brought new cares and duties. The coming of the young lambs first, and afterwards the care of the calves and the dairy, gave Annie and Sarah full employment for a time. Annie's cheeks, that had grown thin and pale during the winter's confinement, began to get back their bright colour again.

From this time the care of her father devolved almost entirely on Christie. Her aunt was, in one respect, better than she used to be. She rarely suffered such intense pain as during the first part of the winter; but every day was making it more apparent that she could never hope to have full use of her limbs again. To an affliction like this, Aunt Elsie could not look forward submissively. She came at last to acknowledge, in words, that her trouble was sent by God, and that she ought to submit, believing that out of the present trial He could bring blessing. But in her heart she murmured bitterly. She could not bear to think that her helplessness added greatly to the burden of care that their father's illness had brought on these young girls. Yet her murmuring and repining spirit added to their troubles more than her helplessness did. Those days were very dreary to Aunt Elsie.

And on none of the family did the burden of her great unhappiness rest so heavily as upon Christie.

Not that she had very much to do for her. After she was dressed by Annie and settled in her low chair for the day, she asked and needed little further care. Indeed, in the first misery of her helplessness she rather shrank from all assistance that was not absolutely indispensable, and almost resented all attempts to add to her comfort or relieve her pain. Christie was never quite sure that her aunt was satisfied with anything that was done for her. She never complained; but her acceptance of service seemed always under protest, as though she would fain have refused it if she had had the power. Her very sympathy with the child in her weariness was so expressed as to seem like a reproach.

In her attendance upon her father it was very different. All that was done for him was right; and his gentle thanks for her constant ministrations made the service sweet to his weary little daughter. No doubt he passed many a sorrowful day during that long and painful winter; but he suffered no murmur of his to add to the distress of those dear to him. In the silence of many a long and wakeful night, he could not but look in the face the possibility that his children might be left orphans, and the thought could not be otherwise than one of great pain. But he suffered no expression of doubt or fear to discourage them. He wished to live for their sakes; and for a long time he believed that he should live. But the hope passed away with the winter. As the days began to grow long, and the time approached when his children hoped he would be well again, the conviction gradually dawned upon him that the summer air would bring no healing. He felt that he had taken his last look of the snows of winter, that the willow buds and the pale spring blossoms that his little ones brought to him so lovingly were the last he should ever see. For himself it would be well; but for his children—— ! None but He who knoweth all things knew the pang that rent his heart at the thought of them! Orphans and strangers in a strange land, what was to become of his young daughters? Some of those bright May days were dark enough, as he groped amid the gloom of his great fear for them.

But the faith of the Christian triumphed. Before the time came to speak the words which were to chase all hope from their hearts, he could speak them calmly and even hopefully. The voice that never speaks in vain had said to the ear of faith, ' Leave thy fatherless children with *Me* ; ' and he was thenceforth at peace. He sometimes sighed when he noticed the look of care that could not always be chased from the brow of his elder girls ; but almost always he was at peace about them and their future.

As for them, they were altogether hopeful. They never saw the cloud that was growing darker and drawing nearer during those bright spring days. In after days, they wondered at their strange unconcern, and said to one another, ' How could we have been so blind?' They were grave and anxious many a time, but never with the fear of death. They held long consultations together when Effie was at home ; but it was always how they might arrange their affairs so that they need not vex nor annoy their father while he was not strong. They did not apprehend how near was the time when no earthly care should have power to vex him. Even Effie, more thoughtful and anxious than the rest, cheated herself with the hope that time alone was needed to restore him. Whatever Aunt Elsie saw in her brother's changing face, she said nothing of her fears till the time for self-deception was past with them all.

When the time of his departure drew very near, they even thought him better, because he suffered less, and because a far greater part of his time was spent in his arm-chair, or in moving about the room. More than once, too, he was able, by the help of his staff and of a daughter's willing arm, to go into the garden, or to the turf seat at the end of the house; and his enjoyment of the pleasant spring air and the pleasant spring sights and sounds beguiled them into the belief that he was becoming himself again. But, alas! it was not so. When the suffering passed away, there came in its place a feeling of restlessness that could not be controlled. There was rest for him nowhere. He grew weary of the bed, weary of the arm-chair, weary of his aimless wanderings up and down. At such times, Christie's voice, singing or reading, had, now and then, a power to soothe, sometimes to quiet, sometimes even to put him to sleep. And, indeed, she grew very skilful in her efforts to soothe and amuse him; and at any hour of the night or day a movement of his would bring her to his side. A softly-spoken word, or the loving touch of his hand upon her head, was enough to make her forget all her weakness and weariness; and during her whole life, or, at least, since her mother's death, Christie had passed no happier days than in that last month of her father's life.

'Your voice is like your mother's, Christie, my lassie,' he said one night, when all but themselves were sleeping.

Christie gave a quick look into his face. He smiled.

'Yes, and you have reminded me of her in various ways during the last few weeks. I hope you will be as good a woman as your mother was, Christie.'

She was not a demonstrative child, usually; but now she dropped her face upon her father's hand, and he felt the fall of her warm tears. It was gently withdrawn, and laid upon her head, and in words that Christie never forgot, he prayed God to bless her. But even with the joy that thrilled her there came upon her a shudder of awe—a fearful certainty that she was listening to the words of a dying man. For a time she lay quite motionless, and her father slumbered with his hand still upon her head. He breathed quite softly and regularly, and in a little time Christie found courage to raise herself and to look into his face. There was no change on it, such as she had heard comes always to the face of the dying, and gradually the quick beating of her heart ceased. As she stood gazing, he opened his eyes and met her look.

'You are weary and wan, poor child,' he said. 'You should have let Annie or Sarah be with me to-night. Lie down and rest.'

'Are you worse, father? Would you like to have me call Annie or Sarah?'

He looked surprised.

'No; I am very comfortable. I think I shall sleep. Lie down and rest, my poor, weary lamb.'

She moved the light so that his face might be in the shadow, and then laid herself down on the low bed near him. She did not mean to sleep; she thought she could not, but weariness overcame her, and she did not waken till Annie lifted the window-curtain and let the light stream in on her face. She woke with a start and a cry; but a glance at her sister's serene face reassured her.

'You frightened little creature! What makes you jump out of your sleep in that way? I doubt if you have slept much, and yet father says he has had a good night.'

'Oh, yes, I have,' said she, with a sigh of relief. 'I think I have been dreaming.'

Looking into her father's face for confirmation of Annie's assurance that he was better, he met her look with a smile which quite banished her fears, saying he was very comfortable and had slept well. Once or twice during the day her fears came back; but she strove to chase them away, calling herself foolish and unthankful. And she could easily do so; for he did seem really better. He conversed more than usual with Aunt Elsie—though Christie did not understand all they said. She only knew that they spoke earnestly, and that her father spoke cheerfully. Aunt Elsie looked grave and doubtful enough. 'But she always does,' thought Christie. 'I can judge nothing by that.'

He went farther down the garden-walk than he had ever gone yet; and he looked so cheerful, sitting in the sunshine, that Christie smiled at her unreasonable fears. Alas! that day was to be ever memorable to the Redfern children, as the last on which the sunshine ever rested on their father's face. He never trod the garden path again.

That night Effie came home, and did not go away again till all was over. Christie never knew very well how those days passed. She remembered running down the lane to meet her sister in the twilight, and the irresistible impulse that came over her to tell of the

F

terrible fear that had come upon her as she sat that night with her father's hand on her head. She called herself foolish and weak, and hastened to tell her sister how much better he had been through the day, how he had walked down the garden and enjoyed the sunshine, and how easy and peaceful he had been since then. But the shadow that had fallen on Effie's face at her first words did not pass away as she continued to speak; and it was with eyes opened to see 'the beginning of the end' that she came into her father's chamber.

She did not leave him again. Christie slept on the couch near him; but all night long Effie sat with her eyes fixed on her father's changing face. He did not bid her lie down, as he was wont to do. He always smiled when he met her look, and once he said, 'I have much to say to you, Effie;' but, while she listened for more, he slumbered again. And so the night passed.

The light of the morning made the change more visible. Sarah saw it when she came in. They did not need to tell each other what they feared. When Christie awoke, it was to see the anxious faces of the three sisters bending over their father. She rose mechanically, and stood beside them.

'Is he worse?' she asked. 'He seems sleeping quietly.'

She did not need to say more.

'Annie,' said Effie, in a little time, beckoning her sister away from the bed, 'Aunt Elsie must have her breakfast before she is told this; and the bairns—' Effie's voice failed her for a moment. 'We must try and keep them quiet.'

Annie said something in a low voice about the doctor; Effie shook her head.

'It's of no use,' said Effie. 'Still, we might send. I'll tell James.' And she went out.

A little after daybreak he seemed to rouse himself for a moment; but he soon slumbered again. By and by their neighbours, who had heard from the messenger sent for the doctor that Mr. Redfern was worse, came dropping in. They looked in for a moment upon the group of girls gathered round their father's bed, and then, for the most part, seated themselves in the outer room with Aunt Elsie. Mrs. Nesbitt and her son John lingered in the room, and whispered together. In a little while the mother beckoned to Effie.

'My poor bairn,' she said, 'if you have anything to say to your father, or anything to ask of him, it had better be now.'

Effie gave a quick, startled look.

'Now?' she said. 'So soon?'

'Effie, my bairn, for the sake of the rest,' whispered her friend.

In a minute or two she was able to take her old place by the pillow. As she bent over her father, the doctor came in. He stood for a moment looking down on him.

'Speak to him,' he said.

'Father,' said Effie, stooping, with her face close to his. 'Father.'

He stirred a little at the sound of her voice, and his fingers wandered aimlessly over the coverlet.

'Is it morning?' he asked.

'Father,' repeated Effie, 'Dr. Grey is here.'

He opened his eyes at that, and met the look of the doctor fixed on him.

'Oh, is the end come?' he asked. 'I didna think it

would be so soon. Did I hear Effie's voice? I have so much to say to her! My poor bairns!'

Effie bent her face again close to his. Her voice was low, but firm and clear.

'Father, don't let any thought of us disturb you now. God is good. I am not afraid.'

'And your aunt, she has suffered much, sacrificed much for us. Consider her first in all things. Be guided by her.'

'Yes, father.'

'There are other things. I didna think this was to be so soon; and now it is too late. But you have some kind friends. Did I hear John Nesbitt's voice?'

'Yes, father; he is here.' And she beckoned to John to come nearer. But he seemed to have forgotten him. John stooped towards him, and said, in a low voice:

'Is there anything I can say that would make it easier for you to leave them?'

The eyes of the dying man turned towards him, slowly.

'John, you are a good man, and true. They will be very solitary. You will be their friend?'

'Always. So help me God!'

The words were spoken like the words of a vow.

The dying man's mind seemed to wander a little after that; for he asked again if it was morning, and what was to be done in the field to-day. But Effie's pale face bending over him seemed to recall all.

'Effie,' he said, 'I leave them all with you—just as I would have left them with your mother. Be to them what she would have been to you all. You will aye be mindful of the little ones, Effie?'

'Father, with God's help, I will,' she answered, firmly.

'Poor little ones! Poor wee Christie!' he murmured.

They brought them to him, guiding his hand till it rested on each head, one after the other.

'Fear God, and love one another.' It was all he had strength to say, now. John Nesbitt read from the Bible a verse or two now and then, speaking slowly, that the dying man might hear. Then an old man, one of the elders of the kirk, prayed by the bedside. The uneasy movement of his head upon the pillow, and the aimless efforts of his hands to grasp something, were the only signs of suffering that he gave; and when Effie took his hand in hers, these ceased.

'If Christie would sing, I think I could sleep' he said. 'Her voice is like her mother's.'

Effie beckoned to her sister.

'Try, Christie; try,' she said.

But Christie's lips could utter no sound. John Nesbitt began, The Lord's my Shepherd;' and in a little time several trembling voices joined. When they came to the verse:

> 'Yea, though I walk through Death's dark vale,
>   Yet will I fear no ill ;
> For Thou art with me, and Thy rod
>   And staff me comfort still,'—

they rose full, clear, and triumphant. They were the last sounds he heard on earth. When they ended, Mrs. Nesbitt's hand was gently laid on their father's eyelids, and at the sight of that the children knew they were orphans.

CHAPTER V.

CLOUDS AND SUNSHINE.

WHEN a great sorrow has just fallen upon us, we find it impossible to feel that all things about us are not changed. We cannot imagine ourselves falling into the old daily routine again. The death of one dear to us gives us a shock which seems to unsettle the very foundation of things. A sense of insecurity and unreality pervades all that concerns us. We shrink from the thought that the old pleasures will charm us again, that daily cares will occupy our minds to the exclusion of to-day's sadness, that time will heal the wounds that smart so bitterly now.

But it does; and as it passes, we find ourselves going the old rounds, enjoying the old pleasures, doing the duties which the day brings; and the great healer does his kindly office, to the soothing of our pain. It is not that our bereavement is no longer felt, or that we have forgotten the friend we loved. But the human heart is a harp with many strings. Though one be broken, there are others which answer to the touch of the wandering breezes; and though the music may be marred in some of its measures, it is still sweet.

The young cannot long sit under the shadow of a great sorrow, if there be any chance rays of sunshine gleaming. Besides, the poor have no time to sit down and nurse their grief. When little more than a week had passed after Mr. Redfern's death, Effie was obliged to return to the ruling and guiding of her noisy little kingdom. She went sadly enough; and many an anxious thought went back to the household at home. But she could not choose but go. They had agreed among themselves that there should be no change till after the harvest should be gathered in, and in the meantime, all the help that she could give was needed. Her monthly wages were growing doubly precious in her estimation. They were the chief dependence at home.

The sowing and planting had been on a limited scale this spring, and all outdoor matters, except what pertained to the dairy, could very well be attended to by James Cairns, their hired man, who was strong and willing. So Annie and Sarah were in the house, and the little ones went to school as soon as the summer weather came.

As for Christie, little was expected from her besides attending to Aunt Elsie, and reading to her now and then. These were easy enough duties, one would think, considering how little attention Aunt Elsie was willing to accept from any one. But light as they were, Christie could not hide, and did not always *try* to hide, the truth that they were irksome to her.

Poor little Christie! How miserable she was, often! How mortified and ashamed of herself! This was all so different from what she had meant to be when Effie went away—a help and a comfort to all. There were times when she strove bravely with herself: she strove to be less peevish, and to join the rest in their efforts to be useful and cheerful; but she almost always failed, and every new failure left her less able and less willing to try again.

But Christie was not so much to blame for these shortcomings as she had sometimes been. The great reaction from the efforts and anxieties before her father's death, as well as the shock of that event, left her neither strength nor power to exert herself or to interest herself in what was passing. Her sisters meant kindly in claiming no help about the household work from her, but they made a mistake in so doing. Active work, that would have really tired her, and left her no time for melancholy musings, would have been far better for her. As it was, she could apply herself to no employment, not even her favourite reading. Her time, when not immediately under her aunt's eye, was passed in listless wanderings to and fro, or in sitting with folded hands, thinking thoughts that were unprofitable always, and sometimes wrong. Fits of silence alternated with sudden and violent bursts of weeping, which her sisters could neither soothe nor understand. Indeed, she did not understand them herself. She struggled with them, ashamed of her folly and weakness; but she grew no better, but rather worse.

She might well rejoice when, at the end of a fortnight, Effie came home. The wise and loving elder sister was not long in discovering that the peevishness and listlessness of her young sister sprang from a cause beyond her control. She was ill from over-exertion, and nervous from over-excitement and grief. Nothing

could be worse for her than this confinement to Aunt
Elsie's sick-room, added to the querulousness of Aunt
Elsie herself.

'You should let Christie help with the milking, as
she used to do,' she said to Sarah. 'It would be far
better for her than sitting so much in Aunt Elsie's
room. She seems ill and out of sorts.'

'Yes, she's out of sorts,' said Sarah, with less of
sympathy in her tone than Effie had shown. 'There's
no telling what to do with her sometimes. She can
scarcely bear a word, but bursts out crying if the least
thing is said to her. I dare say she is not very well,
poor child!'

'She seems far from well, indeed,' said Effie, gravely.
'And I'm sure you, or I either, would find our spirits
sink if we were to spend day after day in Aunt Elsie's
room. You don't know what it is till you try it.'

Sarah shrugged her shoulders

'I dare say we should. But Christie doesna seem
to mind much what Aunt Elsie says. I'm sure I
thought she liked better to be there than to be working
hard in the kitchen or dairy.'

'She may like it better, but it's no' so good for
her, for all that. You should send her out, and try
and cheer her up, poor lassie! She's no' so strong
as the rest of us; and she suffers much from the
shock.'

That night, when the time for bringing home the
cows came, Effie took her sun-bonnet from the nail,
saying carelessly:

'I'm going to the pasture. Are you coming, Christie?'

'For the cows?' said Christie, tartly. 'The bairns
go for them.'

'Oh, but I'm going for the pleasure of the walk. We'll go through the wheat, and down by the brook. Come.'

Christie would far rather have stayed quietly at home, but she did not like to refuse Effie; and so she went, and was better for it. At first Effie spoke of various things which interested them as a family; and Christie found herself listening with pleasure to all her plans. At the side of the brook, where they sat down for a while, as they usually did, they spoke of their father and mother; and though Christie wept, it was not that nervous weeping which sometimes so exhausted her. She wept gently; and when Effie spoke of the love that should bind them all closely together, now that they were orphans, she prayed inwardly that God would make her more patient and loving than she had lately been. Her heart was lighter than it had been for days, when they rose to go.

They went to the kirk together the next day too. They did not walk; so there was no lingering in the kirk-yard or at the half-mile corner. But the day was fine and the air pleasant; and the motion of the great wagon in which they drove, though not very easy, was agreeable for a change, and Christie enjoyed it all. I am afraid she did not enjoy the sermon better than usual. She had a great many wandering thoughts, and she had to struggle against overpowering drowsiness, which she did not quite succeed in casting off. But she enjoyed the kind greetings and looks of sympathy that awaited them in the kirk-yard, though they brought many tears to Effie's eyes, and sent them gushing over her own pale cheeks. She was glad of old Mrs. Grey's sweet, cheerful words, and of the light

pressure of blind Allie's little hand. She was glad
when she heard Mrs. Nesbitt ask Effie to bring her
sister over to pass a week with her, and more glad still
when Effie made the promise, saying the change would
do her good. Altogether, the day was a pleasant one,
and Christie went home better and more cheerful than
she had been since her father's death.

But before the week was over she had fallen back
into the old way again; and when Effie came home on
Saturday, she found her as wan and listless and peevish
as ever. Something must be done without delay,
thought the elder sister. So, that night, as she sat
with Annie and Sarah in her aunt's room, when all the
little ones had gone to bed, she said:

'Aunt Elsie, I am going to take Christie back with
me, to stay a week with Mrs. Nesbitt.'

Aunt Elsie looked astonished and somewhat displeased.

'Why should you do the like of that?' she asked.

'Oh, just for a change. She's not very well, I think,
and a little change will do her good.'

'Folk canna aye get changes when they would like
them,' said Aunt Elsie, coldly. 'I see nothing more
than usual the matter with her. If she's no' well,
home's the best place for her. I see no cause why
Mrs. Nesbitt should be troubled with the likes of
her.'

'Oh, Mrs. Nesbitt winna think it a trouble. Christie
will be no trouble to her. I know she canna well be
spared. You'll miss her; but she'll be all the better a
nurse when she comes home strong and cheerful.'

'I beg you winna think about me in making your
plans for pleasuring,' said her aunt, in a tone which

always made those who heard it uncomfortable. 'I'll try and do without her services for a while. She thinks much of herself; and so do you, it seems.'

There was an unpleasant pause, during which Effie congratulated herself on the forethought that had sent Christie safely to bed before the matter was discussed. Annie, as she generally did in similar circumstances, started another subject, hoping to avert anything more unpleasant. But Effie wanted the matter decided, and Aunt Elsie had something more to say.

'It's my belief you mean to spoil the lassie, if she's no spoiled already, petting and making a work with her as though she were really ill. Ill! It's little any of you ken what it is to be ill.'

'I don't think she's very ill,' said Effie, gently; 'but she's nervous and weary and out of sorts, and I think maybe a change——'

'Nervous!' repeated Aunt Elsie, contemptuously. 'It was better days when there was less said about nerves than I am in the way of hearing now. Let a bairn be cross, or sulky, and, oh! it's nervous she is, poor thing! Let her have a change. I know not, for my part, what the world is coming to. Nervous, indeed!'

'I didna mean to excuse Christie's peevishness—far from it,' said Effie. 'I know you have not a cheerful companion in her. But I do think she is not well; and as Mrs. Nesbitt asked her, I thought perhaps you wouldna mind letting her go for a while.'

'It matters little what I may think on that or any other subject,' said Aunt Elsie, in a tone which betrayed that anger was giving place to sadness. 'Helpless as I am, and burdensome, I should take what consideration

I can get, and be thankful. I needna expect that *my* wishes will govern any of you.'

This was very unjust, and the best way to make her feel that it was so was to keep silence ; and not a word was said in reply. In a little time she said, again—

'I dinna see how you can think of taking the child away anywhere, and a printed calico all that she has in the way of mourning, and her father not buried a month yet.'

'It would matter very little at Mrs. Nesbitt's,' said Effie, congratulating herself on her aunt's softening tone, but not seeming to notice it.

'Times are sorely changed with us, when the price of a gown more or less is felt as it is,' said Aunt Elsie, with a sigh. 'I have seen the day—' And she wandered off to other matters. Effie chose to consider the affair of Christie's going settled. And so it was. No further objection was made ; and they went together the next afternoon.

If Effie could have chosen among all the pleasant homes of Glengarry, she could have found no better place for her young sister than Mrs. Nesbitt's. It was quiet and cheerful at the same time. Christie could pursue her own occupations, and go her own way, no one interfering with her, so long as her way was the right way and her occupation such as would do her no injury. But there were no listless wanderings to and fro, no idle musings, permitted here. No foolish reading was possible. If a shadow began to gather on the child's brow, her attention was claimed immediately, either by Jean, the merry maid-of-all-work, or by Mrs. Nesbitt herself. There were chickens to feed, or vegetables to be gathered, or the lambs were to be counted.

or some other good reason was found why she should betake herself to the fresh air and the pleasant fields or the garden.

The evenings were always bright. There was no danger of being dull where Mrs. Nesbitt's merry boys were. Her family consisted of four sons. John, the eldest, was just twenty-three—though, for some reason or other, the young Redferns were in the habit of thinking him quite a middle-aged man. Perhaps it was because he was usually so grave and quiet; perhaps because of a rumour they had heard that John meant, some day, to be a minister. He taught a Sabbath-class too, and took part in meetings, like a much older man than he was.

The other lads were considerably younger. Lewis, the second son, was not yet eighteen; Charles was twelve, and little Dan not more than nine. They were neither grave nor quiet. The house was transformed into a very different place when they crossed the threshold from the field or the school. In a fashion of her own, Christie enjoyed their fun and frolic very much. She told Effie, when she came to see her, that she had heard more laughter that week than she had heard in Canada in all her life before. As for them, they wondered a little at her shyness and her quiet ways; but they were tolerant, for boys, of her fancies and failings, and beguiled her into sharing many a ramble and frolic with them.

Once she went to her sister's school, which was three miles from the Nesbitt farm, and once she spent a day with Mrs. Nesbitt at old Mrs. Grey's, and they brought little Allie home with them. The little blind girl was a constant wonder and delight. She was as cheerful and happy as were any of the merry Nesbitt boys; and if there was less noise among them when she was one of the circle, there was no less mirth. To say that she was patient under her affliction would not be saying enough; she did not seem to feel her blindness as an affliction, so readily and sweetly did she accept the means of happiness yet within her reach. To Christie, the gentle, merry little creature was a constant rebuke, and all the more that she knew the little one was unconscious of the lesson she was teaching.

There was no service in the kirk the next Sabbath, so, instead of going home as usual, Effie, for Christie's sake, accepted Mrs. Nesbitt's invitation to spend it at her house. She saw with delight the returning colour on her little sister's cheek, and noticed the change for the better that had taken place in her health and spirits, and inwardly she rejoiced over the success of her plan. 'She shall have another week at this pleasant place, if possible—and more than that.' And she sighed to think how much the poor girl might have to try both health and spirits when these pleasant weeks should be passed. But she did not let Christie hear her sigh. She had only smiles and happy words for her.

It was a very pleasant Sabbath for Christie—the very pleasantest she could remember to have passed. She could not agree with Charlie Nesbitt that it was 'a little too long.' She enjoyed every moment of it. She enjoyed the early walk, the reading, the singing, and the walk to John Nesbitt's Sabbath-class in the afternoon. It was rather far—three miles, nearly—and the walk tired her a little. But all the more for that did she enjoy her rest on the low sofa after tea.

It was a very pleasant place, that parlour of Mrs.

Nesbitt's—so neat, so cool, so quiet. There was not much to distinguish it from other parlours in Laidlaw; and, in general, they were prim and plain enough. There was a small figured carpet, crimson and black, upon the floor. It did not quite reach the wall on one side, for Mrs. Nesbitt's Scottish parlour had been smaller than this one; and the deficiency was supplied by a breadth of drugget, of a different shade of colour, which might have marred the effect somewhat to one more fastidious than Christie. For the rest, the chairs were of some common wood and painted brown, the sofa was covered with chintz to match the window-curtains, and there was a pale blue paper on the walls. For ornaments, there were two or three pictures on the walls, and on the mantel-piece a great many curious shells and a quaint old vase or two. There was a book-case of some dark wood in the corner, which was well filled with books, whose bindings were plain and dark, not to say dingy. There were few of Christie's favourites among them; so that the charm of the room did not lie there. There was another small cabinet, with a glass door—a perfect treasury of beautiful things, in Christie's estimation, old china and glass, and an old-fashioned piece or two of plate; but the key was safely kept in Mrs. Nesbitt's pocket.

Perhaps it was the charm of association that made the place so pleasant to Christie. Here, every day, she had been made to rest on the chintz sofa, and every day she had wakened to find a kind face beaming upon her and to hear a kind voice calling her by name. I think almost any place would have been pleasant with Mrs. Nesbitt going about so gently and lovingly in it. Some thought of this came into Christie's mind, as she lay musing there that Sabbath afternoon. The fading light fell on the soft gray hair that showed beneath the widow's snowy cap, and on the placid face beneath, with a strangely beautifying power. The sweet gravity that was on her silent lips was better worth seeing, Christie thought, than other people's smiles. Her eyes had no beauty, in the common acceptation of the term. They seemed like eyes that had been washed with many tears. But the sadness which must have looked from them once had given place to patience and gentle kindness now.

'How nice and quiet it is here!' whispered Christie to her sister, who sat beside her, leaning her head upon her hand.

Effie quite started, as she spoke.

'Yes; it is a very peaceful place. I get rid of all vexing thoughts when I come in here.' And she turned her eyes to Mrs. Nesbitt's placid face.

'Vexing thoughts!' repeated Christie. 'I dare say Effie has many a one.' And she sighed too; but almost before she had time to ask herself what Effie's vexing thoughts might be, she was asleep. A voice, not Effie's nor Mrs. Nesbitt's, soon awoke her. The twilight had deepened, and up and down the darkening room John Nesbitt was walking, with a step quicker than was usual. Christie fancied there was something like impatience in his step. He soon came and leaned on the window, close to the place where Effie sat, and Christie heard him say, in a voice which was not quite steady :

'Is it all over, then, Effie?'

Effie made a sudden movement of some kind, Christie could not tell what, and after a moment she said :

'It would be better for you, John.'

He did not wait to hear more. Soon, however, he came back again.

'And will it be better for you, Effie?' he asked, gravely and gently, yet with strong feeling.

'I must think of many a one before myself in this matter,' she said; and soon after added, 'Don't make this trouble harder to bear, John.'

There was a long silence; but John did not resume his walk, and by and by Effie spoke again.

'Do you never think of your old wish to finish your studies?'

'My father's death put an end to that,' he answered, sadly.

'I don't know why,' said Effie. 'Of course at the time it must have done so; but you are young, and your brothers are growing up to take your place with your mother and on the farm, and I think it would be like putting your hand to the plough and looking back, to give up all thought of entering the ministry. You have your life before you, John.'

He did not answer.

'If it were for no other reason than that,' continued Effie, 'I could not consent to burden you in the way you propose; and besides—your mother——'

She turned, and caught the astonished eyes of Christie peering out of the darkness, and paused.

'Effie,' said Christie, when they were in their own room, and the candle was out, 'what were you saying to John Nesbitt to-night?'

'Saying?' repeated Effie.

'Yes—in the parlour. Does he want us to come and live here? I thought he did by what he said.'

'Some of us,' said Effie, after a pause. 'John is very kind, and so is his mother. But of course it is not to be thought of.'

'Must we leave the farm, Effie?' asked Christie, anxiously.

'I hardly know; I cannot tell. Aunt Elsie must decide.'

'Is it not ours, Effie? Was my father in debt?'

'Not for the farm; but it was paid for, or partly paid for, with money that belonged to Aunt Elsie. I canna explain it. She sold her annuity, or gave up her income, in some way, when we came here. And in the letter that father wrote, he said that he wished that in some way, as soon as possible, she should get it back.'

'But how?' asked Christie, wondering.

'I hardly know. But you know, Christie, Aunt Elsie is not like other people—mean; it would make her more unhappy to feel that she was dependent than it would make most people. And we must, in some way, manage to do as father wished. If he had lived, it would have been different. She doesna think that I know about it. She didna see father's letter.'

'Then the farm will be Aunt Elsie's?' said Christie.

'Yes; and if we could manage it well, we might live on as we have been living; but I am afraid we canna.'

Christie had her own thoughts about all living on Aunt Elsie's farm; but she said nothing.

'I suppose we shall have to let the farm, or sell it, and get the money invested, in some way, for Aunt Elsie.'

'And what then?' asked Christie, in a suppressed tone.

'I am sure I canna tell,' said Effie; and the tone of her voice betrayed more anxiety than her words did. 'Not that there is any great cause for anxiety,' she added. 'There is always work to do for those who are willing; and we'll try and keep together till the bairns are grown up.'

'Will Aunt Elsie go home to Scotland, do you think, Effie?' asked Christie.

'Oh, no! I don't think she will. She doesna like this country altogether, I know; but now that she has grown so helpless, she will not care to go back. She has no very near friends there now.'

'Do you think Aunt Elsie would take the money if the farm was sold?' asked Christie, again.

'As to that, it has been partly hers all along. When the farm was bought, my father gave Aunt Elsie a mortgage, or something—I don't understand exactly what but it was as a security that her money was to be safe to her. If we had been able to carry on the farm, there would have been little difference; though there are some other debts too.'

'And if we leave the farm, where can we go?' asked Christie.

'I don't know; I lose myself thinking about it. But God will provide. I am not *really* afraid, when I have time to consider. The bairns must be kept together in some way. We must trust till the way is opened before us.'

But there was something very unlike Effie's usual cheerfulness in her way of speaking. Christie could plainly see that. But she mistook the cause.

'Effie,' she said, after a little pause, 'it winna be

very pleasant to think that we are depending on Aunt Elsie. I dinna wonder that you sigh.'

'Whisht, Christie! It's not that, child. I don't think you are quite just to Aunt Elsie. She has done much, and given up much, for us since mother died. Her way is not aye pleasant; but I think she would be easier to deal with as the giver than as the receiver. I mean, I shall be very glad if it can be arranged that she shall have her income again. But we won't speak more of these things to-night, dear. We only vex ourselves; and that can do no good.'

But Effie did not cease to vex herself when she ceased to speak, if Christie might judge from the sighs that frequently escaped her. Just as she was dropping to sleep, her sister's voice aroused her.

'Christie,' she said, 'you are not to say anything to any one about—about John Nesbitt's wanting me to come here. Of course it's impossible; and it mustna be spoken about.'

'I couldna help hearing, Effie.'

'No; I know, dear. But it's not to be spoken about. You must forget it.'

'Did Mrs. Nesbitt want it too?' asked Christie.

'I don't know. Mrs. Nesbitt is very kind; but you mustna say anything to her about this matter—or to any one. Promise me, Christie.'

Christie promised, wondering very much at her sister's eagerness, and thinking all the time that it would be very nice to live with Mrs. Nesbitt and her sons, far pleasanter than to live on the farm, if it was to be Aunt Elsie's. Christie felt very unsubmissive to this part of their trouble. She thought it would be far easier to depend for a home and food and clothes on their kind neighbours, who were friends indeed, than on the unwilling bounty of her aunt. But, as Effie said, Christie by no means did justice to the many good qualities of her aunt, and was far from properly appreciating her self-denying efforts in behalf of them all.

After that night, Effie did not often allude to their future plans when with Christie. It was best not to vex themselves with troubles that might never come, she said. They must wait patiently till the harvest was over, and then all would be settled.

The summer passed on, with little to mark its course. Christie had more to do about the house and in the garden than in the spring, and was better and more contented for it. But she and her sisters sent many an anxious glance forward to the harvest-time.

They did not have to wait so long, however. Before the harvest-time their affairs were settled. An opportunity, which those capable of judging thought very favourable, occurred for selling it; and it was sold. They might have occupied the house for the winter; but this would only have been to delay that which delay would make no easier. It was wiser and better in every way to look out for a home at once.

About six miles from the farm, in the neighbourhood where Effie's school was, there stood on the edge of a partially-cleared field a small log-house, which had been for several months uninhabited. Towards this the eyes of the elder sister had often turned during the last few weeks. Once, on her way home from school, she went into it. She was alone; and though she would have been very unwilling to confess it, the half-hour she passed there was as sorrowful a half-hour

as she had ever passed in her life. For Effie was by
no means so wise and courageous as Christie, in her
sisterly admiration, was inclined to consider her.
Looking on the bare walls and defective floors and
broken windows, her heart failed her at the thought
of ever making that a home for her brother and
sisters.

Behind the house lay a low, rocky field, encumbered
with logs and charred stumps, between which bushes
and a second growth of young trees were springing.
A low, irregular fence of logs and branches, with a
stone foundation, had once separated the field from
the road; but it was mostly broken down now, and
only a few traces of what had been a garden remained.
It was not the main road that passed the house, but
a cross-road running between the main roads; and the
place had a lonely and deserted look, which might well
add to the depression which anxiety and uncertainty
as to their future had brought on Effie. No wonder
that very troubled and sad was the half-hour which
she passed in the dreary place.

'I wish I hadna spoken to Aunt Elsie about this
place,' she said to herself. 'She seemed quite pleased
with the thought of coming here; but we could never
live in this miserable hovel. What could I be thinking
about? How dreary and broken-down it is!'

There were but two rooms and a closet or two on
the ground-floor. Above, there might be another made
—perhaps two; but that part of the house was
quite unfinished, showing the daylight through the
chinks between the logs. Floor there was none.

'It could never be made comfortable, I am afraid,'
she said, as she made her way down the creaking

ladder. 'I could never think of bringing the bairns here.' And it was with a heavy heart that she took her way home.

But her courage rose again. Before many days had passed she had decided to try what could be done with the place. The house, such as it was, with a little square of garden-ground, could be got for a rent merely nominal. It was near her school. She could live at home, and the little ones could go to school with her. Thus they could be kept together, and their education not be neglected. With what she and her sisters could earn they could live comfortably for some years in this quiet place. She could not fulfil her promise to her father to keep the little ones together, elsewhere; for she must not give up her school. Her salary was not large, but it was sure; and here they would be under her own eye. The price of the farm had been well invested in her aunt's name, though Aunt Elsie herself was not yet aware of the fact. Effie was not sure whether she would remain with them or return home. But whatever she did, her income must be quite at her own disposal. The sisters must work for themselves and the little ones. If their aunt stayed with them, well; but they must henceforth depend on their own exertions.

When Effie had once decided that the little log-house on the cross-road was thenceforward to be their home, her naturally happy temper, and her earnest desire to make the best of all things for the sake of the others, made it easy for her to look for hopeful signs for the future, and to make light of difficulties which she could not fail to see. Under her direction, and by her assistance, the little log-house' underwent an entire transformation before six weeks were over. Nothing was done by other hands which her own or Sarah's and Annie's could do. The carpenters laid new floors and mended broken windows; the plasterers filled the chinks and covered the walls of what was to be their chamber; but the girls themselves scrubbed and white-washed, papered and painted, cleaned away rubbish from without and from within, and settled their various affairs with an energy and good-will which left them neither time nor inclination for repining. In a little while it would have been impossible to recognize in the bright and cheerful little cottage the dismal place in which, at her first visit, Effie had shed some very bitter tears.

Aunt Elsie did not leave them. She quite resented the idea of such a thing being possible. She had little faith in the likelihood of the children being kept together and clothed and fed by the unassisted efforts of the sisters, and assumed the direction of affairs in the new home, as she had always done in the old. Effie's words with regard to her proved true. She was far easier to do with when she found herself in a position to give rather than to receive assistance. Her income was not large. Indeed, it was so small that those who have never been driven to bitter straits might smile at her idea of a competence. It would have barely kept her from want, in any circumstances; but joined to Effie's earnings it gave promise of many comforts in their humble home. So ample did their means seem to them at first, that they would fain have persuaded each other that there need be no separation—that all might linger under the shelter of the lowly roof. But it could not be. Annie and Sarah both refused to eat bread of

their sister's winning, when there was not work enough
to occupy them at home; and before they had been
settled many weeks, they began to think of looking for
situations elsewhere.

At first they both proposed to leave; but this Effie
could not be prevailed upon to consider right. Helpless as Aunt Elsie was and seemed likely to continue,
there was far more to do in their little household,
limited as their means were, than it was possible for
Christie to do well. The winter was coming, already
the mornings were growing short. She herself could
do little at home without neglecting her school; and
her school must not be neglected. And besides, though
Effie did not say much about it, she felt that almost any
other discipline would be better for her nervous, excitable sister, than that she would be likely to experience
with none to stand between her and the peculiar rigour
of Aunt Elsie's system of training. So she would not
hear of both Annie and Sarah leaving them. Indeed,
she constantly entreated, whenever the matter was discussed, that neither of them should go till winter was
over. There was no fear but that the way would be
opened before them. In the meantime, they might wait
patiently at home.

And the way was opened far sooner than they had
hoped or than Effie desired. A lady who had been
passing the summer in the neighbourhood had been
requested by a friend in town to secure for her the
services of a young woman as nurse. Good health and
a cheerful temper, with respectability of character, were
all that was required. Then Annie and Sarah began
seriously to discuss which of them should go and which
should stay at home. Strange to say, Aunt Elsie was

the only one of them all who shrank from the idea of
the girls 'going to service' or 'taking a place.' It
was a very hard thing for her brother's daughters, she
said, who had been brought up with expectations and
prospects so different. She would far rather that Sarah
who was skilful with the needle, and had a decidea
taste for millinery and dressmaking, should have offered
herself to the dressmaker of the neighbouring village,
or even have gone to the city to look for such a situation there. But this plan was too indefinite to suit
the girls. Besides, there was no prospect of present
remuneration should it succeed. So the situation of
nurse was applied for and obtained by Annie. Sarah's
needle could be kept busy at home, and perhaps she
could earn a little besides by making caps and bonnets
for their neighbours. While they awaited the lady's
final answer, the preparations for Annie's departure
went busily on.

The answer came, and with it a request that another
nurse might be engaged. A smaller girl would do.
She would be expected to amuse, and perhaps teach
reading to two little girls. If such a one could be
found, permission was given to Annie to delay her
departure from home for a week, till they should come
together.

There was a dead silence when the letter was read.
Annie and Sarah looked at each other, and then at
Effie. Christie, through all the reading, had never
taken her eyes from her elder sister's face. But Effie
looked at no one. The same thought had come into
the minds of all; and Effie feared to have the thought
put into words. But Aunt Elsie had no such fear, it
seemed; for after examining the letter, she said, in a

voice that did not betray very much interest in the subject:

'How would you like to go, Christie?'

Christie said nothing, but still looked at Effie.

'What do you think, Effie?' continued her aunt.

'Oh, it's of no use to think about it at all! There's no need of Christie's going. She is not strong enough. She is but a child.'

Effie spoke hastily, as though she wished the subject dropped. But Aunt Elsie did not seem inclined to drop it.

'Well, it's but a little girl that is wanted,' she said. 'And as for her not being strong enough, I am sure there canna be any great strength required to amuse two or three bairns. I dare say it might be the very place for her.'

'Yes; I dare say, if it was needful for Christie to go. There will be many glad to get the place. You must speak to the Cairns' girls, Annie.'

'Would you like to go, Christie?' asked her aunt, with a pertinacity which seemed, to Effie at least, uncalled for.

But Christie made no answer, and looked still at Effie.

'There is no use in discussing the question,' said Effie, more hastily than she meant to speak. 'Christie is far better off at home. There is no need of her going. Don't speak of it, Aunt Elsie.'

Now Aunt Elsie did not like to have any one differ from her—'to be dictated to,' as she called it. Effie very rarely expressed a different opinion from Aunt Elsie. But her usual forbearance made her doing so on the present occasion the more disagreeable to her aunt; and she did not fail to take her to task severely for what she called her disrespect.

'I didna mean to say anything disrespectful, Aunt Elsie,' said she, soothingly, and earnestly hoping that the cause of her reproof might be discussed no further. But she was disappointed.

'Wherefore should I no' speak about this thing for Christie? If it's no disgrace for Annie to go to service, I see no season why it should not be spoken of for Christie.'

'Disgrace, aunt!' repeated Effie. 'What an idea! Of course it is nothing of the sort. But why should we speak of Christie's going when there is no need?'

'For that matter, you may say there is no need for Annie's going. They both need food and clothes as well as the rest.'

Effie took refuge in silence. In a little while her aunt went on:

'And as for her being a child, how much younger, pray, is she than Annie? Not above two years, at most. And as for health, she's well enough, for all that I can see. She's not very strong, and she wouldna have hard work; and the change might do her good. You spoil her by making a baby of her. I see no reason why the bread of dependence should be sweeter to her than to the rest.'

'It would be bitter enough, eaten at your expense,' were the words that rose to Christie's lips in reply. Effie must have seen them there, for she gave her no time to utter them, but hastily—almost sharply—bade her run and see what had become of the girls and little Willie. Christie rose without speaking, and went out.

Aunt,' said Effie, quietly, when she was gone, 'I

don't think it is quite kind in you to speak in that way to Christie about dependence. She is no more dependent than the rest of the children. Of course, when she's older and stronger she'll do her part. But she is very sensitive; and she must not be made unhappy by any foolish talk about her being a burden.'

Effie meant to soothe her aunt; but she failed, for she was really angry now, and she said a great many words in her anger that I shall not write—words that Effie always tried to forget. But the result of it all was that Annie's departure was delayed for a week, till Christie should be ready to go with her.

But I should be wrong in saying that this decision was the result of this discussion alone. There were other things that helped Effie to prevail upon herself to let her go. It would be better and pleasanter for Annie to have her sister near her; and Christie was very desirous to go. And, after all, the change might be good for her, as Aunt Elsie said. It might improve her health, and it might make her more firm and self-reliant. Going away among strangers could hardly be worse for her than a winter under the discipline of her aunt. Partly on account of these considerations, and partly because of Christie's importunities, Effie was induced to consent to her going away; but it was with the express understanding that her absence was to be brief.

As the time of their departure drew near, she did not grow more reconciled to the thought of her sister's going. She felt that she had been over-persuaded; and in her heart there was a doubt as to whether she had done quite right in consenting.

The last night, when all the others had gone to bed,

and Effie was doing some household work below, Christie slipped down-stairs again.

'Effie,' she said, eagerly, 'do not take my going away so much to heart. I am sure it is for the best, and I shall grieve if you grieve. Do think that it's right.'

'You foolish lassie! Did you come down-stairs with bare feet to tell me that? How cold your hands are! Come and sit down by the fire. I want to speak to you.'

Christie sat down, as she was bidden, but it was a long time before Effie spoke—so long that Christie said at last:

'What is it, Effie?'

Her sister started. 'I have nothing to say but what I have said before, Christie. You are not to stay if you don't like. You are not to let any thought of any one or anything at home keep you, unless you are quite content and quite strong and well. And, at any rate, you are to come home in the spring.'

Effie had said all this before; and Christie could only repeat her promise.

'I am afraid you think I am wrong to go away, Effie?'

'No, dear; I don't think you are wrong. I am sure your motives are good. I wish you were not going; but there is no use in saying so now. I hope it will turn out for the best to you and to us all. I will try and not be anxious about you. God will keep you safe, I do not doubt.'

'Effie,' said Christie, 'do you remember what you said to me once about God's hearing prayer, and how He always hears the prayers of His people in the best way, though not always in the way they wish and expect?'

'Yes, I mind something about it. And how all things work together for good to His people and for His glory at the same time. Yes, I mind.'

'Well,' said Christie, softly, 'if folk really believe this, it will be easy for them to leave their friends in God's hands. They can ask Him for what they need, being sure that they will get what is best for them, and that He canna make a mistake.'

There was a few minutes' silence; and then Effie said:

'Christie, if I were sure that you are one of God's people—one of the little lambs of His flock—I would not fear to let you go. Do you think you are?'

'I don't know, Effie. I am afraid not. I am not like what the Bible says God's people ought to be. But I am sure I wish to be.'

'Christie,' said her sister, earnestly, 'you must never let anything hinder you from reading your Bible every day. You must not rest till you are sure about yourself.'

'Effie,' she said, in a low voice, and very seriously, 'I think God did once hear a prayer of mine. It was a good while ago—before father died. It was one of my bad days; I was worse than usual; and when I came back from the pasture I sat down by the brook— under the birch-tree, you mind—and I went from one thing to another, till I said to myself, "I'll see if there's any good in praying." And so I prayed Aunt Elsie might not scold me when I went home; and she didna. But I didna care for that, because you were at home that night. But I prayed, too, that you might bring me a book. I meant "The Scottish Chiefs," or something; but you brought my Bible. I have thought, sometimes, that was one of the prayers answered in a better way than we ask or expect.'

The last few words were spoken in a very husky voice; and as she ceased, her head was laid on Effie's lap. There were tears in Effie's eyes too—she scarcely knew why. Certainly they were not for sorrow. Gently stroking her sister's drooping head, she said:

'Perhaps it was so, Christie. I believe it was; and you are right. We need not fear for one another. We will trust in Him.'

CHAPTER VI.

So Annie and Christie went away; and the days that followed their departure were long and lonely at the cottage. They had never been long separated, and the absence of two of their number made a great blank in their circle. All missed them, but none so much as Effie; for mingled with regret for their absence was a feeling very like self-reproach that she had permitted Christie to go. It was in vain that she reasoned with herself about this matter, saying it was the child's own wish, and that against her aunt's expressed approbation she could have said nothing to detain her.

She knew that Christie was by no means strong, that she was sensitive (not to say irritable), and she dreaded for her the trials she must endure and the unkindness she might experience among strangers. She was haunted by a vision of her sister's pale face, homesick and miserable, with no one to comfort or sympathize with her; and she waited with inexpressible longing for the first tidings from the wanderers. The thought of her was always present. It came with a pang sometimes when she was busiest. She returned from school night by night with a deeper depression on her spirits, till Aunt Elsie, who had all along resented in secret her evident anxiety, could no longer restrain the expression of her vexation.

'What ails you, Effie?' said she, as the weary girl seated herself, without entering the house. 'You sit down there as if you had the cares and vexations of a generation weighing you down. Have matters gone contrary at the school?'

'No. Oh, no,' said Effie, making an effort to seem cheerful. 'Everything has gone on as usual. I had two new scholars to-day. They'll be coming in, now that the autumn work is mostly over. Have not the bairns come in?'

'I hear their voices in the field beyond,' said her aunt. 'But you havena told me what ails you. Indeed, there's no need. I know very well. It would have been more wise-like to have kept your sisters at home than to fret so unreasonably for them now they are away.'

Effie made no answer.

'What's to happen to them more than to twenty others that have gone from these parts? It's a sad thing, indeed, that your father's daughters should need to go to service, considering all that is past. But it can't be mended now. And one thing is certain: it's no disgrace.'

'No, indeed,' said Effie. 'I don't look on it in that light; but——'

'Yes; I ken what you would say. It's aye Christie you're thinking about. But she'll be none the worse for a little discipline. She would soon have been an utter vexation, if she had been kept at home. You spoiled your sister with your petting and coaxing, till there was no doing with her. I'm sure I dinna see why she's to be pitied more than Annie.'

Effie had no reply to make. If she was foolish and unreasonable in her fears for Christie, her aunt's manner of pointing out her fault was not likely to prove it to her. She did not wish to hear more. Perhaps she was foolish, she thought. Good Mrs. Nesbitt, who was not likely to be unjust to Christie, and who was ready to sympathize with the elder sister in what seemed almost like the breaking-up of the family, said something of the same kind to her once, as they were walking together from the Sabbath-school.

'My dear,' she said, 'you are wrong to vex your-self with such thoughts. Your aunt is partly right. Christie will be none the worse for the discipline she may have to undergo. There are some traits in her character that havena fairly shown themselves yet. She will grow firm and patient and self-reliant, I do not doubt. I only hope she will grow stronger in body too.'

Effie sighed.

'She was never very strong.'

'If she shouldna be well, she must come home; and, Effie, though I would never say to an elder sister that she could be too patient and tender to one of the little ones—and that one sometimes wilful and peevish, and no' very strong—yet Christie may be none the worse, for a wee while, no' to have you between her and all trouble. My dear, I know what you would say. I know you have something like a mother's feeling for the child. But even a mother canna bear every burden or drink every bitter drop for her child. And it is as well she canna do it. If Christie's battle with life and what it brings begins a year or two earlier than you thought necessary, she may be all the better able to conquer. Dinna fear for her. God will have her in His keeping.'

Effie strove to find a voice to reply; but she could only say :

'Perhaps I am foolish. I will try.'

'My dear,' continued her friend, kindly, 'I dinna wonder that you are careful and troubled, and a wee faithless, sometimes. You have passed through much sorrow of late, and your daily labour is of a kind that is trying to both health and spirits. And I doubt not you have troubles that are of a nature not to be spoken of. But take courage. There's nothing can happen to you but what is among the " all things " that are to work together for your good. For I do believe you are among those to whom has been given a right to claim that promise. You are down among the mist now; I am farther up the brae, and get a glimpse, through the cloud, of the sunshine beyond. Dinna fret about Christie, or about other things. I believe you are God-guided; and what more can you desire ? As the day wears on, the clouds may disperse; and even if they shouldna, my bairn, the sun still shines in the lift above them.'

They had reached the cross-road down which Effie was to take her solitary way; for the bairns had gone on before. She stood for a moment trying to make sure of her voice, and while she lingered Mrs. Nesbitt dropped a kiss, as tender as a mother's, on her brow, and said, 'Good-night!' A rush of ready tears was the only answer Effie had for her then. But she was comforted. The tears that spring at kind words or a gentle touch bring healing with them; and when Effie wiped them away at last, it was with a thankful sense of a lightened burden, and she went on her way with the pain that had ached at her heart so many days a little softened.

Yes; Effie had trials that would not bear speaking about, and least of all with John Nesbitt's mother. But they were trials that need not be discussed in my little tale. Indeed, I must not linger longer at the cottage by the wayside. I may not tell of the daily life of its occupants, except that it grew more cheerful as the winter passed away. The monthly letter brought them good tidings from the absent ones; and with duties, some pleasant, some quite otherwise, their days were filled, so that no time was left for repining or for distrustful thoughts.

I must now follow the path taken by Christie's weary little feet. Sometimes the way was dusty and uneven enough, but there were green spots and wayside flowers now and then. There were mists and clouds about her, too, but she got glimpses of sunshine. And by and by she grew content to abide in the shadow, knowing, as it was given her to know, that clouds are sent to cool and shelter and refresh us. Before content, however, there came many less welcome visitors to the heart of the poor child.

Can anything be more bewildering to unaccustomed

eyes than the motley crowd which business or pleasure daily collects at some of our much-frequented railway stations? To the two girls, whose ideas of a crowd were for the most part associated with the quiet, orderly gatherings in the kirk-yard on the Sabbath day, the scene that presented itself to them on reaching Point St. Charles was more than bewildering; it was, for a minute or two, actually alarming. There was something so strange in the quick, indifferent manner of the people who jostled one another on the crowded platform, in the cries of the cabmen and porters, and in the general hurrying to and fro, that even Annie was in some danger of losing her presence of mind; and it was with something like a feeling of danger escaped that they found themselves, at last, safe on their way to the house of Mrs. McIntyre, a connection of some friends of that name at home.

The sun had set long before, and it was quite dark as they passed rapidly through the narrow streets in the lower part of the town. Here and there lights were twinkling, and out from the gathering darkness came a strange, dull sound, the mingling of many voices, the noise of carriage-wheels and the cries of their drivers, and through all the heavy boom of church-bells. How unlike it all was to anything the girls had seen or heard before! And a feeling of wonder, not unmingled with dread, came upon them.

There was no time for their thoughts to grow painful, however, before they found themselves at their journey's end. They were expected by Mrs. McIntyre, and were very kindly received by her. She was a widow, and the keeper of a small shop in a street which looked at the first glimpse dismal enough. It was only a glimpse they had of it, however; for they soon found themselves in a small and neat parlour with their hostess, who kindly strove to make them feel at home. She would not hear of their trying to find out their places that night, but promised to go with them the next day, or as soon as they were rested. Indeed, she wished them to remain a few days with her. But to this Annie would by no means agree. The delay caused by Christie's coming had made her a week later than her appointed time, and she feared greatly lest she should lose her place; so she could not be induced to linger longer. Her place was still secure for her; but a great disappointment awaited Christie. The lady who had desired the service of a young girl to amuse her children had either changed her mind or was not satisfied with Christie's appearance; for after asking her many questions about her long delay, as she called the three days beyond the specified week, she told her she was afraid she could not engage her. She added to the pain of Christie's disappointment by telling her that she did not look either strong enough or cheerful enough to have the care of children; she had better apply for some other situation.

'She's weary with her journey—poor thing!' suggested Mrs. McIntyre, kindly. 'And she's a stranger here, besides—poor child!'

'A stranger!' Yes, Christie had just parted from Annie at the door of a large house in the next street, bravely enough; but it was all the poor girl could do now to restrain an outburst of tears.

'How old are you?' asked the lady, again.

Christie had just courage enough to tell her; but it was Mrs. McIntyre who answered the next question.

'Are your parents living?'

'No—poor thing! She is an orphan. There is a large family of them. She came down with her sister, hoping to get a place. The elder sister is trying to keep the little ones together.'

Christie made a movement as if to silence the speaker. The lady looked at a gentleman who sat at a distant window seeming to read.

'What do you think?' she asked.

He rose, and walked in a leisurely manner down the room, nodding to Mrs. McIntyre as he passed. As he returned, he paused, and said something in an undertone to the lady. Christie caught the words.

'If anything was to happen to her, she would be on your hands. She seems quite without friends.'

Christie was on her feet in a moment. Her chair was pushed back with a motion so sudden that the gentleman turned to look at her. She was anything but pale now. Her cheeks were crimson, and there was a light in her eyes that bade fair to be very soon quenched in tears.

'I am very sorry that I——' She could utter no more. Laying her hand on Mrs. McIntyre's arm, she said, huskily, 'Come.' Her friend rose.

'Perhaps if you were to try her for a month——' she suggested.

But Christie shook her head.

'But where can you go? What can you do?' said Mrs. McIntyre, in a low voice.

Where, indeed? Not to the house she had just seen

Annie enter; she had no claim there. Not home again, that was not to be thought of. She turned a helpless glance to the persons who seemed to hold her destiny in their hands. The lady looked annoyed; the gentleman, who had observed the girl's excitement, asked:

'Were you ever at service before?'

'Oh, no!' said Mrs. McIntyre, intending to serve Christie's cause. 'The family looked forward to something very different; but misfortunes and the death——' She stopped, intending that her pause should be more impressive than words.

Other questions followed—Could she read and write? Could she sew? Had she ever been in the city before? —till Christie's courage quite rose again. It ended in nothing, however, but a promise to let her know in a day or two what was decided.

In the silence that followed the closing of the street-door after them, Christie felt that Mrs. McIntyre was not well pleased with the termination of the interview: and her first words proved it.

'You needna have been so sensitive,' she said. 'It will be a long time before you get a place where everything will be to your mind. You needna expect every lady to speak to you as your own sisters would. I doubt you'll hear no more from these people.'

But she was a good-natured and kind-hearted woman; and a glance at Christie's miserable face stopped her.

'Never mind,' she added; 'there are plenty of folk in the town will be glad to get a well-brought-up girl like you to attend to their children. But you must look cheerful, and no' take umbrage at trifles.'

Christie could not answer her. So she walked along by her side, struggling, with a power which she felt was giving way rapidly, with the sobs that were scarcely suppressed. She struggled no longer than till she reached the little chamber where she and Annie had passed the night. The hours that she was suffered to remain there alone were passed in such an agony of grief and home-sickness as the poor child never suffered from before. She quite exhausted herself at last; and when Mrs. McIntyre came to call her to dinner, she found her in a troubled sleep.

'Poor child!' she said, as she stood looking at her, 'I fear we must send her home again. She is not like to do or to get much good here.'

But she darkened the room, and closed the door softly, and left her. When Christie awoke the afternoon was nearly gone. Her first feeling was one of utter wretchedness; but her sleep had rested and refreshed her, and her courage revived after she had risen and washed her face and put her dress in order. When she was ready to go down, she paused for a moment, her hand resting on the knob of the door.

'I might try it,' she murmured; and she fell on her knees by the bedside. It was only a word or two she uttered:

'O God, give me courage and patience, and help me to do right.'

Her tears fell fast for a moment; but her heart was lightened, and it was with a comparatively cheerful face that she presented herself in the little back parlour, where she found Mrs. McIntyre taking tea with a friend.

'Oh, you are up, are you?' she said, kindly. 'You looked so weary, I couldna bear to call you at dinner-time; but I kept your dinner for you. Here, Barbara; bring in the covered dish.' And she placed a seat for the girl between her and her friend.

Christie thanked her, and sat down, with an uncomfortable feeling that the friends had been discussing her before she had come in. And so it soon appeared. The conversation, which her entrance had interrupted, was soon resumed.

'You see, I don't well know what his business is,' said the visitor. 'But, at any rate, he doesn't seem to have much to spend—at least in his family. His wife —poor lady!—has her own troubles. He's seldom at home; and she has been the most of the time, till this illness, without more than one servant. When she's better, I dare say she'll do the same again. In the meantime, I have promised to look for one that might suit. The one she has leaves to morrow. My month's out too, then, and she's to let me go; though how she's to battle through, with that infant and all the other children, is more than I can tell.'

Mrs. McIntyre shook her head.

'She would never do for the place. She doesna look strong; and the house is large, you say?'

'Far larger than they need. I said that to her, one day. But she said something about keeping up a certain appearance. She's not one that a person can speak freely to, unless she likes How old are you, my girl?' she suddenly asked, turning round to Christie.

'I was fourteen in June,' she replied; and turning to Mrs. McIntyre, she asked, 'Is it a place for me?'

Mrs. McIntyre looked doubtful.

'It's a place for some one; but I doubt it's too hard a place for you.'

Christie sent a questioning look to the visitor, who said:

'Well, in some respects it's a hard place. There is plenty to do; but Mrs. Lee is a real gentlewoman, mindful of others, and kind and pleasant-spoken. I should know; for I have sick-nursed her twice, besides being there, now and again, when the children have been ill.'

'But think upon it. The only nurse, where there's an infant and four other children as near each other as they can well be. She's not fit for the like of that,' said Mrs. McIntyre.

'The eldest is but seven,' said Mrs. Greenly. 'But, for that matter, Mrs. Lee is nurse herself; and Nelly, the housemaid, is a kind-hearted girl. She might make a trial of it, anyway.'

'We'll see what your sister says,' said Mrs. McIntyre to Christie. 'She'll be round on the Sabbath. Or maybe you might go there and see her before that time.'

Mrs. Greenly shook her head.

'But I doubt if I can wait for that. I must see the other girl this afternoon; and if she should suit the place there would be no more to be said. What do you think yourself, my girl?'

Christie had been too little accustomed to decide any matter for herself, to wish to decide this without first seeing her sister. So she only asked if Mrs. Greenly passed near the street where Annie lived. Not very near, Mrs. McIntyre said; but that need not interfere. Barbara should go with her there, if Mrs. Greenly would consent to put off seeing the other girl till the next morning. Mrs. McIntyre could not take the responsibility of advising Christie to accept the situation. It was better that her sister should decide. But Christie had decided in her own mind already. Any place would be better than none. But she needed Annie's sanction that Effie might be satisfied—and, indeed, that she might be satisfied herself; for she had little self-reliance.

She saw Annie, who shrank from the thought of Christie's having to trespass long on Mrs. McIntyre's hospitality; and Christie dwelt more on Mrs. Greenly's high praise of Mrs. Lee than on the difficulties she might expect among so many children with insufficient help. So the next afternoon Christie and her little trunk were set down before the door of a high stone house in St. —— Street. She had to wait a while; for Mrs. Greenly, the nurse, for whom she asked, was engaged for the time; but by and by she was taken up-stairs, and into a room where a lady was sitting in the dress of an invalid, with an infant on her lap. She greeted Christie very kindly; but there was a look of disappointment on her face, the girl was sure.

'She seems very young, nurse, and not very strong,' she said.

'She is not far from fifteen, and she says she has good health. She has been very well brought up,' said Mrs. Greenly, quickly, giving Christie a look she did not understand.

'How old are you?' asked Mrs. Lee, seeming not to have heard the nurse.

'I was fourteen in June. I am very well now, and much stronger than I look. I will try and do my best.'

There was something in the lady's face and voice that made Christie very anxious to stay.

'Have you ever been in a place before?' the lady asked again.

Christie shook her head; but Mrs. Greenly took upon herself in reply.

'Dear, no! It's only lately that her father died. There is a large family of them. The oldest sister is trying to keep the little ones together, Mrs. McIntyre tells me; and two of the sisters have come to the city to take places. The elder one is at Mrs. Vinton's, in Beaver Hall.'

Remembering the consequences of such a communication on a former occasion, Christie trembled; but she was soon relieved.

'Poor child!' said the lady. 'So you have never been from home before?'

'No, ma'am,' said Christie, eagerly. 'But I was very glad to come. I was sorry to leave them all; but I wished to do my part. I will do my best for you and the children.'

'You needn't fear that the children will learn anything wrong from her, ma'am,' she heard Mrs. Greenly say. 'She has been well brought up.'

But she heard no more; for the pattering of little feet on the stairs told of the approach of children. The door opened, and a little girl, six or seven years old, entered, followed by two little boys, who were younger. The girl went directly to her mother, and began stroking the baby's face. The boys, looking defiantly at Mrs.

Greenly, as though to assure her that they would not submit to be sent away, took their stand behind their mother's chair. The mother's hand was gently laid on the little girl's head.

' Where is Harry ? ' she asked.

' He's asleep in Nelly's clothes-basket. She said we were not to make a noise to wake him, so we came up here. Bridget has gone away.'

' Yes, I know. And has Letty been trying to amuse her brothers, to help mother ? '

The child shook her head.

' Harry played with the clothes-pins, and then he fell asleep. And Tom and Neddie are both bad boys. They wouldn't obey me. Won't you let me take the baby now ? '

' Baby's asleep, and you mustn't make a noise to wake her,' said the nurse, in an ominous whisper. ' And your mother's very tired, and must lie down and sleep too. And you are going, like a nice young lady, into the nursery, to see how quiet you can keep them.'

She laid her hand on the child's arm as she spoke ; but it was shaken off abruptly, and the pretty face gathered itself into a frown. Her mother's hand was laid on her lips.

' Mother,' entreated the child, ' I will be so good if you will let me stay. There's nothing to do in the nursery, and I'm so tired of staying there ! '

' But your brothers,' said Mrs. Greenly. ' They won't stay without you, and your mother will be worse if she don't get rest. Indeed, ma'am, you are quite flushed already,' said she, looking at Mrs. Lee ; ' quite feverish.

You are no more fit to be left than you were a fortnight ago. You must have rest. The children must go.'

'Let us go to the yard, then,' pleaded one of them.

'It has been raining. Neddie must not go out,' said the weary mother. 'Is not my little daughter going to be good?' she pleaded.

'Oh, do let me stay. I will be so good. Send the boys away to Nelly in the kitchen, and let me stay with you.'

On a table near the bed stood a tray, with several vials and glasses on it. At this moment the whole was put in jeopardy by the enterprising spirit of little Tom, who was determined to make himself acquainted with their various contents. Neddie was endeavouring to raise himself to the window-seat, using the curtains as a ladder to assist his ascent. There was a fair prospect of confusion enough.

'This will never do,' said the nurse, hastily, as she removed the tray and its contents, and reached the window just in time to save the wilful Neddie from a fall. 'Do you know,' she added, suddenly changing her tone, 'what Nelly brought from market to-day? Apples! They are in the side-board down-stairs. And here are the keys. Who would like one?'

The boys suspended their mischievous operations, and listened. Letty did not move.

'Let me stay,' she whispered.

'Come, Miss Letty, like a good child. Your mother *must* sleep, or she will be ill, and the baby too. Come! I know what your quietness is—fidgeting about like a mouse. Your mother would have a better chance to sleep with all the boys about her. Come away.'

I

'Go, Letty; go with nurse. Be a good child,' pleaded her mother, on whose cheek a bright colour was flickering. 'My darling would not make mamma ill, and baby sister too?'

'Nurse, try me this once. I will be so quiet.

But nurse was not to be entreated; and the reluctant child was half led, half dragged from the room, screaming and resisting. Her mother looked after her, weary and helpless, and the baby on her lap sent up a whimpering cry. Mrs. Lee leaned back on her chair, and pressed her hands over her eyes.

Christie rose.

'Will you trust me with the baby? I will be very careful.'

The lady started; she had quite forgotten her. Christie stooped over the baby with eager interest.

'Are you fond of children?' asked Mrs. Lee.

'I love my brother and my little sisters. I have never been with other children.' There were tears in Christie's eyes as she raised them to look in Mrs. Lee's face, called forth quite as much by the gentle tones of her voice as by the thought of 'the bairns' at home.

'I am afraid you could do nothing for baby,' said Mrs. Lee. 'Nurse will be here presently. Perhaps you could amuse the children; but they miss me, and are fretful without me.'

'I will try,' said Christie, eagerly. 'Are they fond of stories? I am very good at telling stories. Or I can read to them. I will do my best.'

She went down-stairs, and guided by the sound of children's voices, entered the dining-room. The little girl had thrown herself on the sofa, where she was sobbing with mingled grief and rage. The boys, on the contrary, were enjoying the prospect of eating the apples which Mrs. Greenly was paring for them.

'The baby is crying. The lady wants you. She says I am to try and amuse the children,' said Christie.

'Well, I wish you joy of your work,' said Mrs. Greenly, whose temper was a little ruffled by her encounter with Miss Letty. 'For my part, I have no patience with children who don't care whether their mother gets better or not. Children should love their parents and obey them.'

'I do love my mamma!' cried Letty, passionately, between her sobs. 'Go away, naughty nurse!'

'I'm just going, my dear,' said the nurse. 'And mind, my girl,' she added, to Christie, 'these children are to be kept here, and they are to be kept quiet too. Mrs. Lee's wearied out of her very life with their noise. That useless Bridget was just as good as nobody with them.'

So she went up-stairs, and Christie was left to manage with the children as best she might. While the apples lasted there was little to be said. Letty did not heed hers, though it lay on the sofa, within reach of her hand, till Tom made some advances in that direction. Then it was seized and hidden quickly, and Tom's advances sharply repelled. Tom turned away with a better grace than might have been expected, and addressed himself to Christie.

'Are you Bridget?' he asked.

No,' she said, gravely; 'I'm Christie.'

'Are you going to stay here?'

'Would you like me to stay?'

'No,' said the boy; 'I wouldn't. I like my mamma to dress me. Biddy brushes too hard.'

'But I am Christie. I'll brush very gently till your mother gets better again. Wouldn't you like me to stay? My home is very far away.'

'How far?' asked Neddie, coming forward and standing beside his brother.

'Oh, ever so far—over the river, and over the hills, and past the woods; away—away—away down in a little hollow by the brook.'

The children looked at her with astonished eyes. She went on:

'There are birds'-nests there, and little birds that sing. Oh, you should here how they sing! And there are little lambs that play all day long among the clover. And there are dandelions and butter-cups, and oh! I can't tell you how many pretty flowers besides. Whose dog is that?' she asked, suddenly, pointing to a picture on the wall.

'It's my mamma's,' said Neddie.

'Is it? He's a very pretty dog. What's his name?'

'He hasn't got any name. He's a picture,' said Tom.

'Oh, yes; he has a name. His name is—Rover. Is not that a pretty name? Come and sit down by the window, and I will tell you a story about a dog named Rover. You like stories, don't you?'

They came slowly forward and stood beside her.

'Well, Neddie,' she said to Tom. 'Are you Neddie?'

'No; I'm Tom. That's Neddie.'

'Oh! that's Neddie, is it? Well, Tom and Neddie, I'm going to tell you a story about Rover. Only we must speak low, and not disturb your mamma and baby sister. What's the baby's name, I wonder?'

'It's baby,' said Neddie.

Yes; but she must have another name besides baby.'

'No, she hasn't,' said Tom.

'Her name's going to be Catharine Ellinor,' said Letty, forgetting her trouble for a moment. 'That's grandmamma's name.'

'Oh, that's a very pretty name!' said Christie. 'She's a dear baby, I am sure.' But Letty had no more to say.

'Tell us about Rover,' said Tom.

'Oh, yes! I must tell you about Rover. "Once upon a time—"' And then came the story. Never did dog meet with such wonderful adventures before, and never was a story listened to with greater delight. Even Letty forgot her vexation, and listened eagerly. In the midst of it Nelly entered, carrying little Harry in her arms. At the sight of him every trace of ill-humour vanished from Letty's face. Running to meet them she clasped her arms round her little brother.

'Where are his shoes, Nelly?' she said, stooping to kiss his rosy little feet.

'What a sweet child!' exclaimed Christie. 'I hope he won't be afraid of me.'

He *was* very lovely, with his flushed cheeks and tangled curls, and not in the least afraid of anything in the world. He looked out of his bright blue eyes as frankly and fearlessly at Christie as if she had been his nurse all his life. She placed him on her knee while Letty tied his shoes.

'Are you to be nurse?' asked her fellow-servant Nelly.

'I don't know. I would like the place,' said Christie.

'You'll have your hands full,' said Nelly, emphatically. Christie had nothing to say to this; and the boys became clamorous for the rest of the story.

In the meantime, the October sunshine, though it was neither very warm nor very bright, had dried up the rain-drops on the paved court behind the house, and Mrs. Greenly, showing her face for a moment at the dining-room door, told Christie she might wrap the children up and take them out for a little time. With Nelly's help, the wrapping up was soon accomplished. The yard was not a very pleasant place. It was surrounded by a high wall, and at the foot of the enclosure was a little strip which had been cultivated. There were a few pale pansies and blackened dahlia-stalks lingering yet. In two corners stood a ragged and dusty fir-tree; and all the rest of the yard was laid over with boards.

'The children are not to sit down, for they would take cold,' called out Mrs. Greenly from an upper window. In a little while Christie had them all engaged in a merry game, and greatly were they delighted with it. Some tokens of disorder and riot were given by Tom and Letty; but on the whole the peace was kept. Their enjoyment was complete, and it was a merry and hungry group that obeyed Nelly's summons to the tea-table.

Christie's first afternoon was a decided success. There was nothing more said about her staying. She fell very naturally into her place in the nursery, and she and the little people there soon became very fond

of each other. It was a busy life, and so far a pleasant
one. When her position and duties were no longer
new to her, she accommodated herself to them with an
ease which would have surprised Aunt Elsie, and even
Effie, who had a higher opinion of Christie's powers
than her aunt had. She was very earnest and conscientious in all she did, and Mrs. Lee soon trusted her
entirely. She must have left the children much to her
care, even though she had less confidence in her; for
she did not gain strength very fast. The baby was a
fragile little creature, and rarely, night or day, during
the first three months of her life, was her mother's care
withdrawn from her. So the other children were quite
dependent on their young nurse for oversight as well as
for amusement; and considering all things, she did
very well, for she tried to do everything as in the sight
and fear of God.

CHAPTER VII.

'CLOSER THAN A BROTHER.'

BUT all the days of that dreary autumn were not so happy. Indeed, there were many times when Christie felt ready to give up in despair. Once it happened that for weeks together the rain kept the little ones in the house, and the only glimpse of the outer world which Christie could get was from the nursery window. For one accustomed to a country life this was no small deprivation, and though she was hardly conscious of the cause, her spirits (never very lively) were ready to sink under it. She became used to the confinement after a while, or rather, as she told Annie, she did not mind it. But the constant attention which the little ones claimed was a great strain on her cheerfulness. From early morning till the hour when the unwilling eyes of the last of them were closed in slumber, she had not a moment's respite. There was always something to be done, some one to be coaxed or cautioned or cared for.

The little Lees were not naughty children. On the contrary, they were very loving, affectionate little creatures. All of them, except, perhaps, Letty, were easily amused and governed. But, as is the case with all over-indulged children, they were inclined to be exacting when they had the power; and it was no wonder that, among so many of them, Christie sometimes grew weary even to exhaustion, and fancied that her strength and courage were quite spent.

And worse than all, there were times when homesickness, that could not be resisted or reasoned away, assailed her. Almost always it was at night—in the evenings, now growing so long, when no sound save the gentle breathing of the sleeping children broke the reigning silence. It was not so bad at such times, however, for she could then let her weary head fall, and weep a part of her troubles away. But sometimes in broad daylight, when in her walks with the children she crushed beneath her feet the dead leaves of the trees, while the autumn wind sighed drearily through their bare boughs, a pang of bitter loneliness smote her. Among the crowds she met she was always fancying familiar faces. More than once she sprang forward with a cry to grasp the hand of one who looked on her with the unheeding eyes of a stranger. If at such a time any one had come to her with a message from Effie, saying, 'Come home,' she would probably have gone at all hazards—so dreary and lonely her life seemed to her.

It was not so with Annie. She made friends easily. She and Christie went to church; and but few Sabbaths passed before they met many who nodded and smiled to her bright faced sister But Christie was shy and quiet, and shrank from the notice of strangers; and up to the very last time that she passed through them, the busy streets of the city seemed a lonely place to her.

Christie never quite forgot the remedy tried for the first time beneath the boughs of the birch-tree by the brook. There were hours when it seemed to her now, as it seemed to her then, a cure for all the ills of life, a help in every time of need. There were times when, having nowhere else to go, she carried her burden to Effie's chief Friend, and strove to cast it from her at His feet. She did not always succeed. Many a time she lay down in the dark, beside little Harry, altogether uncomforted. It seemed to her that nothing could help her but going home again. But it was only now and then, at rare intervals, that it seemed possible for her to go. Almost always she said to herself, 'I canna go home. I must stay a little while, at least.' Sometimes she said it with tears and a sorrowful heart, but almost always she had courage to say it with firmness.

But now she was beginning to feel herself wrong in coming ; or, rather, she began to see that her motive in coming was wrong. It was less to help Effie with the little ones, as she was now satisfied, than to escape from dependence on Aunt Elsie. Not that, even in her worst moments, Christie could make herself believe that her aunt did not gladly share the little that she had with her brother's orphans, or that she would share it less willingly with her than with the others. The unwillingness was on her part. And the root of this unwillingness was pride, and an unforgiving remembrance of what she called her aunt's harshness to her. Aunt Elsie had been at times more or less hard with all her nieces. But she had been so to Christie in a way different from the rest ; and the child was willing to believe that the cause lay less in her waywardness than in her aunt's unjust partiality. With such feelings

permitted, nay, at times willingly indulged, no wonder
that she too often failed to find the peace she sought.

But gradually the home-sickness wore away. Daily
she became more useful and more valued in the nursery.
She felt that Mrs. Lee trusted her, and this did much
to make her content. She almost always was patient
when the children were in their exacting moods, and
was always firm in refusing any forbidden pleasure.
From her 'your mamma would be displeased,' or her
'it is not right,' there was no moving her; and of this
the children soon became aware. She never assumed
authority over them. They would have resented this
quickly enough. But if the reward of a story or a
merry game before bed-time was forfeited by ill-conduct,
it was felt as a severe disappointment. For any disobedience or other naughtiness in the nursery, the
refusal of a kiss for good-night was punishment enough.
All children are not so easily guided or governed as the
little Lees were; and few children are placed so entirely
apart from evil influences as they were in those days.
They were quick and restless, and full of spirit, but, as
I have said, they were affectionate and tractable; and
though often, before the last little busybody was safely
disposed of for the night, Christie believed her strength
and patience to be quite exhausted, her love for them
increased day by day.

So the first three months of her absence from home
wore away, and the merry Christmas-time drew nigh.
Till now, Christie had seen little of the master of the
house. He was rarely in for many days together. His
business took him here and there through the country;
and even when he was in the city he was not much at
home. Once or twice he came into the nursery. He

seemed fond of his children in a careless, indifferent way; but the children were shy and not very happy in his presence. If Mrs. Lee was not happier when he was at home, she was certainly more sad and silent for a few days after he went away, and sighed often when she looked at her children, as though she were burdened with many cares.

About Christmas-time a great change took place in the household. In the course of one of his many journeys Mr. Lee met with a serious accident. It was not pronounced serious at the time of its occurrence, but it became so through neglect. It was painful as well as dangerous, and confined him to the house during the greater part of the winter. From this time Christie's duties became more arduous. Mrs. Lee's time and attention were frequently required by her husband, and the fragile little Ellinor then became the special care of Christie. The nursery, too, was removed to a room in the attic; for Mr. Lee at first could not, and at last would not, bear the noise of the children; and Christie's glimpse of the outer world extended only to roofs and chimneys now. The brief daily airings of the children were taken in a sleigh; and the doctor insisted that their mother should always share them. She was very delicate; and her husband, thoughtless and exacting, failed to perceive that her strength was too much tried. Mrs. Greenly was engaged as his sick-nurse; but she could not be on the alert both night and day, and when she failed her place must be supplied by his uncomplaining wife. Night or day it was all the same. She was never sure of an hour's respite.

So Christie reigned alone in the attic-nursery, and controlled and amused the children, and mended, and

managed, and looked cheerful through it all, in a way
that excited the admiration and astonishment of Mrs.
Greenly, and the thankful gratitude of Mrs. Lee. How
she got through it all she hardly knew. On the days
when the baby was her exclusive care, it was bad
enough. But by teaching the children to hail the
coming of the little one as a mark of their mamma's
great confidence in them, she succeeded in making
them share the responsibility with her. The boys
would amuse themselves quietly for hours rather than
disturb little Ellinor; and Letty (usually the most
restless and wayward of them all) never grew weary of
humming little songs, and otherwise amusing the baby,
as she lay in the cot. So they went on better than
might have been expected. But what with the close
confinement in the house, and the climbing of two or
three long flights of stairs, Christie grew pale and thin,
and was many a time very weary.

She had one pleasant hour in the week. At ten on
every Sabbath morning she called for her sister, and
they went to church together. Not to the church they
would have chosen at first. There they had difficulty
in finding seats together; so they went elsewhere, with
a friend of Annie's, and after a time they had no desire
to change. They rarely saw each other during the
week. Annie sometimes came into Christie's nursery;
but the only real pleasure they had together was in the
walk to and from church on Sabbath morning.

March was passing away. The snow was nearly
gone, but there had been a shower during the night,
and the pavements were wet, as Christie set out on her
accustomed walk one morning. The wind blew freshly,
too, and weary with the work of six days, she shrank

from facing it, even for a little while, with her sister, so, at the street by which she usually went to the house where Annie lived, she paused.

'I'll wait in the church for her to-day,' she said to herself. 'I'm tired, and it's later than usual. She'll know if I'm not there by half-past ten, and she'll come down. At any rate, I'm too tired to go up the hill.'

Yes, she was very tired. The fresh air did not brighten and enliven her as it usually did. The warm, moist wind that came in gusts from the south was not invigorating, and she went slowly up the church-steps, glad that her walk was over. There was no one in the church. Even the sexton was not visible; and Christie placed herself in her accustomed seat under the gallery, near the door, glad to rest in the pleasant stillness of the place. How quiet and peaceful it seemed! The sound of the moaning wind seemed to come from far away, and the stillness within was all the deeper. After the noise and turmoil of six days, the silence was more grateful to her weary sense than the sound of sweetest music would have been; and closing her eyes, she leaned back, not to think, but to rest and be at peace.

Soon the congregation began to assemble, but her repose was too deep to be disturbed by the sound of footsteps or the rustling of garments. She neither stirred nor heard a sound till Annie laid her hand upon her arm. Then she awoke with a start, coming back to a realization of time and place, with a flutter of confusion and pain.

'What ails you? Have you been sleeping? Are you not well?' whispered Annie, in alarm.

'Oh, yes, I'm well enough. I think I must have

been sleeping, though,' said Christie, scarcely able to restrain a laugh at Annie's astonishment.

'Sleeping! at this time of day, and in the kirk too!' exclaimed Annie.

'Well, never mind,' said Christie, smiling, and holding down her head to hide her confusion. 'Did you see David McIntyre? I'm almost sure I saw him in the street.'

'Yes, I saw him. He brought this letter from Effie.' Christie took it from her.

'Don't read it now, in the kirk. There's nothing in it that will not keep. There is a little note for yourself inside. They are all well. Why didna you come up to-day? I have something to tell you.'

Christie listened eagerly.

'I canna tell you now,' said her sister. 'See, the people are nearly all in. But I'll come down to-night, if I can.'

At that moment a hard-featured man, a little in front, turned his sharp eyes towards them, with a look that was intended to warn and reprove; so nothing more was said.

As Annie was walking home with Christie, 'I'm thinking of changing my place,' she said.

'Changing!' repeated Christie. 'I thought you were quite content.'

'Oh, it's not that. Mrs. Vinton wishes it. Her younger sister is going to be married, it seems, and her mother, who is an invalid—something like Aunt Elsie, I should think—wants some one to be with her always. She lives with a son, somewhere in the far West. Miss Emma—that's the sister—has been down. She thinks I should suit her mother, and Mrs. Vinton is willing to

spare me. I think I should like to go, for some things.
The wages are higher.'

'But so far away,' said Christie, in consternation;
'and to leave me!'

'Yes, that's what disturbs me. You mustna stay
when I go.'

Christie shook her head. 'I suppose there's the
same need of my staying now that there was before,'
said she, quietly.

'But Effie was never quite willing that you should
come, you know; and besides, your place is too hard
for you.'

'Just now it is, perhaps,' interrupted Christie; 'but
Mr. Lee is better, and we'll soon get into our old way
again.'

'But what I want is this,' said Annie; 'I want Sarah
to come and take my place at Mrs. Vinton's. I have
told her about Sarah. And then you could go home
and be with Effie.'

'But *I* never could do what Sarah does at home,'
said Christie; 'taking care of Aunt Elsie and all. It
would be far harder than what I have to do now.'

'But you would be at home, and you would have
some one to look after you. I could never think of such
a thing as leaving you here alone.'

'But, Annie, Sarah would be alone,' remonstrated
Christie.

'Yes, I know; but it's quite different with Sarah.
She's strong and healthy, and will hold her own with
anybody; and besides, I'm sure Effie will never hear
of your staying here alone. But there's time enough
to think about it. If I go, I shall spend a week at
home first. No; I can't go in,' said Annie, as they

came to Mrs. Lee's door. 'I must go home. I shall write to Effie. Now, don't fret about this, or I shall wish I hadna told you;' for Christie looked very grave indeed.

'We'll wait and see what Effie thinks,' said she, sadly.

'Well, you have her letter; and I'll come down to-night, if I can, and we'll talk it over. But, for any sake, dinna look so glum, as Aunt Elsie would say.'

Christie laughed a little at her sister's excitement, but it was a very grave face that bent over the baby's cot that afternoon. The south wind had brought rain, and when night came, the drops dashed drearily against the window-panes. Listening to it, as she sat with the baby in her arms and the others sleeping quietly about her, Christie said to herself, many times, that Annie could never venture out in such a night. Yet she started at every sound, and listened eagerly till it had died away again. Effie's letter had told her nothing new. They were all well and happy, and the old question was asked, 'When is Christie coming home again?' But the letter, and even the little note, more precious still, could not banish from her mind the thought of what Annie had said to her; and it seemed to her that she could not possibly wait for another week to hear more. The baby was restless, its mother was detained down-stairs, and Christie walked about and murmured softly to still the little creature's cries. But it was all done mechanically, and wearily enough. Through the baby's cries and her own half forced song, and through the dreary sounds of the wind and rain, she listened for her sister's foot upon the stairs. She could not have told why she was so impatient to see

K

her. Annie could tell her no more than she had already told her during their walk from church. But since the possibility of getting home had been suggested, the old feelings had started within her. A sudden rush of home-sickness had come over her, and with it the old unwillingness to go home and be a burden. She could fix her thoughts on nothing else. Even after the baby had fallen into an uneasy slumber, she wandered up and down the room, hushing it in her arms as before.

There was a step on the stairs at last. It was not Annie, however, but Mrs. Lee.

'I am afraid the baby has been fretful,' she said, kindly, as she took the child in her arms. 'You look tired, Christie.'

'No; I'm not very tired.' But she moved about the room, putting aside little frocks and shoes, keeping her face all the time from the light. She was very much afraid that if Mrs. Lee were to speak so gently again her tears must flow; and this must not be if she could possibly help it. In the meantime, Mrs. Lee had taken up a book, which lay on a table beside her. It was Christie's Bible; and when she had finished putting away the children's clothes worn through the day, and seated herself at a little distance, Mrs. Lee said:

'You are fond of reading, Christie?'

Christie had many times asked permission to take a book into the nursery, when the children were asleep, and she answered:

'Yes, ma'am; I like to read, very much.'

'And do you like to read the Bible? Some people seem to take great pleasure in it.'

'Yes; I read it every day. I promised Effie I would.'

Mrs. Lee continued to turn over the leaves.

'Whose marks are these on the margin?' she asked.

'I suppose they are Effie's. John Nesbitt marked one or two for me, when I was staying at his mother's last summer. The rest are Effie's.'

Mrs. Lee read, 'He shall cover thee with His feathers, and under His wings shalt thou trust.'

'That was John's,' said Christie, quickly. 'One day a hawk came very near, and we saw the chickens run to take shelter with their mother; and in the evening John marked that passage, because, he said, it was just the right one for a feeble, frightened, faithless little creature like me. I was not well at the time.'

Christie paused, partly because she thought she had said enough, and partly because it would not have been easy for her to say more just then.

'I don't think your friend could have known you very well,' said Mrs. Lee, smiling. 'He would never call you feeble, or frightened, if he knew all you have done, and what a comfort you have been to me, this winter.'

'Oh, he meant that I was not brave and cheerful, like Effie; and I am not.'

'It is pleasant to have these tokens of your friend, any way,' said Mrs. Lee, musingly.

'There are other of his marks:—"Under the shadow of Thy wings will I make my refuge, until these calamities be overpast,"—and another about rejoicing under the shadow of His wings.'

It was a troubled, tearful face that Christie laid down on her hands as she said this. Mrs. Lee was still turning over the leaves, and took no notice of the sigh that escaped the little nurse.

'You read it to please your sister and your friend, do you? Or do you really love to read it? I have heard of those who find their chief happiness in believing what the Bible teaches. Do you?'

There was a pause, during which Christie slowly raised her face from her hands and turned it towards Mrs. Lee. Then she said, with some hesitation:

'I don't know. I wouldn't be without the Bible for all the world; and yet I know I don't find all the comfort in it that some people do. I suppose it is because I am not sure that I am a Christian.'

'A Christian?' repeated Mrs. Lee.

'Yes; a child of God,' said Christie, with a sigh. 'If I were sure that I am a child of God, then all the promises in His Holy Word would be mine.'

'I suppose you mean if you were always good and never committed any sin?' said Mrs. Lee, inquiringly.

'No; not that, exactly. Even God's people fall into sin sometimes.'

'What do you mean by being a child of God, then? We are all His children in a certain sense, are we not?'

Christie glanced doubtfully at Mrs. Lee.

'I mean one who loves God supremely—one who is at peace with God, who has no will but His—one whose sins are forgiven for Jesus Christ's sake.'

'And you think you are not one of these?' said Mrs. Lee.

'I don't know. Sometimes I hope; but I am afraid not. I am sure I wish to be.'

Mrs. Lee looked as though she did not quite understand her; but she said nothing more. She laid down the book and rocked the baby gently on her knee. Her thoughts were not very happy, Christie fancied, if she might judge by her face, which grew grave and sad as she gazed on the child. One of the little boys made a sudden movement. Christie rose to replace the coverlet on him.

'How peacefully they sleep!' said their mother. 'Ah me!' she added; 'if they could always be as free from care! If I could get but one glimpse into their future! And yet perhaps it is better as it is.'

'It is better to trust than to know, I once heard Effie say.' Christie spoke shyly, and with hesitation, as though she were not quite sure that she should speak at all.

Mrs. Lee smiled, and said, kindly:

'I see you are very fond of your sister Effie.'

Christie's face spoke; but she did not trust her voice.

'I suppose she is the eldest of your family?'

'Yes. She's twenty-two. Oh, I wish you could see Effie! She is very different from what you would think from seeing me—or Annie, even.'

'How so?' asked Mrs. Lee, greatly amused at the eagerness of one usually so quiet and self-restrained.

'Oh, I can hardly tell you. She looks so different— from me, I mean. Annie's more like her. But it's not so much her looks. She is so brave and cheerful and strong. She is not afraid. And yet she is gentle, and has patience with us all.'

'Is she one of those you were speaking about just now—a child of God?'

'Yes; she is,' said Christie, gravely. 'She doesn't say much about it; but I do believe it is that which makes the difference. No wonder that she is strong and brave and cheerful always, when she is quite sure that *all things* will work together for her good.'

Christie spoke the last words rather to herself than to Mrs. Lee. The lady listened with much interest, however. She had long ago learned to value her little nurse for her faithfulness and her desire to do right; but this glimpse she was getting of her inner life was something new.

'It's no wonder I love Effie,' continued Christie, whose heart was opened. 'When my mother died, I was sickly, and different from the rest; and she gave me to Effie as her special care. I think I should have died if it hadn't been for her. Oh, if I could only see her, just for one minute!'

Christie was in danger of forgetting all else for the moment. But she checked herself by a great effort, and said:

'I don't mean that I am discontented here, or that I would go home if I could. I know it is best I should be here.'

'What do you mean by all things working together for good?' said Mrs. Lee, by and by. 'I suppose Christians have trials and sorrows as well as others?'

'Oh, yes! I don't mean that. But a Christian may be sure that even his trials are sent for the best. That is what John Nesbitt said to Effie and me once. He said, if we had a friend of whose love we could be sure, a friend who was wise and powerful and who had promised to bring us safely through our troubles, we should have no cause to fret and despond, though we might not understand all that happened by the way. We might be sure that in the end all would be well.'

'If one could only have such a friend!' said Mrs. Lee, with an audible sigh.

'Well, I suppose Jesus Christ is such a friend to

those who love Him,' said Christie, softly. 'He's loving
and powerful, and He has promised; and He cannot
break His promise, we know. If we would but trust
Him!'

Mrs. Lee said nothing. The look of care that Christie
had seen on her face many times since she came, and
oftener than ever within the last few weeks, was settling
on it now. She leaned her head on her hand, and
sighed many times, as she sat gazing on the face of her
baby, who had fallen asleep on her knee. Christie took
up her book; but she could not help stealing a glance,
now and then, at the mother and child.

Thinking of Mrs. Lee's troubles, Christie for a time
forgot her own; and it was not so difficult to wait till
the next week to see her sister as she supposed it would
be. She had to wait longer than that before their
arrangements were made. Annie wrote to Effie; but
as only a weekly mail reached them, and as even that
one might fail, it was some time before they could
expect to hear from her. The days passed very slowly.
Effie's letter seemed a long time in coming.

In the meanwhile April came in, and as the days grew
longer and milder, Christie's anxiety to hear grew more
intense. It seemed to her that she must get away from
the town and run home for a little while. The longing
never left her. Her stories to the children were all
about the buds that were beginning to show themselves,
and the flowers and birds that would be coming soon.
She told them how all living creatures were rejoicing in
the return of spring, how glad the calves and the young
lambs would be to find themselves in the pastures, that
were now becoming green. She told them how the icy
bands that had bound the little brooks through all the

winter-time were broken now by the bright sunshine, and how by this time the water must have reached the hollow at the foot of the birch-tree and covered the turf seat there. She told them how the waters rushed and murmured when they rose so high that the green buds of the birch-tree dipped into them, and how the wind swayed the young willows, till she seemed to hear the sound, and grew faint with her longing to be there.

The letter came at last. Annie was to do as she thought best, Effie said. She could judge what was wisest, and what she would like, better than they could, who were so far away; but as for Christie, she was to come home. Not to exchange with Sarah, however. Whether one of them would go back, or whether both were to stay at home, was to be decided afterwards; but in the meantime Christie was to come home.

'Think of it!' Effie said; 'six long months away! Aunt Elsie, Mrs. Nesbitt, old Mrs. Gray—everybody said she must come home.'

How the poor girl's heart leaped to meet the welcome that awaited her! Yes, she must go home, for a little while at least. Mrs. Lee was grieved at the prospect of parting with her. Christie was almost vexed with herself that the thought of leaving her and the children should not be more painful to her. But there was too much joy in her heart to leave room for more sorrow.

'I didna think I should be so glad to go,' she said to Annie many times during their last walk from church. Annie laughed.

'You have forgotten Aunt Elsie and all other vexations. Wait till you get home. It won't be all sunshine there, I can tell you.'

But even the thought of Aunt Elsie had not the power of making Christie anything but glad. She was afraid of nothing, except that something might happen to hinder her going home.

'You foolish child!' said Annie, laughing. 'What could happen?'

CHAPTER VIII.

'MAN PROPOSES, GOD DISPOSES.'

BUT something *did* happen. That night, when Christie went home, she found Mrs. Lee ill. She was not very ill, at least, not much more so than she had been for a long time. She had been quite unfit for the fatigue of nursing her husband, and now that he was better, her strength forsook her. There was a dull, low fever upon her. The doctor said Mrs. Greenly must be sent for and the baby must be weaned. Christie's heart sickened as she heard all this. Could she leave the baby to a strange nurse? It would greatly add to the anxiety of the mother, and might hinder her recovery for a time, even to know that the children, and especially the delicate baby, must be left to the care of a stranger. Ought she to go home?

What a wakeful, miserable night she passed! She fancied she could bear to stay; but to disappoint Effie and all at home was very painful. Must she stay? It seemed so hard to change her plans now, both for her own sake and theirs.

But the morrow decided the matter for her. Letty was irritable all day and all night, and when the doctor

came in the morning, he pronounced her symptoms to
be those of scarlet fever. So Christie and the other
children were banished to the attic-nursery again. She
said not another word about going home, except to her
sister.

'Tell Effie I couldna get away. It wouldna be right
to leave; would it, Annie? I will try and not be very
unhappy about it.'

But the tears that rolled down her cheeks told how
bitter the disappointment was to her. Annie would
have lingered a week, even to the shortening of her
visit at home, for the sake of having Christie go with
her; but this was not to be thought of. The fever
might go through the whole family. The doctor thought
that most likely it would do so; and she could not better
leave at the end of a week than now.

'And don't tell them I was so very much disappointed
about it,' she said, trying to smile, when Annie rose to
go. 'They must be all the more glad to see me when I
come. I couldna go, Annie. Now, do you really think
I could?'

They were up in the attic-nursery. Christie sat with
the baby in her lap, while little Harry hung about her,
begging to be taken up. The other boys were engaged
in some noisy play near the window; but the confinement up-stairs had already made them irritable, and
Christie's constant interference was required to keep the
peace between them. How much worse it would be if
an entire stranger were put in the place of her who had
been their kind nurse all the winter! And the poor,
anxious mother down-stairs too, how much worse for her!

'No, Christie, dear; considering all things, I think
you do right to stay. But it is a great disappointment.'

'Make Effie understand how it is.' It was only by a great effort that she restrained a flood of tears till her sister had gone. Then they fell upon the baby's frock like rain. The boys looked on in astonishment, and little Harry burst out into a frightened cry, wakening the baby, who joined her voice to his.

'There! there! Hush, baby! hush! Harry, don't cry. Oh me! what shall I do?'

There was but one thing to do, and she tried faithfully to do it;—it was to forget herself and her disappointment, and devote herself to the little ones for the day. And so she did, for that day and many days, with better success than she had dared to hope for. Letty was in the other nursery, next to her mother's room, and for several days Christie saw neither of them. The baby missed her mother less than might have been expected, and submitted to her privation quietly enough. By passing the day down-stairs in the dining-room, or out in the yard when the weather was fine, Christie contrived to keep the boys amused and happy most of the time. Mr. Lee was absent on one of his business journeys. It was uncertain when he would return; but Nelly was equal to all housekeeping emergencies, and no one spoke of his absence with regret. Mrs. Greenly always considered Christie as under her special patronage, as she had been the means of bringing her to the house, and she strove to lighten her burden as much as possible. But it was a weary time, those first ten days after Annie went away.

Christie did not go to church the first Sabbath. It is doubtful whether she would have found the courage, even if she could have been spared. The next week was not so bad with them. Letty's illness, though severe, proved less so than had been feared at first; and though Mrs. Lee grew no better, she did not grow worse. Before the second Sabbath, Letty was pronounced out of danger, and Nelly, taking pity on Christie's pale, weary face, offered to take her place with the children while she went to church.

She went early, as usual, and had time for the shedding of some very sorrowful tears before the congregation gathered. I am afraid there was a little bitterness mingled with the sorrow. The good she had done by staying did not seem worth the great sacrifice it had cost. Letty had not been very ill after all. The other children were well, and might have done with a stranger, and she might have been going to the kirk at home with Effie that very day. Besides, Mrs. Greenly did not seem to think her staying a great matter—though she had more than once praised her for her care of the children. As for Mrs. Lee, she had scarcely seen her; and when she had, she had not alluded to the change in her plans which sickness had made. What had cost her so much, she thought, was a small matter in their view; and it is no wonder that the pang of home-sickness that smote her, as she looked at her sister's empty seat in the kirk, was all the harder to bear because of this. She did not gain much good from the sermon that day. Heedless of some curious —perhaps pitying—eyes that were turned towards her, she leaned her head on her hand and thought her own dreary thoughts; and when the services were over, she rose and went away with the rest, although uncomforted.

The day passed slowly enough. It needed a greater effort than she could make to amuse the children and

keep them interested, and they were noisy and trouble
some. The baby, too, was fretful, and would by no
means be content to sit still; and Christie wandered
about with her, listless and miserable, till tea-time.
After tea, thankful for the prospect of a little peace, she
put the boys to bed, and seating herself by the baby's
cot, went back to her sad, unprofitable thoughts again.

It was well for her—though she did not think so—
that this moody fit did not last long. Mrs. Greenly's
step upon the stairs aroused her.

'Christie,' said she, 'are you reading? Just take
your book and go and sit down-stairs, will you? Letty's
asleep, and will need nothing, I dare say. If she does,
you can call me. Mrs. Lee will need nothing either.
I don't know how it is that I am so overcome with
sleep. I'll lie down and rest a minute or two, and I'll
hear the children if they wake.'

Christie took her book and went down, but she did
not read. Instead of that, she seated herself in the
dark on the stairs, and began her unprofitable musings
again. Mrs. Lee was not asleep. She was evidently
feverish and uncomfortable, and turned about and
sighed often and heavily. Christie had been told not
to go into her room unless she was called, so she sat
still a little, beguiled from her own sad thoughts as she
took note of the uneasiness of the sick lady.

'Are you there, nurse?' said Mrs. Lee, at last.

Christie rose, and went softly in.

'Oh, is it you, Christie? Are the children asleep?
How's the baby to-night? I feel very weary and
wakeful. I don't know what ails me.'

'Shall I call nurse?' asked Christie.

'No. Oh, no. She could do nothing for me. Are

you reading? Read to me a little. Perhaps it will quiet me and make me fall asleep.'

While Christie brought the light and placed it where Mrs. Lee's eyes would not be troubled by it, she said again :

'The children are quite well, nurse tells me. It was very well that you decided not to go home, Christie. I am very glad you stayed.'

Christie said nothing.

'I am afraid your sister was disappointed,' said Mrs. Lee.

'Yes,' said Christie. She could not say more.

'Do you think you will go soon?'

'I don't know, ma'am.' Poor Christie! Going or staying seemed a small matter to Mrs. Lee. It would not bear talking about; so she said :

'What shall I read to you?'

'Oh, anything. It doesn't matter. Anything to pass the time.'

Christie turned over a book or two that lay on the table, still at a loss what to choose.

'You had a book in your hand when you came in,' said Mrs. Lee, presently. 'Read that.'

It was the Bible; and opening it at random, Christie read. She read softly and slowly, psalm after psalm ; and soothed by her voice, Mrs. Lee lay and listened. After a time, Christie thought that she slept, and made a pause.

'Do you believe what you have been reading?' she asked, suddenly.

Christie started.

'It's the Bible,' said she.

'Yes; I know. Of course you believe it in a general

way. Everybody does. But do you take the good of it? That, for instance—"God is our refuge and strength, a very present help in trouble. Therefore will not we fear, though the earth be removed." Are you never afraid?'

Christie did not answer.

'Do you remember what you said to me the other night about your sister, and all things working for good to those who love God? Are you sure of it? And are you always content with what God sends you?'

Poor Christie! She sat conscience-stricken, remembering her murmuring spirit through the day.

'If I could be sure that I am one of those to whom God has given a right to His promises, I think I should be content with all He sends.'

She spoke humbly, and in a broken voice.

'Oh, if one could be sure!' murmured Mrs. Lee. 'If there was any good or pleasant thing in this world of which one could be quite sure! Oh, how weary I am of it all!'

The charm of the reading was broken. She moved her head restlessly on the pillow. Christie went to her.

'Can I do anything for you? Let me bathe your hands and face.' And she brought some fresh water. 'Sometimes when my head used to ache badly, my mother brushed it softly.'

'I thought your mother was dead,' said Mrs. Lee, raising herself up, and submitting to be tended after Christie's fashion.

'Yes, she died four years ago. I was but a child; but I remember her quite well.'

'My mother is dead too,' said Mrs. Lee, with a sigh. 'I wonder if she would have died if I had not left her?

I was but a child—only sixteen—and we never can tell beforehand how things are to turn out. If I had only known! But, oh me! why do I vex myself with all these things to-night? It is too late now :—too late now !'

Christie was alarmed at her evident excitement. Laying her gently down on her pillow, and smoothing her hair, she said :

'If you please, ma'am, Mrs. Greenly said I was not to speak to you, and that you must be kept quiet.'

With a strange sound between a sob and a laugh, she said :

'Ah, yes! It is easy for her to say, "Keep quiet;" but all her good nursing does not reach my troubles. Oh, me; how weary I am! My mother is dead, and I have no sister; and my brothers have quite forgotten me. But if we could only be sure that what your sister says is true, about the Friend that cares for us, and who will bring us safe through all troubles !'

'It's not Effie that says it,' said Christie, eagerly, 'It's in the Bible; and you may be quite sure it's true.'

'I wouldn't care so much for myself; but these poor little children who have no one but me, and I so weak and helpless. My heart fails when I think of all they may have to bear. I suppose my mother had just such anxious thoughts about me. Oh, if she had known all ! but she could not have helped me here.'

'But the verse says, "A very present help in trouble,"' said Christie, softly. 'That's one difference between a heavenly Friend and all earthly friends.'

'Yes,' said Mrs. Lee, languidly. Christie continued :

'The Bible says, too, "The Lord is nigh unto all them that call upon Him, to all that call upon Him in truth." And in another place, "Wait on the Lord: be of good courage, and He shall strengthen thy heart."'

'Yes; if, as you say, one could be sure that all these words were for us,' said Mrs. Lee. Christie faltered a little; but by and by she said:

'Well, the trust, like all other blessings, comes from Him. We can but ask Him for it. At any rate, it is to those who are in trouble that He promises help. It is to those who labour and are heavy-laden that Christ has promised rest.'

'Rest!' echoed Mrs. Lee, wearily. 'Oh for rest!'

'Yes; and He says He will give it to those who come to Him,' continued Christie. 'We ought not to doubt Him. He has said, in twenty places, that He will hear prayer.'

'I have a prayer-book. My mother gave it to me. But I have neglected it sadly.'

'But the New Testament and the Psalms are full of promises to hear prayer.' And Christie repeated many verses as they came to her mind:

'*Him that cometh unto Me, I will in no wise cast out.*

'*Whatever ye ask in My name, it shall be done unto you.*

'*Ask, and ye shall receive; seek, and ye shall find.*

'*If ye, then, being evil, know how to give good gifts to your children, how much more shall your Father in heaven give His Holy Spirit unto those who ask Him?*

'And the Psalm says:

> "And in the day of trouble great
> See that thou call on Me;
> I will deliver thee, and thou
> My name shalt glorify."'

'Can't you sing?' asked Mrs. Lee, coaxingly.

It was a long time before Christie could conquer her shyness so as to sing even with the children, but she had no thought of shyness now. She began the twentieth, and then the twenty-third Psalm, singing them to old Scotch tunes—rippling notes of strange, wild melody, like what we seldom hear in our churches nowadays. The child's voice had a clear, silvery sweetness, melting away in tender cadences; and breathing words suited to such times of need as come to all, whatever else may pass them by, it did more than soothe Mrs. Lee, it comforted her.

> 'Yea, though I walk through Death's dark vale,
>   Yet will I fear no ill;
> For Thou art with me, and Thy rod
>   And staff me comfort still.'

And so she sang on, her voice growing softer and lower, till Mrs. Lee fell asleep, and slept as she had not slept before for months, calmly as a child; and Christie stood beside her, listening to her gentle breathing, and saying to herself:

'I wonder if I have done her any good?'

Then she went back to her seat upon the stairs, and before she had sat there long in the darkness the blessed knowledge came to her that, whether she had done any good or not, she had gained much within the last two hours. In trying to comfort another she had herself been comforted.

'I can ask for the best blessing that God has to give, and keep asking till I get it. Why should I not?' And no bitterness was mingled with her tears, though they still fell fast. 'I will try and do right, and trust, and have patience, and God will guide me, I know He will.'

And so she sat in the dark, sometimes slumbering, sometimes thinking, till the baby's whimpering cry summoned her back to her usual care.

The next week was better in all respects than the last. Letty grew well rapidly, and her mother improved a little day by day. The doctor, looking now and then into the attic-nursery, gave them hope at last that the little ones might escape the fever for this time; and Christie's thoughts began to turn homeward again. But not so anxiously as before. The pain of parting from the children would be harder now. And during these days she began to feel a strange yearning tenderness for the poor young mother, scarcely less helpless and in need of care than they. It had come to be quite the regular thing now for Mrs. Greenly to take an hour's rest in the attic-nursery when the children had fallen asleep, while Christie took her place in Mrs. Lee's room.

New and wonderful were the glimpses which those twilight hours gave to Christie. She found that Mrs. Lee, sitting in her drawing-room, or even in the nursery, giving directions about the care of the children, was a very different person from Mrs. Lee lying in bed feverish or exhausted, looking back over the days of her childhood, or forward to a future that was anything but hopeful to her disenchanted eyes. Naturally reserved, the lady had made but few acquaintances in the city, and had not one intimate friend; and now, when weak and weary and desponding, it was a relief to her to speak to some one of the times and places and events over which memory had brooded in silence for so many years. She never dreamed what glimpses of her heart she was giving to her little nurse. She only saw the sympathy expressed by Christie's grave face or eager gesture; and she talked to her, sometimes regretfully enough, about her mother and her brothers and her childish days. Yet, sad as those memories were, they were scarcely so sad as the thoughts she sent out into the future. She did not often speak her fears; but her silence and her frequent sighs were to Christie more eloquent than words.

Christie rarely spoke at such times as these—never, except when a question was asked; and then her reply was generally prefaced with, 'I have heard my father say,' or, 'Effie once told me,' or, 'I heard John Nesbitt saying.' Ignorant as she knew herself to be on the most important of all subjects, she was yet far wiser than her mistress. Some of Christie's simple remarks and suggestions made an impression on her heart that wiser and more direct teachings might have failed to make.

As for Christie, in her sympathy for Mrs. Lee's troubles, she almost forgot her own. In striving to relieve her from all anxiety about the children, she was ready to forget even her own weariness; and in the knowledge that she was doing some good to them all, she ceased to regret that Annie had gone home without her.

CHAPTER IX.

LIGHT IN DARKNESS.

THE week passed. Sunday morning came; and out of a broken, uneasy slumber, Christie was awakened by the fall of rain-drops on the window. In the midst of the trouble and turmoil of the week she had striven to be patient; but through it all she had looked forward to the two hours' respite of the Sabbath, and now it seemed to her that she could not be denied. Turning her aching eyes from the light, she did not, for a moment or two, try to restrain her tears. But she could not indulge herself long, if she had been ever so much inclined. For soon arose the clamour of childish voices, that must be stilled. So Christie rose, and bathed her hot eyes, and strove to think that, after all, the clouds were not so very thick, and they might break away in time for her to go.

'At any rate, there is no good in being vexed about it,' she said to herself. 'I must try and be content at home, if I canna go.'

It was an easier matter to content herself than to her first waking thought seemed possible. She was soon busy with the little ones, quieting their noise as she washed and dressed them, partly for little Harry's sake, and partly because it was the Sabbath-day. So earnest was she in all this that she had no time to think of her disappointment till the boys were down-stairs at breakfast with their mother. Then little Harry seemed feverish and fretful and 'ill to do with,' as Mrs. Greenly, who visited the attic-nursery with the baby in her arms, declared. Christie strove to soothe her fretful pet, and took him in her arms to carry him down-stairs. A gleam of sunshine met her on the way.

'It is going to be fine weather, after all,' she said to Nurse Greenly, turning round on the first landing.

But nurse seemed inclined this morning to look on the dark side of things, and shook her head.

'I'm not so sure of that,' said she. 'That's but a single gleam; and I dare say the sky is black enough, if we could see it. And hearken, child, to the wind! The streets will be in a puddle; and with those pains in your ankles you'll never, surely, think of going out to-day?'

Christie's face clouded again; and so did the sky, for the gleam of sunshine vanished.

'I should like to go, indeed,' said she; 'and it's only when I am very tired that my ankles pain me.'

'Tired!' repeated nurse. 'Yes, and no wonder; and yet you will persist in carrying that great boy, who is far better able to carry himself. I don't wonder that you want to go even to the church, to be out of the reach of trouble for a while.'

Christie laughed a little—she could not help it—at nurse's energy.

'I am afraid it *is* partly for the quiet that I want to go,' said she, looking grave enough for a minute,

And she did go, after all, though the weather was so forbidding.

Christie's first thought, when she entered the church, was that their hall-clock had gone wrong and made her late; for already there was scarcely a vacant seat, and it was not without difficulty that she found her way to the place she was accustomed to occupy. There were strangers in the pew, and strangers before her and around her; and with a shy and wondering feeling Christie took up her hymn-book.

The great multitude that filled the seats and thronged the aisles were waiting impatiently to hear the sound of a voice hitherto unheard among them. Christie sent now and then a curious glance over the crowded seats and aisles, and up to the galleries, from which so many grave, attentive faces looked down; but even when the stillness which followed the hum and buzz of the coming in of the congregation was broken by the clear, grave tones of a stranger's voice, it never occurred to her that it was the voice of one whose eloquence had gathered and held many a multitude before. In a little while she forgot the crowd and everything else. At first she strained her short-sighted eyes in the direction of the voice, eagerly but vainly. But this soon ceased; and by the time the singing and the prayers were over, she only listened.

To many in the house that day, the word spoken by God's servant was as 'a very lovely song of one that hath a pleasant voice and can play well on an instrument.' To many it was a stumbling-block, and to many more foolishness. But to the weary child, who sat there with her head bowed down, and her face hidden in her hands, it was 'Christ the power of God

and the wisdom of God unto salvation.' She forgot the
time, the place, and the gathered multitude. She
forgot her own weakness and weariness. She forgot
even the speaker in the words he spoke. In a little
while she grew unconscious of the tears she had tried
to hide, and her hands fell down on her lap, and her
wet cheeks and smiling lips were turned towards the
face that her dim eyes failed to see.

I cannot tell what were the words that so moved
her. It was not that the thoughts were new or clothed
in loftier language than she was wont to hear. It was
the old but ever new theme, set forth in the old true
way, reverently and simply, by lips which—long ago
touched by a coal from the altar—had answered to
the heavenly voice, 'Here am I; send me.' It was
God's love, intimated by many a sign and made visible
by many a token, but first and best of all by this, that
'He spared not His own Son, but gave Him up to die
for us all.'

No, the words were neither new nor strange; and
yet they seemed to be both to her. It was not as
though she were listening to spoken words. There
seemed to be revealed to her, as in a vision, a glimpse
of mysteries into which the angels desire to look. Her
eyes were open to see God's plan of salvation in its
glorious completeness, Christ's finished work in all its
suitableness and sufficiency, His grace in all its fullness
and freeness. Oh, that wondrous grace ! Angels gaze
from afar, while ascribing to its Author greatness and
power and glory. But the redeemed have a higher
and more thrilling song put into their mouths.

'Unto Him who loved *us*, and gave Himself for
us !' they sing; and then and there this child had a

foretaste of their unspeakable blessedness. It was as 'the chiefest among ten thousand, and altogether lovely,' that she saw Him now; and love supreme, and entire trust and peacefulness, took possession of her heart. Very sinful, and weak and unworthy she saw herself to be; but she saw also that the grace that can pardon, justify, purify, and save is the more glorious on that very account. Her sins no longer rose between her and God. They were removed from her 'as far as the east is from the west.' They were cast altogether behind His back, to be remembered against her no more for ever.

If before to-day Christie had been one of Christ's little ones—if she had had a place in the fold, and had now and then caught a glimpse of the green pastures and the still waters where the 'Good Shepherd' leads His flock—it was to-day for the first time that she realized the blessedness of her calling. Her little Bible, and her murmured prayer night and morning, amid the sleeping children, had more than any other thing, more than all other things together, helped her quietly and cheerfully through the weary winter. Clinging now to one promise, and now to another, she had never been quite without the light and help that seemed to come from above. But to-day it was not a solitary promise. It was not even the sense that *all* the promises to God's people from generation to generation were hers to rely upon. It was the blessedness of the knowledge that began to dawn, like heaven's own light, upon her, the knowledge that she was no longer her own, but *His* who had bought her with a price—*His* to have and to hold, in sorrow and joy, through life and in death, henceforth and for ever. Now, 'neither life, nor death, nor angels, nor principalities, nor powers, nor things present, nor things to come, nor height, nor depth, nor any other creature, could separate her from the love of God which is in Christ Jesus our Lord.'

Silently, with the thoughtful or thoughtless multitude, she passed from the house of prayer. Yet her soul was sending up a song of praise that reached the heaven of heavens. A forlorn little figure she must have seemed to any chance eye that rested on her as she picked her way among the pools that had settled here and there on the pavement. It was only by a great effort that she held her own against the wind and rain, that threatened to carry away her shawl, and rendered vain her attempts to shield her faded crape bonnet with a still more faded umbrella. If one among the crowd who met or passed her on her way took any notice of her at all, it must have been to smile at or to pity her. Yet over her angels in the high heavens were rejoicing. In her heart was the peace that passeth understanding, soon to blossom forth into joy unspeakable and full of glory.

Heedless alike of smiles and pity, she hastened along, unconscious of discomfort. Even the near approach to the house, and the thought of the peevish children and the dim attic-nursery, had no power to silence the song that her grateful soul was singing. She went up the stone steps without her accustomed sigh of weariness; and the face that greeted Mrs. Greenly as she opened the door, though pale enough, and wet with rain-drops, was a very pleasant face for any one to see.

'You foolish child!' Mrs. Greenly exclaimed, eyeing the little figure that stood on the door-mat. 'You would have been better at home.'

Something in Christie's face kept her from saying more.

'I am very glad I went—very glad,' said Christie, stooping to take off her wet shoes, that she might not soil Nelly's spotless oilcloth; and as she gathered them up and faced Mrs. Greenly again, she repeated, softly:

'I am very, *very* glad! You haven't needed me much, have you? How is wee Harry?'

Nurse took no notice of her question, but looking gravely at her, said:

'I wonder the wind didn't carry you away, poor child!'

'It very nearly did,' said Christie, laughing. 'I am very glad to be safe within doors again; but I am very glad I went, for all that.'

'But you are wet through!' said nurse, laying her hand on her shoulder. 'Go and change your clothes this very moment. Stay,' she added, as Christie began to ascend the stairs. 'If the children get a sight of you there will be an end of your peace. Go down to the kitchen, and I will bring down your things for you.'

Christie looked wonderingly into her face.

'You are very kind. But you need not take the trouble. I'm not so very wet.'

'Do as I bid you,' said Mrs. Greenly, impatiently. 'You'll be ill with those pains in your ankles again. And you have a weary week before you, or I'm mistaken.'

'What is it?' asked Christie, in alarm.

'It may be little, after all; but little Harry seems far from well, and his mother is naturally anxious. At any rate, I'm going to call for the doctor this afternoon, and if it should prove that he has taken the fever, why,

I must stay for a week, and you have the prospect of a longer confinement in the attic-nursery.'

It was too true. Little Harry was very ill—much worse than his sister had been at first. The doctor looked very grave when he saw him that afternoon, and positively directed that the other children should be kept away from the room. But Christie was not sent with them to the attic.

Having caught a glimpse of her passing the door, Harry could not be pacified till he found himself in her arms; and not even his mother could beguile him from her through all that long afternoon. He was very feverish, and seemed to suffer much, poor little fellow. Sometimes she soothed his restlessness by singing to him in a low voice, or by telling him the tales that had amused him many a time during the long winter. Sometimes she walked about with him in her arms; but she was not able to do this very long, and so she sat on a low chair, rocking him gently in her arms. The other children were down-stairs with Nelly. Mrs. Greenly had gone out to make arrangements for a longer stay; and poor Mrs. Lee, anxious and unhappy, went in and out of the nursery, unable to quiet herself or to take the rest she so much needed.

It was nearly dark when the doctor came in again, and the little boy had fallen into an uneasy slumber. The doctor started slightly when he saw Christie, and said, rather hastily—

'I thought I told you to keep away?'

The child stirred and murmured as the light was brought in, and Christie hushed him softly; but she made no reply. Mrs. Lee spoke for her:

'But he was so restless, doctor, and seemed so

uncomfortable after you went away; and we could do nothing to quiet him till Christie took him. He is very fond of her.'

The doctor laid his hand on the hot forehead of the little patient, but his eye was on Christie.

'Have you ever had the fever?' he asked.

'I am not sure. I think I had it when I was a child. But I am not afraid of it.'

'When you were a child! That could not have been a long time ago, I should imagine,' said the doctor, smiling a little, as he looked into the earnest face turned towards him. 'But I dare say you will do as well for Harry as Nurse Greenly herself could do.'

'Is he in danger? Is he worse than Letty was?' asked his mother.

'Oh, no! He is by no means so ill as she was at one time,' said the doctor, cheerfully. 'And a fine rugged little fellow like Harry may get through much better than his sister. But, at the same time, this fever sometimes becomes more severe as the season advances, and it is as well to keep the other children away. Not that I think there is any particular danger for any of them—even the baby; but being weaned so young, and her teeth coming, it is as well to be cautious. So if Christie is to nurse Harry, she may as well have nothing to do with the baby—or the boys.'

Mrs. Lee looked still harassed and anxious.

'There is no harm done,' continued the doctor, soothingly. 'If Christie has to be with the other children, she should not be with Harry. But if Harry is so fond of her, perhaps she had better stay with him to-night, at any rate. I dare say you can manage without her up-stairs for one night?'

'Oh, yes! we can do very well,' said Mrs. Lee.

'When do you expect Mr. Lee home?' asked the doctor.

Mrs. Lee shook her head. 'I have been expecting him every day for a week. He must come soon, now, or write. He has not yet heard of Letty's illness. I was so glad it was over befoie he came! and now Harry, and perhaps the others——' She stopped short, but soon added, 'I hope nurse will not need to go.'

'No, it's not likely; and even if she should, you will manage with some one for the other children. I am quite willing to trust my patients with this careful little person, since she is not afraid. The little fellow seems quite fond of her. I suppose you don't mind being kept awake a little for one night?' he said, as he again stooped over the flushed face of the little boy.

'Oh, no! And even if I go to sleep, I wake very easily. The least movement wakes me. I think you can trust me, ma'am; and I can call you or Mrs. Greenly at any moment, you know.'

'I have trusted her all the winter, as I have never been able to trust any one with the children before,' said Mrs. Lee to the doctor. 'Christie has been very good to the children, and to me too. I am only afraid I have put too much on her—such a child as she is.'

Christie's face, which had been pale enough before, crimsoned all over with pleasure at the words of Mrs. Lee.

'I am quite strong; at least, I am much stronger than I look,' she said.

'Well, you are to stay with little Harry to-night, at

any rate, and I hope I may find him much better in the morning,' said the doctor.

He gave some further directions about the child's drink and medicine, and went away. Christie heard him in the passage urging upon Mrs. Lee the necessity of keeping herself quiet and taking rest. The child, he assured her, was in no danger; but he would not answer for the consequences to herself should she suffer her over-anxiety to bring on a return of the illness from which she had only just recovered. He did not leave her till he saw her resting on the sofa in her own room; and Christie did not see her again till the house had become quiet for the night. Mrs. Greenly had paid one brief visit to the sick-room, and then, weary with the exertions of the week, betook herself to the attic-nursery to rest. Christie was left quite alone but her solitary musings were not so sad as they had been many a time. And sitting there in the dim light of the night-lamp, she said to herself, 'I can never, never have such sad thoughts again.'

CHAPTER X.

IT was past midnight when Mrs. Lee entered the nursery again. Little Harry was on the bed, and his weary nurse was preparing to lie down beside him.

'He seems to be sleeping quietly,' said his mother, as she bent over him.

'Yes, ma'am—much more quietly than he did last night. I think he will have a good night,' said Christie.

Mrs. Lee seated herself on the side of the low bed, and listened to his quick, irregular breathing.

'I was beginning to hope that all the others might escape, now that Letty is so well,' she said; 'but if Harry gets over it I shall be glad. It is always well that children should have these diseases while they are at home, if they must have them—poor darlings!'

She looked grave, and even sad as she spoke; but her face was not so pale, and she did not look so hopeless as she had done when the doctor was present.

'I feel quite rested and refreshed,' she said, after a few moments. 'I have been asleep two or three hours. You had better go up-stairs and lie down awhile, and I will stay with Harry the rest of the night. You look very tired, Christie.'

'I was just going to lie down here,' said Christie. 'Do you think you need to sit up, ma'am? He seems sleeping so quietly, and the least movement he can make will wake me. I can keep a light burning, and call you at any moment. I do not think you need to sit up.'

'I am afraid you will not rest much with him, if his least movement will wake you,' said Mrs. Lee, doubtfully.

'Oh, I wake and sleep again very easily,' said Christie, cheerfully. 'I am used to it now.'

Still Mrs. Lee lingered, watching the child with anxious eyes, and now and then sighing deeply Christie sent many a pitying glance towards her wondering if any trouble that she knew nothing of was added to the anxiety with which she regarded her child. She longed to be able to comfort her. Her heart was full of sympathy for her—sympathy which she did not venture to express in words. She did not even let her looks express it, but took up her Bible, that she might not seem to be watching her. Mrs. Lee roused herself at last, and turning to Christie, said:

'Mrs. Greenly tells me that Mr. G., the famous preacher, was in town to-day. And, by the bye, you must have heard him. He preached in —— Church this morning. You were there, I suppose?'

'Yes; I was there,' said Christie, with great interest. 'There was a strange minister preached; but I didn't know that he was a great man. That was the reason there was such a crowd of people, I suppose. I wondered why it was.'

'You didn't like him, then? or you didn't think him a great man?' said Mrs. Lee, smiling.

'Oh, yes,' said she, eagerly; 'I liked him. But I wasn't thinking about him as a great man; I wasn't thinking of him at all—only of what he said.'

'He told you something new, then?' said Mrs. Lee.

'No! Oh, no! Nothing new; nothing that I had not heard many times before. And yet it seemed to come to me as new!' she added, a strange, sweet smile passing over her face.

'What did he say that was new to you?'

'Some things he said that I shall never forget. He was telling us of God's love to man, shown in many ways, but most and best of all in the work of redemption. It wasn't new, what he said; and yet—I don't know how it was—I seemed to see it as I never saw it before.' And again the same bright smile flashed over her countenance.

'The work of redemption?' repeated Mrs. Lee; and there was a questioning tone in her voice that made Christie look at her doubtfully before replying.

'Yes; you know, "God so loved the world that He gave His only begotten Son, that whosoever believeth on Him might not perish, but have eternal life." And "All we like sheep have gone astray. We have turned every one to his own way; and the Lord hath laid on Him the iniquity of us all." And there are many more verses in the Bible like this. One of them says, "When there was no eye to pity, or hand to save, God's eye pitied, and His own arm brought salvation." I'm not sure that these are the exact words, but that is the meaning of the verse.'

'Brought salvation!' repeated Mrs. Lee. 'That means that God's people will be saved, and will go to heaven when they die?'

'Yes,' said Christie, hesitatingly. 'It means that; but it means something more. We don't have to wait till we die to get the good of salvation. We shall be saved from the punishment of sin when we die, but we are saved here from its power. We come to hate what we once loved, and to see beauty and worth in things that before were uninteresting to us. What was hard to do and hard to bear becomes easy for Christ's sake. Somehow or other, everything seems changed. "Old things pass away. All things become new."'

She paused, and letting her cheek rest on the hand that held her Bible, she gazed into the glowing embers with eyes that seemed to see pleasant things far away. Mrs. Lee looked at her with wonder for a time, and then said:

'Has all this happened to you—this change you speak about?'

A sudden flow of tears was the only reply her question received at first. But soon she raised her head, and said:

'Sometimes—now and then—I have hoped so; and to-day, when God's great love to sinners was set forth, and the way of salvation shown to be so wise, so free, so suitable, it seemed foolish and unreasonable to doubt any more. I had heard all about it many and many a time before, but the words seemed to come home to my heart to-day. It was like the sudden shining out of a light in a dark place. Maybe I'll go back again to my old doubts and discontent. But I hope not; I believe not. I know He is able to keep me; and I think He will.'

Mrs. Lee had laid herself down by Harry, and was

listening now, with her eyes shaded by her hand. She lay so long and so quietly that Christie thought she must have fallen asleep, and began softly to turn over the leaves of her Bible again; and she quite started when, in the course of half an hour, she spoke again.

'You said something about God's love in redemption. What did you mean by it? Tell me more of what the preacher said.'

Christie hesitated a moment, and was at a loss what to say: 'I can't mind all he said. That is, I can't mind the exact words. But he told us what a blessed thing it is for us that our salvation, from beginning to end, is God's own work, and how impossible it is that we could be saved if it depended on ourselves.'

'Yes; even if one could begin one's life again. It would be all the same. We might avoid some errors and keep from falling into some mistakes; but after all, it would come to the same thing in the end, I dare say. There is no use in wishing for another chance.'

Mrs. Lee sighed; and Christie hesitated a moment, and then said: 'We can do nothing to save ourselves, ma'am, and all else that we have to do grows easy, because of the grace which God gives, and because of a knowledge of Christ's love to us. It is easy to do the will of One who loves us, and whom we love.'

There was a long pause after this, which Mrs. Lee broke by saying: 'What was it you said about "no eye to pity, and no arm to save"?'

'Here it is,' said Christie; and she eagerly read the words from her Bible, and many more besides—a verse here and a verse there, as her own judgment or Effie's marginal marks suggested: such as, '*Surely He hath borne our griefs and carried our sorrows.*

'*He was wounded for our transgressions, and bruised for our iniquities.*

'*For when we were without strength, in due time Christ died for the ungodly.*

'*For scarcely for a righteous man will one die; yet peradventure for a good man some would even dare to die.*

'*But God commendeth His love toward us, in that, while we were yet sinners, Christ died for us.*

'*Who shall lay anything to the charge of God's elect? It is God that justifieth. Who is he that condemneth? It is Christ that died; yea, rather, that is risen again, who is even at the right hand of God, who also maketh intercession for us. Who shall separate us from the love of Christ?*'

'If we could be sure that we are among the children of God,' said Mrs. Lee, with a sigh. And soon after she added: 'There are a great many things in the Bible that are hard to understand.'

'Yes; I suppose so—I am sure of it,' said Christie, gravely. 'But the things most necessary for us to know and understand are easy for us; at least, with the help of the Holy Spirit they grow easy, I think. It is very plainly told us we are sinners and need a Saviour, that a Saviour has been provided, and those who come to Him He will in no wise cast out. These are the chief things; and besides these, we are assured of help and guidance and peace, all the way through to the end.'

Christie spoke slowly, striving to put into as few words as possible these precious truths of the Bible.

'You seem to know a great deal about these things, and to take a pleasure in them,' said Mrs. Lee.

Christie shook her head. 'I take pleasure in them, but I know very little. It is only lately that I have cared to learn. I am very ignorant.'

Ignorant though she was, the child knew more of God's truth than her mistress; and many a word in season she spoke to her anxious heart during the long watches that they shared together in the sad times that followed that memorable day. They were words very simply and humbly spoken—rarely Christie's own. They were passages of Scripture, or bits from the catechism, or remembered comments upon them made, in her hearing, by her father, or by Effie and her friends.

Nothing could have been farther from Christie's thoughts than any intention of teaching. She did not dream how strange and new to her listener were the blessed truths that were beginning to present themselves so vividly to her own mind. She would have shrunk from the thought of presuming to teach, or even to suggest new trains of thought. In ordinary circumstances she might have found it difficult to converse long on any subject with Mrs. Lee. But watching and anxiety, shared in the chamber over which hangs the shadow of a great dread, soon break down the barriers of reserve which a difference of age or position raises; and there seemed no inappropriateness in the grave, earnest words that now and then fell from the lips of the little maid. Indeed, weak in body and exhausted in mind as the troubles of the winter and spring had left her, Mrs. Lee found positive rest and refreshment in the society which might at another

time have seemed unsuitable; and mingled with the
gratitude with which she saw Christie's devotion to
the sick child was a feeling of respect and admiration
for the character which was gradually developing before
her eyes.

How long the days and nights seemed! Little
Harry's robust frame and fine constitution availed him
little. The fever raged with great violence; and the
close of the week found the doctor still in doubt as to
how it might end with him. His mother's strength
and hopefulness had held out wonderfully till this time;
but when the baby, the fair and fragile little Ellinor,
was stricken down, faith, strength, and courage seemed
to fail her. It was not long, however. The child's
need gave the mother strength; and the baby needed
nothing long. The other children were sent away to a
friend's house in the country; and silence, broken only
by the moans of the little ones or the hushed voices of
their anxious nurses, reigned through the house, lately
echoing to far other sounds.

Before three silent days had passed, the mother
knew that her baby must die. In the presence of her
unutterable sorrow Christie was mute. The awe which
fell upon her in the dread presence left her no words
with which to comfort the stricken mother. But in
her heart she never ceased through all that last long
night to pray, 'God comfort her.'

And she *was* comforted. Though her tears fell fast
on the folded hands of her child as she said the words,
they were humbly and reverently spoken:

'"Thy will be done." It would have been harder to
leave my child than to let her go!—and now one of
my darlings is safe from all sorrow for ever!'

The father came home just in time to lay his little
daughter in the grave; and then both father and
mother sat down to wait. For what? For the gradual
return of the rose to the cheek and the light to the
eye of little Harry? Alas, no! It was not to be.
A keener pang was to pierce the heart of the stricken
mother. For to part with little Harry was a far harder
trial to anticipate than even the loss of her baby had
been to bear. But day by day it became more apparent
to all that Harry's end was hastening. The fever went
away, but there seemed to be no power to rally in the
little worn-out frame of the child. His father, for a
little while, spoke hopefully of a change of air, and
the sea-side; but he could not long so cheat himself
with false hopes. The restlessness and irritability,
which they had said to one another were hopeful signs,
passed away. His smiles were more languid and
constrained, and he soon failed to recognize the anxious,
loving friends who ministered to his wants.

Before this the mother's strength had quite failed;
and the father, unused to the sight of suffering, shrank
from looking on the last agony of his child. Through
all his illness the little boy had clung to Christie—
never quite at rest, even in the arms of his mother,
unless his Christie was near. Her voice had soothed
him, her hands had ministered to his comfort, her care
had been lavished on him, through all those lingering
days and nights. And now it was Christie who met
his last smile and listened to his last murmured 'Good-
night!' Yes, it was Christie who closed his eyes at
last, and straightened his limbs in their last repose.
She helped to robe him for the grave, and to lay him
in his little coffin; and all the time there was coming

and going through her mind a verse she had learned
long ago—

> ' Now, like a dew-drop shrined
>   Within a crystal stone,
> Thou'rt safe in heaven, my dove ;
> Safe in the arms of Jesus,
>   The everlasting One ! '

CHAPTER XI.

AND now a sad silence fell on the household. The
children were not to be brought home for some time,
the doctor said; and their mother was not able to go
to them; so Christie was left to the almost unbroken
quiet of her forsaken nursery. She needed rest more
than she was aware, and sank into a state of passive
indifference to all things which would have alarmed
herself had not her kind friend, Mrs. Greenly, been
there to insist that she should be relieved of care till
her over-tasked strength should be in some measure
restored. In those very quiet hours, thoughts of home
came to her only as a vague and shadowy remembrance.
The events of the winter, and even the more recent
sufferings of the last month, seemed like a dream to
her. Dearly as she had loved her little charges, she
was hardly conscious of regret at their loss. It seemed
like something that had happened long ago—their long
suffering and departure. The very promises which
had of late become so sweet to her, soothed her merely
as a pleasant sound might do. She scarcely took note
of their meaning or power during those days.

But this soon passed away, and with returning

strength came back with double force the old longing
to go home. She had sent a line to Effie when little
Harry was taken ill, telling her how utterly impossible
it would be for her to leave her place. Since then,
about the time of the baby's death, a neighbour had
called, and by him she had sent the same message,
assuring her sister that she was quite content to stay.
But her old eagerness to get home came back, now
that she found herself with little to occupy her, and
she waited anxiously for the time when Mrs. Lee might
be spoken to on the subject.

In the meantime, Mrs. Greenly was called away,
and the duty of attendance upon Mrs. Lee once more
devolved on Christie. If anything could have banished
from her heart all thought of home or all wish for
change, the days that followed would have done so.
Not an hour passed in which she was not made to feel
that she was a comfort to her friend—for *friends*, in
the highest sense, the mistress and her little maid were
fast becoming. The readings and conversations which
had been begun during their long watches together
were renewed; and blessed seasons they proved to
both. Christie never knew—never could know on
earth—all the good she did Mrs. Lee in those days.
She was only conscious of an ever-increasing love for
her and an ever-increasing desire to serve her.

If in the first agony of her bereavement there had
been in the mother's heart murmuring and rebellious
thoughts, they were all stilled now. With more than
the submission of a chastened child—with joy that had
in it a sense of reconciliation and acceptance—she was
enabled to kiss the Hand that had smitten her. She
seldom spoke of her children; but when she did, it

was with gratitude that they had been hers, and were still hers, in heaven. Seen by the new light that was dawning on her soul, the world, its hopes and fears and interests, looked to her very different. Humble submission and cheerful trust took the place of her old, anxious forebodings. Scripture truths, which formerly conveyed no distinct idea to her mind, came home to her now with power. They were living truths, full of hope and comfort. The promises were to her a place of rest and refuge—a strong tower, into which she could run and be safe. By slow degrees the light of the glorious Gospel of Jesus Christ dawned upon her soul ; and to one fearful and doubtful of the future, as she had been, what blessed rest and refreshment was in the trust, that gradually grew strong, in the embrace of an Arm mighty to save ! To know herself one of those to whom Jesus has given a right to say, ' I will fear no evil, for *Thou* art with me,' was all that she needed for her consolation ; and during those days the blessed knowledge came to her.

What part the simple words and earnest prayers of her little nurse had in bringing about this blessed change, God knows. The girl herself had little thought of the good which her entrance into the household had wrought. It might have helped her to a more patient waiting had she known how often her name was mingled with the thankful praises of Mrs. Lee. She was not impatient, but a longing for home that would not be stilled mingled with the gladness that filled her heart at the thought of being useful.

Summer had come. June was half over, and the only glimpse of green she had had was the top of the mountain, far away, Now and then Nelly brought home from the market a bunch of garden-flowers. But the sight of them only made her long the more for the fields where so many flowers that she knew had blossomed and faded unseen. More than once, when sent out by Mrs. Lee to take the air, she had tried to extend her walk in one direction or another, till she should reach the country. But partly because she did not know the way, and partly because she grew so soon weary, she never succeeded. She had to content herself with the nearest street where there were trees growing, and now and then a peep through open gateways upon little dusty strips of grass or garden-ground.

Oh, how close and hot and like a prison the long, narrow streets seemed to her! How weary the street noises made her! It was foolish, she knew, and so she told herself often, to vex herself with idle fancies. But sometimes there came back to her, with a vividness which for the moment was like reality, the memory of familiar sights and sounds. Sometimes it was the wind waving the trees, or the ripple of the brook over the stepping-stones; sometimes it was the bleating of the young lambs in the pastures far away. She caught glimpses of familiar faces in the crowd, as she used to do in the home-sick days when she first came; and she could not always smile at her folly. Sometimes her disappointment would send her home sad and dispirited enough. Almost always the smile that met her as she entered Mrs. Lee's room brought back her content; but often it needed a greater effort to be cheerful than an on-looker could have guessed. Still, the effort was always made, and never without some measure of success.

One morning she rose more depressed than usual.
A quiet half-hour with her little Bible was not sufficient
to raise her spirits, though she told herself it ought
to be; and she said to herself, as she went down-stairs,
'I will speak to-day about going home.'

Mrs. Lee was able to go down-stairs now. On this
particular day a friend was to visit her, and Christie
determined to say nothing about the matter till the
visitor should be gone. But the prospect of a long
day in the solitary nursery did not tend to brighten
her face, and it was sadly enough that she went slowly
down the street on an errand for Nelly when breakfast
was over.

She did not look up to-day in her usual vain search
for a 'kenned face,' or she would never have passed by
the corner so unheedingly. A pair of kind eyes, for
the moment as grave and sad as her own, watched her
as she came on, and after she passed. In a little while
a very gentle hand was laid on her shoulder.

'What's your haste, Christie, my lassie?'

With a cry she turned to clasp the hand of John
Nesbitt. Poor little Christie! She was so glad, so
very glad! It was almost like seeing Effie herself, she
told him, amid a great burst of tears that startled the
grave John considerably. For a moment her sobs came
fast. The open streets and the wondering passers-by
were quite forgotten.

'Whisht, Christie, my woman, said John, soothingly,
'that's no' the way we show our gladness in Glengarry.'

Drawing her hand under his arm, he held it firmly
in his own. Christie made a great effort to control
herself, and the face which she soon turned towards her

friend had grown wonderfully brighter for the tears that fell.

'Effie bade me notice how you looked and what you said; and I'm afraid she'll no' be pleased to hear that I got such a tearful welcome,' said John, with his grave smile.

'Oh, Effie will understand. Why, it's almost like seeing Effie herself to see you, John!' she repeated, giving him a tearful smile. She felt sure it was a true friend's hand that pressed hers so warmly as she spoke.

'But where are you going, Christie?' asked John.

'Oh, I forgot; we are past the place.' But her face grew grave in a moment. 'When did you come, John? and how long are you going to stay?'

'I came yesterday, and I shall stay no longer than I can help. I have had enough of this dusty town for once. I wonder how you ever stayed so long in it, Christie.'

'I wonder myself, whiles,' she said gravely; 'but it won't be long now.'

'Are they better at your house? Will they spare you to go home with me?'

'There is no one ill now. Did you hear——' But Christie's voice was lost in the remembrance of little Harry and the baby.

'Yes, we heard. You must have had a sad time, poor lassie! But the remembrance of these precious little ones cannot be altogether sorrowful, Christie?'

'No; oh, no, indeed!' But she could say no more. As they drew near the house, she added:

'And shan't I see you again, John?'

'Ay, lass, that you will. I'm by no means done with you yet. Are you busy to-day? because I would like

your help. I promised to get some things for my
mother, and I'm not good at choosing. Will you come
with me? Do you think you can be spared?'

'I don't know. I should like it. I can ask.'

In a minute she returned, with a face made radiant
by Mrs. Lee's cheerful consent to spare her for as much
of the day as she pleased; and it was arranged that
John should call for her in half an hour.

If anything could have marred the delight with
which her preparations were made, the sight of her
faded bonnet and shawl might have done so. The rain
and the snow had wet them, the sun had done its work
on them, and the wind had taken liberties with them,
many a time. And besides, they seemed too hot and
heavy for such a summer day, even if they had not been
shabby and gray. For Christie had had other things
to think about of late than the getting of summer
garments. Just for a minute a wish that they had been
newer and fresher-looking, for John's sake, came to her
mind. It was only for a moment that she thought
about it at all.

'For John cares little for such things,' she said to
herself; 'and there's no matter for the shop-people and
the rest.'

She was right. Looking into the brightened face
that met him at the door, John failed to discover that
the bonnet above it was dingy and brown. And if the
rustiness of the little shepherd's-plaid shawl that covered
her shoulders marred in any degree the pleasure with
which he drew her hand beneath his friendly arm, he
gave no token that it did so. Christie gave a little sigh
of satisfaction as she found herself out on the street
once more.

'I have got so many things to ask about,' she said; 'but I suppose I may as well wait till we have done with the shops. If I once begin, I'm afraid I shan't be able to attend to anything else.'

The purchases were soon made. Indeed, Mrs. Nesbitt's commissions had not been very extensive. Christie had more to do on her own account. But she had planned so many times just what she was to get for each one at home, that it did not take her long to choose. Besides, her purse was not one of the fullest. Still, the little she had to do involved a good deal of running here and there; and her parcels increased in number and size to such an extent, that Christie at last said, laughing, she would have to forego the pleasure of taking them home herself, as her box would never hold half of them; John would need to try to find room for them in his.

'And are you not afraid they may call you extravagant at home, getting so many braw things?'

Christie laughed.

'I'm no' sure. But then—unless it's Aunt Elsie's gown—there's nothing dear. They are just prints; the frocks and the other things are all useful, except perhaps the playthings for the bairns; and they are useful too, for things that give pleasure have a use, I am sure.'

'It canna be doubted,' said her friend, laughing.

Christie's face grew a little grave, after a rather lengthened examination of the pieces left in her purse.

'There is just one other thing; but I fear I ought not to have left it to the last. It's for blind Alice. I have thought about it so long. It's not very far, we might ask the price of it, anyway.'

It was true, the place was not very far; but it was a

shop of greater pretensions than any they had entered yet. Christie had set her heart on a musical-box, which she knew would be a treasure to the blind child. But the cost! It was altogether beyond her means, even if she were to stay another month.

The disappointment was very great.

'Allie must have something that she can hear, you ken; and I had no thought that it would be so dear.'

'Why not send her a bird—a real canary?' said John, as they made a pause at a low window in a narrow street, where a great variety of cages were hanging.

'A bird?' repeated Christie. 'I never thought of that. Are they very dear?'

'We can ask,' said John; and as Christie stood admiring the gay plumage of some strange bird, he put the question to the person in waiting. Christie did not hear his answer. John did not mean that she should.

'Could you spare two dollars, Christie?' said he.

'Two dollars!' she repeated. It was the wages of half a month.

'I have cheaper ones,' said the man, 'but he is the best singer I have had for a long time. Or maybe you would like a pair?'

'A pair!' thought Christie to herself. If she could manage to get one she would be content! As if to verify the words of his owner, the bird, after hopping quickly from perch to perch, poured forth such a flood of melody as Christie had never heard from a bird's throat before.

'Oh, how sweet!' exclaimed she. 'To think of little Allie having music like that all the winter long! But how can you carry it, John?'

Oh, John could carry it easily—no fear; and touched by Christie's eager delight, or by some more powerful cause, the man let the cage go with the bird.

So that was settled.

'We're done now, I suppose,' said Christie, with a sigh, as they passed along the shady side of the street. The excitement of pleasure was passing out of her face; and more than ever before, since the first glimpse he got of it, did John Nesbitt realize what a pale, weary little face it was.

'I wish you were going home with me, Christie!'

'I wish I was, indeed! I wish I had spoken to Mrs. Lee before! But I couldna leave her, John, till she got some one else, she is so delicate now. Sometimes I think I never could get courage to leave her at all, if she were to ask me to stay.'

'Ay, lass; but there's more to be said about that. They'll think at home that you're forgetting them, if I tell them what you say.'

Christie laughed.

'I'm not afraid. I don't think it would be right to leave her now; and seeing you has given me courage for another month at least. You can tell Effie that.'

'I shall have two or three things to tell her besides that,' said John, looking down on her with the grave smile which she liked so much to see. 'I shall be sorry to tell her how pale and ill you look,' he added, his face growing grave as he looked.

'Oh, that's only because I am tired just now; and besides, I was always "a pale-faced thing," as Aunt Elsie used to say. You are not to vex Effie by making her think that I am not well,' she said, eagerly. 'I have not been used to walking far, lately, and I get tired very soon.'

They were entering the large square at the moment, and John said:

'Can we go in there among the trees? I see seats there. Let us sit down and rest a while.'

'Oh, yes! I have been here before. Nothing reminds me so much of home as the flickering of these shadows—not even the leaves themselves. And how sweet the flowers are! Do you ken, John, I didna see the leaves this year till they were full-grown? I can hardly believe that the spring has come and gone again.'

John Nesbitt was looking and listening, and all the time he was considering something very earnestly. He had not many dollars at his disposal, and the few he had he was not inclined to part with but for value received. He was saying to himself, at the moment, that if it should be decided that he was qualified for the work to which he had set himself apart, he should need them all, and more too, before his course of study should be finished. He had a vision, too, of a set of goodly volumes, bound in calf, on which his heart had been set a year or more. Untouched in his pocket-book lay the sum he had long ago set apart for their purchase; and there was very little in it besides.

'There must be a limit to the pleasure a man gives himself. I can only choose between them,' said the prudent John to himself. To Christie he said: 'Have you ever been round the mountain? Would you like to go to-day?'

'Never but once—in the winter-time; but I should like to go, dearly.' And the eager, wistful look in the eyes that through all the pleasant spring-time had seen no budding thing, won the day.

'Well, I have never been round it either. So let us take one of these carriages that seem so plenty here, and go together. It is well worth the trouble, I have heard.'

Christie's first look was one of unmixed delight, but soon it changed into one a little doubtful. She did not like to speak her thoughts; but in a little while she said, half smiling:

'Are you no' afraid that they may think you extravagant at home?'

'Indeed, no! At least, I'm sure Effie wouldna, if she saw your face at this moment. It was well we had all those things sent home. Come.' And like a foolish fellow, he determined not to make a bargain for the carriage while the prudent little Christie was within hearing, and so had, I dare say, double to pay when he dismissed it. But the pleasure was not spoiled, for all that.

'How pleasant it is!' said Christie, as the absence of street-noises and the fresher breeze upon her cheek told her that they were leaving the city behind them. Her short-sighted eyes could not take in the view that charmed John so much. But she did not know how it could be more pleasant than the fresh air and the gentle motion of the carriage made it to her; and so she said, when at last she started up and looked about her:

'Is not this the way to the cemetery? Oh, let us go there a little while.'

And so they did. The carriage was dismissed. They were to stay a long time—as long as they liked; and then they could walk home, or perhaps they might get the chance of a returning carriage. At any rate, they would not be hurried.

How lovely the place looked to Christie's unaccustomed eyes! They were not alone. There were groups here and there among the graves — some of them mourners, as their dress showed, others enjoying the loveliness of the place, untroubled by any painful remembrance of the loved and lost. Slowly they wandered up and down, making long pauses in shady places, lingering over the graves of little children which loving hands had adorned. Christie wandered over the little nameless graves, longing to find where her dear ones lay.

'How beautiful it is! It is a very sweet resting-place,' she said to herself, many times.

Yes, it was a very lovely spot. A strange feeling of awe stole over Christie's spirit as she gazed around on the silent city. As far as the eye could reach it extended. Among the trees and on the sunny hill-sides rose many a stately monument of granite and marble, with, oh, so many a nameless grave between! Close at their feet lay a large unenclosed space, where the graves lay close together, in long, irregular lines—men and women and little children—with not a mark to tell who slumbered beneath. It was probably the burial-place of strangers, or of those who died in the hospitals. To Christie it had a very dreary and forsaken look. She shuddered as she gazed on the place.

'A friend's grave could never be found among so many,' said she. 'See! there are a few with a bit of board, and a name written on it, but most of them have no mark. I would far rather be laid in our own kirk-yard at home—though that is a dreary place, too, when the sun doesna shine.'

They moved on together; and in a place which was half in the sunshine and half in the shade, they sat down. In a little while the pleasant influence of the scene chased the dreariness from Christie's thoughts, and she looked about with eyes that did not seem able to satisfy themselves with its beauty.

'How lovely it is here!' she repeated. 'How green and fresh everything is! The very grass seems beautiful!' And she caressed with her hand the smooth turf on which they were seated.

'It's a wonder to me how people can choose to live in the midst of a town, with nothing to see that's bonny but a strip of blue sky now and then.'

'It's a wonder to me,' said John, smiling.

'Oh, but I mean people that may live wherever they choose. There are people that like the town best. Where it is right to stay, I suppose one can be content in time. I think if I hadna home and the rest to think about and wish for, I might be willing to live here always. But at first—oh, I thought I could never, *never* stay! But I am not sorry I came. I shall never be sorry for that.'

There was something in her earnest manner, and in the happy look that came over her face as she spoke, that arrested the attention of John; and he said:

'You have been happy here, then, upon the whole?'

'Yes; upon the whole,' repeated she, thoughtfully; 'but it wasna that I was thinking about.'

'Christie, do you know I think you have changed very much since you used to come and see my mother? You have changed; and yet you are the very same: there's a paradox for you, as Peter O'Neil would say.'

His words were light, but there was a meaning in his

grave smile that made Christie's heart leap; and her answer was at first a startled look, and then a sudden gush of happy tears. Then came good John Nesbitt's voice entreating a blessing on 'his little sister in Christ'; and this made them flow the faster. But, oh, they were such happy, happy tears! and very happy was the hour that followed.

Now and then there comes an hour, in the intercourse of friends with each other, which reveals to each more of the inner and spiritual life of the other than years of common intercourse could do; and this was such an hour. I cannot tell all that was said. The words might seem to many a reader tame and common-place enough, but many of them Christie never forgot while she lived, and many of them John Nesbitt will not cease to remember to his dying day.

Christie had no thought of showing him all that was in her heart. She did not think that the friend who was listening so quietly to all the little details of her life among strangers—her home-sickness, her fears and weariness, her love and care for the children and their mother—was all the time thanking God in his heart for all the way by which this little lamb had been led to take refuge in the fold. She knew by the words he spoke, before he rose to go, that he was much moved. They came back to her many a time afterwards, brightening the sad days, and comforting her when she was in sorrow. They helped her to the cheerful bearing of a disappointment near at hand.

As for John, he was far from thinking the day lost that he had devoted to the pleasure of Christie. If in the morning the hope of possessing at once the much-desired books had been given up with a sigh, it was the sigh, and not the sacrifice, that was regretted now. With a sense of refreshment unspeakable there came to his remembrance the Saviour's promise that the giving of a cup of cold water to one of His little ones should have its reward. To have supported those weary feet, if ever so little, in the way, to have encouraged the faint heart or brightened the hope of this humble child, was no unworthy work in the view of one whose supreme desire it was to glorify Him who came from heaven to earth to speak of hope to the poor and lowly. Nor was this all. He was learning, from the new and sweet experiences which the child was so unconsciously revealing to him, a lesson of patient trustfulness, of humble dependence, which a whole library of learned books might have failed to teach him.

The shadows were growing long before they rose to go.

'You'll be very tired to-morrow, I'm afraid,' said John, as they went slowly down the broad, steep way that leads from the cemetery. 'I'm afraid your holiday will do you little good.'

'It has done me good already. I'm not afraid,' said Christie, cheerfully. 'Only I'm sure I shall think of twenty things I want to ask you about when you are fairly gone.'

'Well, the best way will be to collect your wits and ask about them now,' said John, laughing.

And so she did. Matters of which her sister's letters and chance callers had only given her hints were recalled, and discussed with a zest that greatly shortened the way. They were not very important matters, except as they were connected with home life and home friends; but if their way had been twice as long, the interest would not have failed.

'But, John,' said Christie, at last, 'what was it that Davie McIntyre was telling me about Mr. Portman's failure ? Is it really true ? and has he left his wife and little children and gone—nobody knows where ?'

'Yes, it is too true,' John said, and added many painful particulars, which he never would have given if he had had his wits about him. Christie's next question recalled them, with a shock which was not altogether pleasant.

'Was it not Mr. Portman who had Aunt Elsie's money ? Then she has lost it, I suppose ?'

'Yes, it's too true,' said John, with an uncomfortable conviction that Effie would far rather her little sister had not heard of it yet. He did not say so, however, and there was a long silence.

'I wonder what Effie will do ?' said Christie, at last.

'Now, Christie, my woman,' said John, rather more hastily than was his habit, 'you are not going to vex yourself about this matter. You know, if anybody can manage matters well, your sister Effie can ; and she has a great many friends to stand between her and serious trouble. And I don't believe she intended that you should know anything about this—at any rate, until you were safe at home.'

Christie was sure of that. There was no one like Effie. John could tell her nothing new about her goodness. But if it had been needful that they should be separated before, it was still more necessary now that she should be doing her part; and she intimated as much to John.

'But you must mind that Effie was never clear about your leaving home. If she had had her way, you never would have left.'

'I am very glad I came,' was all that Christie replied, but in a little while she added, 'John, I think, on the whole, you may as well take all the things home with you, if you can. The sooner they get them the better; and something may happen to hinder me.'

'Christie,' said John, gravely, 'Effie has set her heart on your coming home this summer. It would grieve her sorely to be disappointed. You are not going to disappoint her?'

'I don't know,' said Christie, slowly. 'I'm sure Effie would rather I should do what is right than what is pleasant.'

'But you are not well, Christie. You are not strong enough to live as you have been living—at least, without a rest. It would grieve Effie to see how pale and thin you are.'

'I am not very strong, I know, but I shall have an easier time now; and if Mrs. Lee should take the children to the country or the seaside, I should be better. I am sure I wish to do what is right. It is not that I don't wish to go home.'

Christie's voice suddenly failed her.

'It seems like a punishment to me,' she added, 'a judgment, almost. You don't know—Effie dinna ken even—how many wrong feelings I had about coming away. I thought nothing could be so bad as to have to depend on Aunt Elsie, and now——' Something very like a sob stopped her utterance.

'Whisht, Christie!' said John. 'God does not send trouble on His people merely to punish; it is to do them good. You must take a more comforting view of this trouble. I am afraid the pleasure of the day is spoiled.'

'No! oh, no!' said Christie eagerly. 'Nobody could do that. There are some pleasures that canna be spoiled. And besides, I am not going to vex myself. It will all come right in the end, I am quite sure. Only just at first——'

'Thou shalt keep him in perfect peace whose mind is stayed on Thee, because he trusteth in Thee,' whispered John.

'I know it;' and that was all she could say.

CHAPTER XII.

SISTERS IN CHRIST.

CHRISTIE found, on reaching home, that Mr. Lee had returned, and when John called in the morning she was able to tell him it was decided that the family should go to the sea-side for a month.

'And considering all things, John, I am glad that Mrs. Lee wants me to go too. I shall have time for a long visit at home when I come back again, before summer is over. The sea air will make me strong. You know we lived near the sea at home. And I should like to take a pair of red cheeks home to Glengarry.'

John was not altogether satisfied with her cheerful words; but there seemed nothing better for any of them but to make the best of it.

'It might be far worse for you, my lassie,' he said, cheerfully. 'I would have liked to take you home with me to Glengarry, for your sake and theirs. But if you'll promise not to let the look come back that I saw first in your face, I'll leave you with a good heart, and tell no sad tales to Effie and the rest.'

It was all that she could do, even now, to keep a

bright face, but she did; and John went away, taking with him the remembrance of it at its very brightest.

The next few days were too busy to give time for regretful thoughts. The children came home, and there was the making of their dresses, and all the necessary preparations for a journey and a lengthened absence from home.

Christie had only time for a hurried letter to Effie, telling her of their plans. She wrote quite cheerfully. She was not strong, and the runnings to and fro of the day often made her too weary to sleep at night. But she was useful, she knew, and Mrs. Lee's gentle kindness proved that she appreciated her efforts to do her duty, and that helped to make her work pleasant and easy. And there was, besides, an excitement in the prospect of a change of scene. Looking forward to a sight of the sea, to feeling the sea-breeze again, to getting away from the heat and dust and confinement of the city, was enough to help her through the day's toils and troubles. And so she felt and wrote cheerfully, notwithstanding the disappointment that had been so hard to bear.

But a disappointment which she was to feel still more bitterly awaited her. The preparations for departure were nearly completed. Mrs. Lee had so far recovered as to be able to go out, and they looked forward to leaving within a day or two.

One afternoon, while Mrs. Lee was superintending the packing that was going on in the nursery, her husband came in. Christie had hardly seen him since little Harry died. He looked grave enough as he came in. He did not speak to her, but in a little while she heard him mention her name, and her heart stood still, as she heard him say:

'You don't mean to tell me that you are to have no one to take care of the children and wait on you while you are away, but that child? Why, she looks as though she needed to be taken care of herself. I can never think of permitting such a thing.'

Christie felt, rather than saw, the look of entreaty that passed over Mrs. Lee's face as she laid her hand upon her husband's arm. Meeting Christie's startled gaze, she said:

'Go down and ask Nelly if the clean things are ready for this other trunk. I will ring when I want you.'

Very quietly Christie obeyed; but before she closed the door, she heard Mr. Lee say, in his quick, careless manner:

'It is quite absurd to think of it! A rush of a girl like that!'

Christie's heart failed. She knew that Mrs. Lee seldom found courage to differ from her husband in any point where yielding was possible, and she felt that there was little hope that she would do so now.

She was mistaken, however. Mrs. Lee spoke very earnestly to her husband. She told him of all that Christie had been to her and the children through all the long, dreary winter and spring. She told him of the faithful, loving service that had never flagged through weakness and weariness. She assured him of the perfect confidence she placed in her, saying she could not name one, even among her friends, to whom she would so willingly leave the children in case of illness or absence from them. She spoke with tears of little

Harry's love for her, and of Christie's untiring devotion to him through all his long illness, till her voice lost itself in sobs of sorrow at the memories thus awakened.

Mr. Lee did not listen unmoved. All unconsciously, his wife was giving him a glimpse of her own sad experiences during the last few months. Careless as he had grown, he could not listen without a pang, which was half sorrow and half shame.

'My poor Letty!' he said, gently; 'you have had a sad time. You have indeed suffered much.'

'Yes,' she said, tearfully; 'it has been a sorrowful time. But it is over now. I would not have my loved ones back again even if I could. I am glad for their sakes. Nothing can harm them where they are; and I shall see them again.'

There was a long pause. Then Mr. Lee returned to the subject:

'But about your nurse. She really is a very sickly-looking girl. She seems to me like one far gone in a decline. I am very sorry, as you have found her so useful. But I cannot consent that you should go with no more efficient help.'

'But I don't think she is ill,' said Mrs. Lee, doubt-fully. 'She never complains. She was always delicate-looking. I remember when she first came, I quite hesitated about engaging her, she looked such a fragile little creature. But no one would have thought her otherwise than strong, and efficient too, who saw her through all our troubles.'

'Well, to me she looks frightfully ill just now,' said Mr. Lee. 'You must at least speak to the doctor about her.'

'She is tired now,' replied Mrs. Lee. 'She has' worn

herself out—first with me when I was ill and then with the children. A month at the sea-side will quite revive her.'

Mr. Lee was not convinced.

'I feel that I ought to take her. She has wearied herself for us—injured her health, perhaps. I ought to take her, even if we take another servant.'

Mr. Lee alluded to the additional expense.

'Besides,' he added, 'it is doubtful when we may return. We may not return here at all. We may see England before we see this place again. It would never do for you to take the responsibility of such a girl as that—to say nothing of taking her so far from her home and friends.'

Mrs. Lee sighed. She had become accustomed during her married life to frequent and sudden changes. She had learned not to be surprised at them now. Her sigh was for the little graves she must leave behind her, perhaps never more to look on them again. And Christie! Would it be right, in view of these possibilities, to take her away? Knowing them, would she be willing to go? Yes; she felt sure that Christie would not leave them willingly. But she must not think of herself in this matter; she must consider what was best for the poor girl. Would Christie's friends, would that sister she loved so well, consent to let her go away, uncertain where she was to go or when she was to return? No; even if Christie herself was willing, she must not think of taking her away.

Yet who was to supply her place? Oh, how wearily she sighed! how she shrank from this new trial! She knew that to her husband this would seem a very little thing indeed; and she kept her sad thoughts to herself, as she had done many a time before.

'I don't know how I can tell her,' she said. 'It seems so unkind to change our plans at this late hour. She will be disappointed, I am sure.'

'Oh, I will tell her, if that will do,' said her husband. 'I dare say she will be sorry to part from the children and you. You have been very kind to her, I am quite sure. You must make her some little present—a frock, or something; and I'll tell her our plans.'

'How little you can know about it!' sighed Mrs. Lee.

But the matter was considered settled. Nothing more was said about it till the following day, when Mr. Lee told his wife he had engaged a woman to go with them—a very suitable person, highly recommended to him by one of his friends.

In the meantime, Christie, having heard no more of the matter, let the remark which had so startled her quite pass out of her mind; and she was in no way prepared for the announcement which Mr. Lee made on the second morning, of the change in their arrangements. She was grieved and hurt; so grieved that she could hardly restrain her tears, so hurt that she had the power to do so, and to answer, quietly, 'Very well, sir.'

She finished what she was doing in the room and then went out, without another word and without looking towards Mrs. Lee.

'You see, she takes it very quietly,' said Mr. Lee. 'Be sure and make her some little present, as I said before, and it will be all right.'

Mrs. Lee sighed.

'It is I who have the most cause for regret,' she said, sadly; 'but it is vain to speak of it. You could never, *never* know.'

Christie went about the house all day very quietly, but no less busily than usual. Her thoughts were by no means pleasant, however.

'It was my vanity that made me think I was of use to her and that she cared for me,' she said to herself, bitterly. 'And now I must go home, when I was growing content to stay. If I had only taken John's advice, and gone with him! Well, I suppose I was too full of my own plans, and this is the way I am to be taught wisdom and humility. I will try to be content. But it will not be very easy, I am afraid.'

Mrs. Lee was out a good deal during the day, so that she scarcely saw her till the children had gone to bed. Then she came into the nursery to make some last arrangement of little garments; and in spite of herself, Christie trembled to find herself left alone with her.

'I *must* speak to her,' she said. 'Oh, if I only need not! If I could just say good-bye, and nothing more!'

Mrs. Lee sat lost in thought, not seeming to heed her, and Christie stitched away as though there were nothing in the world more important than that little Ned's buttons should be sewed on firmly. They were finished at last, and the little garment laid with the rest. Instead of coming to her seat again, she stood a little behind Mrs. Lee, and said, in a low voice:

'Is it to-morrow, ma'am?'

'Yes; we leave to-morrow, early in the day,' said Mrs. Lee.

By a great effort, Christie said, hurriedly :

'About my things, ma'am—my frock and hat? I am afraid I have not enough to pay for them and take me home.'

She had not time to say more. Suddenly turning, Mrs. Lee laid her hand on her arm.

'Hush, Christie! It is not a matter of wages between you and me to-night. Money could not pay what I owe to you. We'll speak of that by and by. Sit down, now, my poor, weary child.'

She placed herself on a low stool at a little distance, and let her head fall on her hand.

'Are you thinking to go home?' asked Mrs. Lee.

'I don't know. I suppose so. I have nowhere else to go.' Christie's voice was husky, but she was able to command it.

'And did you think I would leave you with nowhere to go?' asked Mrs. Lee, gravely. 'But would it not be best to go? You are not strong, Christie.'

'Perhaps it would be better to go, but I wish I could get a place for a little while.' And Christie told her of the new misfortune that had befallen them, in the loss of her aunt's income.

Mrs. Lee sighed, and after a pause, said :

'I was at Mrs. Seaton's to-day, near the mountain. There is illness in the family, and a young infant. More help is required in the nursery. You remember the twins, the pretty boys we used to see in the carriage. One of them is ill—never to be better, I fear. The other you will have the care of for the present. They are quite in the country. I think it will be good for you to be there. I think you will like it too.'

Christie thanked her as well as she was able.

'It seems unkind to you that we should change our plans at so late an hour. I should have considered sooner. But I thought more of my children, and of having you still with them, than I did of what would be best for you.'

Christie tried to say how glad she would be to go even now. Mrs. Lee shook her head.

'You are not strong, and you are very young. It would be wrong to take you I know not where. It may be a long time before we return here. We may never return.' She was silent for a moment, and then continued:

'Yes, it would be wrong to take you so far from your home to share our uncertain fortunes. If you were but as strong as you are faithful and patient! But it cannot be.'

Christie ceased to struggle with her tears now, but they fell very quietly.

'As for wages,' said Mrs. Lee, lifting the lid of Christie's work-box and dropping in it a little purse, 'money could never cancel the debt I owe you. I am content to owe it, Christie. I know you will not grudge your loving service to my darlings.

'And I owe you more than that,' she added, after a pause. 'Christie, when the time comes when all these chafings and changes shall be over, when seeing the reason of them we shall bless God for them, we shall be friends then, I humbly hope. And you must tell your sister—no, you could never tell her. I wish I had seen your friend, John Nesbitt, when he was here; but I will write. And Christie, my brave girl, look up. See what I have for you.'

Something glistened in the light, and Christie received into her hand a locket, hung by a black ribbon. Upon being opened, there was a face—a lovely child's face—'little Harry!'

Yes, it was little Harry's face, copied from a miniature taken about the time when she first saw him. On the other side, encircled by a ring of the baby's golden hair, was written, in fair characters, by the mother's hand:

'To Christie. From the children.'

And now, Christie,' said Mrs. Lee, when the tears that would come at the sight of the picture had been wiped away, 'our good-bye to-morrow must be a brief and quiet one. To-night I must say, "God bless you." Don't let the world spoil you as you grow older. You won't, I know. You have a talisman against its power. May God make you a blessing to many, as He has made you a blessing to me! Good-bye, my dear child. If we never meet on earth, I humbly hope we may meet in heaven!'

It was not like a parting between mistress and maid. Mrs. Lee kissed her earnestly, while her tears fell on her face, and when Christie said 'Good-bye,' she clung to her as she had not clung even to Effie. It was like the farewell of sisters who know that they must meet death before they look on each other's faces again.

Not one of the many grateful thoughts which filled Christie's heart had she the power to utter. But they were not needed. After so many months of loving service—after so many nights of anxious watching, shared so gladly for the love she bore to her and her little ones—words could have been of little value.

The 'good-bye' in the morning was brief and quiet, as Mrs. Lee had wished—so brief that not till the carriage that took them away had disappeared, did Christie realize that they were gone; and the walls of the deserted nursery echoed to many a bitter sob ere she bade farewell to the place where she had passed so many changeful hours.

CHAPTER XIII.

CHRISTIE'S NEW HOME.

It was a very lovely scene, and all the lovelier for
the light of a fair summer morning upon it. There
was a broad, sunny lawn, with a margin of shade, and
just one mass of flitting shadows beneath the locust-
tree near the gate. Beyond, there were glimpses of
winding walks and of brilliant garden-flowers, and
farther on, the waving boughs of trees, and more
flitting shadows; the cedar hedge hid the rest. The
house that stood beyond the sunny lawn was like a
house in a picture—with a porch in front, and galleries
at the sides, and over the railings and round the pillars
twined flowering shrubs and a vine, with dark shining
leaves. A flight of stone steps led up to the open
porch, and on the uppermost one sat a young girl,
reading. One hand rested on her book, while the other
slowly wound and unwound the ribbon of a child's hat
that lay beside her. Her head was bent low over her
book, and Christie could not see her face for the long,
bright curls that shaded it. So intent was she on her
reading that she did not hear the sound of footsteps;
and Christie stood admiring the pretty picture which

the young girl and the flowers and the drooping vine-leaves made, without caring to speak.

She might have stood long enough before the young reader would have stirred, had not some one advanced from the other side.

'Miss Gertrude, the carriage will be round in ten minutes.'

'Yes, I know,' said the young girl, without raising her eyes. 'I am quite ready to go.'

'But Master Clement is going; and nurse is busy, and he won't let me dress him; and if you please, Miss Gertrude, Mrs. Seaton begs that you will come and coax him, and try to get him away without waking his brother.'

The young lady rose, shutting her book with an impatient gesture; and then she saw Christie.

'Good morning,' she said. 'Do you wish to see any one?'

'I wish to see Mrs. Seaton. Mrs. Lee sent me,' said Christie.

'Oh, the new nurse for Clement. I dare say he won't go into town to-day, Martha. It was only to get him out of the way—the young tyrant. Show this girl to Mrs. Seaton's room. She wished to see her as soon as she came.' And then she sat down and took up her book again.

'If you please, Miss Gertrude, Mrs. Seaton wishes to see you at once. Perhaps you will be so obliging as to go up-stairs with her. Master Clement has kept me so long that I fear I shall not have the things ready to send with Peter.'

Miss Gertrude rose, but with not the best grace in the world, and Christie followed her into the house and up stairs. At the first landing a door opened, and a little boy, half-dressed, rushed out.

'Tudie, let me go with you; I want to go.'

'Naughty boys who won't let Mattie dress them mustn't expect to be taken anywhere. You are not to come with me. You will wake Claude.'

'Oh, Claude's awake, and crying to be dressed. Let me go with you,' pleaded the child.

'No; you are not to come. Remember, I tell you so; and I am not Mattie, to be trifled with.'

Miss Gertrude spoke very gravely. Her brother, a spirited little lad of five or six years of age, looked up into her face with defiance in his eyes. Then he gave a glance down the long hall, as if meditating a rush in that direction; but he thought better of it.

'I'll be good, Tudie. I won't make a noise,' said he.

'Stay where you are,' said Miss Gertrude, decidedly.

She led the way down the long hall, then up a flight of steps, and opened the door of a large room. It seemed quite dark at first, but soon Christie was able to distinguish the different things in it. The furniture of the room was covered with green stuff, and there was on the floor a soft green carpet, with bright flowers scattered over it. The curtains on the windows and on the bed were of white muslin, but the hangings above were green. The paper on the walls was white, with a border of brown acorns and green oak-leaves. It was a very pretty room; and the coolness and the softened light made it seem altogether delightful to Christie after her long, dusty walk.

On the bed was a lady, dressed for an outdoor walk, but her hands were pressed over her eyes as though she were in pain. A little boy lay tossing fretfully on the sofa, but his peevish cry ceased for a moment as they entered the room. Miss Gertrude seated herself beside him, and said, without approaching the bed—

'Here is the young girl that Mrs. Lee sent.'

The lady took her hand from her eyes, and raised herself up. Seating herself in a large chair by the bed, she beckoned to Christie to come towards her.

'You came from Mrs. Lee, did you?' said she.

Christie came forward. The lady observed her for a moment.

'Mrs. Lee told me you were young, and not very strong,' said she; 'but I had no idea you were quite such a child.'

'I am past fifteen,' said Christie.

'And do you mean to tell me that Mrs. Lee trusted her children to you—that infant too—through all her illness?'

'Mrs. Greenly was in the house nearly all the winter, and she was in the nursery very often. That was all the help I had,' said Christie, with a slight change of colour.

'And was it you who took care of little Harry, and who was with him when he died?'

The remembrance of that sorrowful time was too vivid for Christie to bear this allusion to it unmoved. She grew quite pale, and took one step forward towards a little table, and laid her hand upon it. Miss Gertrude, who had been watching her with great interest, rose and brought forward a chair, looking towards her mother, without speaking.

'You look tired,' said Mrs. Seaton. 'Did you walk? Sit down and rest.' Christie gladly obeyed.

'Mrs. Lee speaks very highly of you—very highly

indeed. You must have been very useful to her; and I dare say she was very kind to you.'

Remembering all they had passed through together, Christie could hardly restrain her tears. But, as the lady seemed to expect an answer, she said, with some difficulty—

'She was very kind to me, and I loved her dearly— and the children.'

It is possible Mrs. Seaton did not consider much love necessary between mistress and maid. She did not look as though she did, as Christie could not help thinking as she glanced towards her.

'And you got on nicely with the children, did you? Of course you will have little to do here in comparison with what you must have had there. But my wilful Clement, I am afraid, you will find too much for you. He is a masterful lad.'

She did not speak regretfully, as though the child's wilfulness grieved her very much, but rather the contrary. And, indeed, one could hardly wonder at the pride in her voice as Master Clement rushed in among them. He was a child that any mother would own with pride—a picture of robust health and childish beauty. His brown curls were sadly disordered. One arm was thrust into the sleeve of his frock, in a vain attempt to finish the dressing which Mattie had commenced. One foot was bare, and he carried in his hand his stocking and shoe. He walked straight up to his sister, saying gravely :

'Baby is crying, and I came to tell mamma.

She did not answer him, but laying down Claude's head on the pillow, she began to arrange his disordered dress. He submitted quite patiently to the operation, only saying, now and then, as he turned round to look in her face :

'Am I naughty, Tudie ? Are you going to punish me ?'

She did not answer him. Indeed, there was no occasion. He did not seem at all afraid of the punishment, whatever it might be. When she had tied on his shoe, he slipped from her, and flung himself on the sofa beside his brother. He did not mean to be rough with him, but the little fellow uttered a peevish cry, and pushed him away.

'I didn't mean to hurt you. Don't cry.'

His little brown hand was laid softly on Claude's pale cheek, and their brown curls mingled as their heads were laid on the same pillow. What a contrast they presented ! Christie could hardly persuade herself these were the little lads that she and the Lee children used to admire so much—partly because they were so pretty, and partly because they were so much alike. They were alike still. One could hardly have told, as they lay together, to which head the tangled mass of brown curls belonged. Their eyes were the same, too, but little Claude's were larger, and they drooped with a look of weariness and pain sad to see in any eyes, but very, *very* sad to see in the eyes of a child. His forehead was larger, too,—or it seemed larger, above his thin, pale cheeks. But not even his wan cheeks or weary eyes struck so painfully to Christie's heart as did the sight of his little, wasted hand, white as the pillow on which it lay. It seemed whiter and more wasted still when it was raised for a moment to stroke his brother's rosy cheek. Oh, how very sad it seemed ! And his mother ! She closed her eyes, and laid herself back in her chair, with a sigh that was almost a groan.

Clement was very gentle, or he meant to be very gentle, with his brother. He stroked his cheeks, and kissed him, calling him 'little brother,' and 'poor Claudie.' And the little fellow hushed his peevish cry, and tried to smile for a moment.

'I am going into town,' said Clement; 'and then we are going to spend the day at Aunt Barbara's. They are making hay there. May Claude go? It would make him quite well to play among the hay with me and Fanny and Stephen. Mamma, mayn't he go? Tudie, do let Claudie go.'

'Mamma, mamma, let me go. Let Mattie dress me. Oh, I want to go among the hay!'

He came down from the sofa, and went towards his mother as fast as his trembling limbs could carry him. She met him and received him in her arms.

'My darling cannot go. He is not strong enough. Oh, Gertrude, how could you let Clement come in here?'

'Mamma, I am quite well. I should be quite well if I could play among the hay, as we used to do.'

Memories of health and strength enjoyed in summer sunshine were doubtlessly stirring at the boy's heart, to which he could give no utterance. The look of wistful entreaty in his weary eyes went to his mother's heart.

'My dear boy, if you only could? Oh, Gertrude! how could you be so thoughtless?' she repeated.

'I desired Clement to stay in the nursery, and he disobeyed me,' said Gertrude, gravely.

'And now are you going to punish me?' he asked.

'Go into the nursery, and I will tell you. Go at once.'

'Go away, naughty boy, and not vex your little brother,' said his mother, rocking in her arms the child, who was too weak and weary to resist.

'I didn't vex Claude. Let him go with us. I'm not a naughty boy.' He looked as though he meditated taking up a position on the sofa.

'Go,' said his sister.

'How will you punish me, then?'

'I will tell you when I come to the nursery,' she said, opening the door for him.

Not very willingly, but quietly, he went; and in a little while they heard his merry voice ringing along the hall.

'I am very sorry,' said the young lady, coming back; 'give me Claude. I will walk about with him; you are not able.'

'No, no,' said Mrs. Seaton, though the little boy held out his arms to go to her. 'Go; the carriage is waiting. You should have gone long ago.'

'Need we go?' she asked, looking at Christie. 'Clement can be kept out of the way now.'

'Yes, yes; go,' answered she, hastily. 'We have had vexation enough for one day. And I thought this dear child was so nicely settled for the day; and now he is getting quite feverish again.'

Miss Gertrude urned and went out without reply.

'My boy, my poor boy!' murmured the mother, as she rocked him in her arms, and her lips were pressed on his feverish brow. 'Will he ever play among the hay again?'

She rocked him till his crying was hushed, and

weary with struggling, he begged to be laid down. Christie arranged the pillows, and his mother placed him on the sofa. She would fain have lingered near him; but, weak from recent illness, she was obliged to lie down. In a little while he asked for water, and to his mother's surprise, was willing to take it from Christie's hands. He even suffered her to bathe his hands and feet, and when he grew restless again, let her take him on her lap. He was quite contented to stay there; and the last object the mother saw before she sank to sleep was her sick boy nestling peacefully in the arms of the little stranger maid. And it was the first object she saw when she waked, some three hours afterwards. Christie had not moved, except to let her hat and shawl fall on the floor, and little Claude was slumbering peacefully still. He awoke soon, however, refreshed and strengthened, and not at all indignant at finding himself in a stranger's arms, as his mother feared he might be. He suffered her to wash and dress him, as he had suffered no one but his mother to do for the last three weary weeks. It was very well that he was inclined to be friendly, for Mrs. Seaton found herself much too ill to do the accustomed duty herself; and it was with something very like gratitude stirring at her heart that she said to Christie, when all was done:

'You are fond of children, are you not? You are very gentle and careful, I see.'

The little boy quarrelled with his dinner, as usual; but upon the whole the meal was successful, his mother said; and as a reward for being good, he was promised a walk in the garden by and by.

In the meantime Christie went down-stairs to her

P

dinner, under the care of the friendly Mattie, whom she had seen in the morning. She was very kind, and meant to make herself very agreeable, and asked many questions, and volunteered various kinds of information as to what Christie might expect in her new place, which she might far better have withheld. Christie had little to say, and made her answers as quietly and briefly as possible.

When she went up-stairs again, she found affairs in not quite so cheerful a state as when she had left them. The doctor had been in, and though he had greatly applauded the scheme for sending little Claude into the garden, he had utterly forbidden his mother to leave her bed to go with him. It could not be permitted on any account; and she had so entirely devoted herself for the last few weeks to the care and amusement of the child that he could not, at first, be prevailed on to go without her. He would not look at Mattie, nor at Mrs. Grayson, the housekeeper. After much gentle persuasion on her part, and many promises as to what he would see and hear out in the pleasant sunshine, he suffered Christie to bring his hat and coat and put them on.

'I think you may trust me with him, ma'am,' said Christie. 'I will be very gentle and careful with him. Poor wee boy!' she added, looking into the face that seemed more wan and thin under the drooping plumes of his hat. But his mother dismissed them with a sigh.

It was not a very easy thing to amuse the exacting little fellow for a long time, but it was perhaps a very good thing for Christie that it fell to her lot to do so. A longer indulgence in the musings which had occupied her during three hours passed in the darkened room would not have been good for her, at any rate; and there was no chance for that here. She was suffering very keenly from her parting with Mrs. Lee and her children, and as she had felt the clinging arms of little Claude about her neck, she had said to herself, almost bitterly, that she would not allow herself to love any one—any stranger—so dearly again. Yes, the pain was very hard to bear, and she felt very lonely and sad as she paced slowly up and down the long walks of the garden.

It was a very quiet place, however, quite out of reach of all disturbing sounds, and Christie could not help wondering that she did not enjoy it more, till she remembered what good reason she had for being very weary, and she was content to wait for a full enjoyment of the pretty garden.

'I dare say I shall like to stay here after a little,' she said to herself. 'There is one thing sure, it was no plan of mine to come. I have had enough of my own plans. I'll just try and be as useful and happy as I can, and wait till I see how things will turn. I am afraid Effie may not like my staying, but I can only just wait, and it will all come right.'

And she put her good resolutions into practice then and there. She was very patient with her little charge. She amused him, till he quite forgot his shyness with her. She brought him flowers, and translated the talk of the two little birds who were feeding their young in the old pear-tree, till he laughed almost merrily again. The time soon passed, and it was a very weary but very happy little face that he held up to kiss his mother that night, and he was soon slumbering quietly in his little cot by her side

Then Christie betook herself to her place in Master Clements nursery. She found that noisy young gentleman quiet for the night, and gladly laid herself down. In spite of her weariness, her long walk and her afternoon in the open air had done her good. She was asleep before any lonely or home-sick thoughts had time to visit her, and she slept as she had not slept for weeks, without waking till the twittering of the birds in the pear-tree roused her to begin her new life.

Christie had never to measure her strength with that of the 'masterful' Clement. It happened quite otherwise—fortunately for her, though sadly enough for Mrs. Seaton. The doctor, at his next visit, very decidedly assured her that her proposed visit to the sea-side must no longer be delayed, unless she intended to remain an invalid during the rest of the summer. Her health, her life even, depended on a change of air and freedom from anxiety. The good she could do her sick boy by staying at home would be very little in comparison to the harm she would do herself. She ought to have gone weeks since. Her infant and nurse might go with her, but none of the other children. It would do her more harm than good to be troubled with the boys on the journey or at a strange watering-place, and as for them, home was the best place for both. He assured her that her anxiety for Claude was unnecessary. He was in no immediate danger. It might be months, or even years, before he would be quite well again. He might never be so strong and healthy as his brother. But there was no danger for him. Quiet and constant care were what he needed; and they could be found best at home.

'Come here, my little man,' said he, 'and let me

prove to your mother that you are going to be quite well again, and that very soon, too.'

Claude had been sitting on the balcony into which the windows of the green room opened, and he came forward, led by Christie, at the doctor's desire. After a minute's talk with the child, his eye fell on her.

What! are you here? I thought you had been far enough away by this time. How came you to leave your charge?'

Christie came forward shyly, looking at Mrs. Seaton.

'Mr. Lee thought her not strong enough,' said Mrs. Seaton. 'There was no other one to go; and she hardly seemed fit for the charge of all.'

'Humph! He has made a mistake or two before in his lifetime—and so has she, for that matter,' said the doctor, with a shrug of his shoulders.

'Mrs. Lee didn't know when they would come back again, and she didn't like to take me so far away,' said Christie; 'and I was very sorry.'

'And so you are to be Claude's nurse, it seems?'

Christie looked at Mrs. Seaton.

'She came, in the meantime, to go out with Clement and to help in the nursery generally. I have kept Claude with me altogether of late.' And as Christie took the little boy to the balcony again, she added, 'I don't see how I can leave him. Poor little fellow! He will let no one care for him but me.'

The doctor shook his head.

'That may be very well for him, but it is very bad indeed for you. Indeed, it must not be. Let me make a plan for you. You can quite safely leave him with this new nurse. I would recommend her among a thousand——'

'A child like that!' interrupted Mrs. Seaton.

'A child in appearance, I grant, but quite a woman in sense and patience. She has surprised me many a time.'

'But she has had no experience. She cannot know——'

'Oh, that is the best of it. She will do as she is bidden. Save me from those "experienced" persons who have wisdom enough for ten! I can trust this little maid that she will do exactly as I bid her. She is a very conscientious person—religiously inclined, I should think. At any rate, she is just the nurse I should choose from all the sisterhood for your poor little boy—just the firm and gentle attendant he needs now. Trust me. I know her well.'

It is possible that in speaking thus the doctor's first wish was to set the mind of the mother at rest about leaving her child, but he could say what he did without doing any violence to his conscience. He really had admired and wondered at Christie's management of the little Lees during his frequent visits to their nursery.

'And besides,' he added to himself, 'the poor little fellow will be better when away from his mother's unbounded indulgence for a while. It will be better for all concerned.'

So the matter was arranged—not without many misgivings on Mrs. Seaton's part, however. Her directions as to Christie's management of the boy were so many and so minute that the poor child was in danger of becoming bewildered among them. To all she could only answer, again and again:

'I will be very careful, ma'am;' or, 'I will do my best.'

It was well for Mrs. Seaton that there was but little time left, or her heart, and Christie's too, might have failed. At the very last moment the mother had a mind to change her plans.

'After all,' she said, 'perhaps it would have been wiser to send him to his aunt's. Her children are noisy and troublesome, to be sure; but I should have felt easier about him. Mind, Gertrude, you are to write every day till your father returns. And, Christie, remember, you are to obey the doctor's directions in all things. He is to call every day. And don't let Clement fret him. And, Gertrude, be sure to write.'

CHAPTER XIV.

THE house seemed very quiet after Mrs. Seaton went away. For that day and the next, Christie and her little charge were left to the solitude of the green room and the garden. Miss Gertrude and Clement had gone to visit their aunt, and not knowing when they might return, Christie was beginning to wonder what she should do during the long hours that her little charge slept or amused himself quietly without her. There were no books in the green room—at least, there were none she cared for. In the nursery there were a few story-books for little children—fairy tales, and rhymes, with pictures of giants and dwarfs and little old women, among which Christie recognized some that had been great favourites long ago. But after the first glance she cared no more for them.

On the morning of the third day, when Claude was taking his nap, the time began to hang heavy on her hands. She took her Bible and read a chapter or two, but in spite of herself she grew dull and dreary. The stillness of the house oppressed her. The other servants were busy in a distant apartment. She seemed quite shut in from all the world. Just opposite the window was a large locust-tree, which hid the garden from her; and the only sound that reached her was the murmur of the wind among its branches, and the hum of the bees that now and then rested a moment among the few blossoms that still lingered on them. Her thoughts turned homewards.

'I might write to Effie,' she said to herself. But she was not sufficiently in the mood for it to go to her trunk for her small store of paper and pens; and she sat still, with her head leaning on her hands and her eyes fixed on the swaying leaves, vaguely conscious that the indulgence of her present mood was not the best thing for her.

She was not permitted to indulge it long, however. The little boy stirred and tossed in his crib, and she went to arrange the coverlet over him; and as she was moving listlessly about the room, something glistened in a stray sunbeam and caught her short-sighted eyes, and from the cushions of the great easy chair, where it had lain since the first day of her coming, she drew the book that Miss Gertrude had been reading when she watched the pretty picture she made as she sat beneath the drooping leaves.

With a cry of delight, she recognized her old favourite, 'The Lights and Shadows of Scottish Life.' The very same! though this was glittering in blue and gold, a perfect contrast to the little, brown-covered book, with the title-page lost, which had made Christie forget her bread and her cooling oven on that unhappy day. But the remembrance of the old time and the old favourite came back all the more vividly because of the contrast. The memory of the old times came back. Oh, how long ago it seemed since that summer afternoon when she lay on the grass and read it for the first time! Yet how vividly it all came back! The blue sky, with the white clouds passing over it now and then, the sound of the wind among the low fir-trees, the smell of the hawthorn hedge, the voices of the children in the lane beyond, seemed once more above her and around her. And then the sound of her mother's gentle chiding, when she found her sitting there after the shadows had grown long, came back. Her voice, her smile, the very gown and cap she wore, and the needle-work she carried in her hand, came sensibly before her. Yet how long ago it seemed! Christie remembered how many times she had taken it with her to the fields, when the incompleteness of their fences during the first year of their stay on the farm had made the 'herding' of the sheep and cows necessary that the grain might be safe. She had read it in the woods in spring-time, by the firelight in the long winter evenings, and by stealth on Sundays, when the weather had kept her from the kirk. It was associated in her remembrance with many things pleasant and many things sad; and no wonder that for a while she turned over the leaves, catching only here and there a glimpse of the familiar words, because of the tears that hid them.

Sitting on the floor, with the book held close to her face, she read, and forgot all else. The little lad tossed and murmured, and mechanically she put forth her hand and rocked him in his crib; but she neither heard nor saw when the door opened and some one came in.

It was Miss Gertrude. A look of surprise passed over her face as she caught a glimpse of the reader on the floor, but it gave place to interest and amusement as she watched her. Her absorbed look never changed,

even when she rocked and murmured soothing words to
the restless child. She read on—sometimes smiling,
sometimes sighing, but never lifting her eyes—till Miss
Gertrude came forward and spoke.

'Well, how have you been getting on ?'

Christie started, as if it had been Aunt Elsie's voice
she heard; and at the look of astonishment and dismay
that spread itself over her face, the young lady laughed.

'How has Claude been, all these days?' she asked,
softly, as she bent over the crib.

'He has been quite well and quite good, I think,' said
Christie, trying to collect her scattered wits.

'Has the doctor been here?' asked Miss Gertrude.

'Yes; he was here this morning. He asked when
you were coming home, but I couldn't tell him.'

'Well, I'm here now; and I'm going to stay, too!
If the doctor thinks he is going to banish Clement and
me from home for the next month, he will find himself
mistaken. For my part, I don't see the use of his
coming here so often, just to shake his head and look
grave over poor little Claude. Of course the child's
mother wishes it; but it is all nonsense.'

Christie looked at her in astonishment. But that
the words were so quietly and gravely spoken, she
would have thought them uncalled for, not to say
impertinent, from a girl scarcely older than herself.
They needed no reply, however, and she made none.

She did not then know that Mrs. Seaton was not
Gertrude's own mother, and that she was only half-
sister to the two little boys, upon whom she looked as
mere children, whilst she felt herself a young lady.

'Have you been lonely here?' she asked, in a few
minutes.

'A little. It is very quiet,' said Christie, hesitatingly. 'But I like it.'

'Is Claude fond of you?' asked Gertrude, gravely.

Christie smiled a little.

'He does not object to me. I dare say he will be fond of me in time. I am sure he will be very glad to see you and his brother. It is very quiet for him to be left alone with me.'

'But the doctor wishes him to be quiet,' said Gertrude; 'and his mother won't have him vexed on any account. I have seen her quite tremble when his brother has come near him; and after all .it is no wonder.'

'Clement is so strong,' said Christie; 'but he will learn to be gentle with his brother in time. How very much alike they used to be! We used to see them driving together. We didn't know their names, but we always called them the two pretty boys.'

'Yes, they were very much alike; and it will grieve Clement, when he is older, to know—— Did you never hear about it? They were playing together, and Claude fell. The doctor thinks that fall was the cause of his illness. His mother can't bear to think so, it is so sad; and besides, it seems to make his illness more hopeless. I am afraid he will never be strong and well again.'

'Oh, don't say so,' said Christie, sadly, quite shocked at what she heard. 'Please God, he will be well again. He is only a child; and children outlive so much. For two or three years no one thought I should live to grow up. But I am quite well now.'

'You are not a giant yet, nor very strong either. At least you don't look so,' said Gertrude.

'But I shall grow strong here in the country. I am

better already since I came. Do you really think that little Master Claude will never be strong and well again ?'

'I don't know. I cannot tell. But Aunt Barbara says the doctor is not at all hopeful about it, though he speaks hopefully to mother. Aunt Barbara thinks if the poor little fellow should live, he may be deformed, or lame for life. I think it would be much better for him to die now, than to live to be deformed or a cripple.'

'I don't know. I can't tell,' said Christie, looking with a vague wonder from the sleeping child to the sister who spoke so quietly about his great misfortune. 'It is well we have not to decide about these things. God knows best.'

'Yes, I suppose so. It is in vain to murmur, whatever may happen. But there is a deal of trouble in the world.' And the young lady sighed, as though she had her share of it to bear.

Christie's astonishment increased. Looking at the young lady, she said to herself that it was doubtful whether she knew in the least what she was talking about.

'Troubles in the world ? Yes, doubtless there are— plenty of them! But what could she know of them ?'

'Are you fond of reading?' asked Gertrude, after a little time, her eye falling on the book which Christie still held.

'Yes,' said Christie; 'I like to read. This is the book you left the other day. I only found it a little while ago.'

'Have you read much of it ? There are some pretty stories in it, I think.'

Oh, yes; I read the book long ago. It was one of

our favourites at home. I like to read anything about home—about Scotland, I mean.'

'And so do I,' said Gertrude. 'I knew you were Scotch when I heard you speak. Is it long since you came? Have you been here long? Tell me all about it.'

In the short half-hour before Claude awoke, there was not time to tell *all* about it, but the young girls told each other enough to awaken a mutual interest.

Miss Gertrude's mother had died when she was quite young, and she had been committed to the care of an aunt, with whom she had continued to reside for some time, even after the second marriage of her father. She had had a very happy home, and had been educated with great care. Looking back on those days now, she could see no shadow on their calm brightness. She had had her childish troubles, I suppose, but she forgot them all as she went on to describe to Christie her merry life with her young cousins and her friends. Her aunt's death had broken all those pleasant ties, and she had come to Canada, which must be her home till she was grown up. When she should be of age, she told Christie, and could claim the fortune her mother had left her, she was going home again to live always. She did not like Canada. It did not seem like home to her, though she was living in her father's house. She longed for the time when she should be her own mistress.

Christie didn't enjoy the last part of her story very well. She could not help thinking that some of the trials that the young lady hinted at existed only in her own imagination. But she did not say so. She listened to the whole with unabated interest, and in return, told Gertrude the story of her own life. It was given in very few words. She told about her mother's death, and their coming to Canada, and what happened to them afterwards, till they had been obliged to leave the farm and separate.

It is just possible that the young lady, who sat listening so quietly to these simple details, took to herself the lesson which the story was so well calculated to teach. But Christie had no thought of giving her a lesson. She told of Effie's wise and patient guidance of their affairs, of the self-denial cheerfully practised by all, of her own eager desire to do her part to help keep the little ones together, of Effie's slow consent to let her go; all this, far more briefly and quietly than Miss Gertrude had spoken of her childish days that were passed in her aunt's house. By experience the young lady knew nothing of the real trials of life. She had no rule by which to estimate the suffering which comes from poverty and separation, from solitary and uncongenial toil. Yet, as she sat listening there, she caught a glimpse of something that made her wish she had said less about the troubles that had fallen to her lot. Christie faltered a little when she came to speak of the first months of her stay in town, and of the time when her sister went away.

'I was very, very home-sick. If it hadn't been for shame, I would have gone at the end of the first month. And when my sister went away in the spring, and left me here, it was almost as bad. It seems like a troubled dream.to look back upon it. But it has passed now. It will never be so bad again—never, I am sure.'

'You have got over your home-sickness, then? And are you quite contented now?' she asked, with great interest.

'Yes, I think so. I think it is right to stay. I am very glad to stay, especially now that I am out here, in the country almost. There was a while in the spring that I was afraid I should not be able to stay. But I am better now. I shall soon be quite strong.'

The little boy stirred in his crib, and his eyes opened languidly. Christie was at his side in a moment. To the astonishment of his sister, he suffered himself to be lifted out and dressed without his usual fretful cry.

'How nicely you manage him!' she said, at last. 'This used to be a troublesome business to all concerned.'

Christie did, indeed, manage nicely. Her experience with the little Lees stood her in good stead now. She was very quick, and gentle and firm with the little boy, beguiling him from his fretfulness by little tales or questions, or merry childish talk, till the last string was tied and the last of his beautiful curls arranged. Then he was put in his favourite place among the cushions of the great chair, and the chair was drawn close to the window. Gertrude leaned over him for a moment, and then, kneeling down, she kissed his little white hands, and stroked his thin, pale face, her own looking grave enough all the while.

'He scarcely knows me now,' she said. 'He has almost forgotten me since he has been so ill. But we shall be friends again, my dear little brother.'

'Where's Clement?' asked the child. '*He* is *your* little boy.'

'Oh, but I want two little boys. I want a little boy to take care of and love with all my heart—a gentle, patient little boy, who doesn't fret and cry when he is dressed, any more. I want a little boy to take into the garden in his little carriage, and to be my little boy always.'

'Christie takes me into the garden. I like Christie she's good.'

'I'm quite sure of it,' said Miss Gertrude. 'Listen: There is Clement. Shall I open the door and call him in, if he will promise to be good?'

What a contrast they made! The cheeks of one flushed with health, his bright eyes dancing with happiness, the other—oh, so wan and thin and fragile! Miss Gertrude's eyes filled with tears as she tried to restrain Clement's eager caresses. They were very glad to see each other. Climbing up into the chair beside him, Clement put his arms round his brother's neck and stroked his cheeks.

'You'll soon be well now, Claudie,' he said, 'and we'll go and see the pony. Oh, such a fine fellow as he is! You're getting well now, aren't you?' he added, wistfully.

'Yes, I'm well; but I am too tired,' said Claude, laying himself back among the pillows, with a sigh. Miss Gertrude lifted Clement down, and held him firmly, saying :

'Clement is not going to tire you any more. He is going to be very gentle and good when Christie lets us come in here; and by and by we will go and sit under the locust-tree and be very good and happy all together.'

And so they did that afternoon, and many afternoons besides. A very happy time they had. Far from banishing Miss Gertrude and little Clement, the doctor encouraged them to be much with the sick boy. The noisy Clement was permitted to become the almost constant companion of his brother, on certain conditions. He was never permitted to weary him or vex him. A

Q

walk with his brother was made the reward of good behaviour; and banishment from the green room for an entire day was felt to be so severe a punishment that it was not insisted upon more than once or twice during the time of his mother's absence. Upon both the boys this intercourse had a very beneficial effect. The little invalid brightened under the influence of Clement's merry ways, now that the watchful care of Miss Gertrude or Christie kept his mirth within bounds, and prevented him from being wearied with too boisterous play.

The whole of the pleasant summer morning was passed by him in the open air. Up and down the broad garden-walks he was drawn, when the weather was fine. Sometimes he was content to sit for hours in the shadow of the locust-tree near the window, or in the pleasant cedar walk at the other end of the grounds. Sometimes he was permitted to walk a little while on the lawn; and in a few days the dawning colour on cheek and lip was hailed as a hopeful sign of returning health.

Christie grew quite satisfied with her new place, and devoted herself to her little charge with an interest that was untiring; and the increasing affection of the little boy made her service day by day more pleasant to her.

Of Miss Gertrude she scarcely knew what to make. She was always very kind to her, and spent much time with her and little Claude, either in the garden or in the green room. But she was not gentle and pleasant to all the world. She was sometimes full of impatient and discontented thoughts, and now and then let fall words that proved this too plainly. Christie was sometimes pained, and sometimes amused, as she listened to her.

Like too many young people, she had a keener eye for defects than for excellences of character; and she never hesitated to amuse herself at the expense of those with whom she came in contact. Sometimes her remarks were amusing and harmless enough, but too often they were unkind and severe; and more than once she tried to place in a ludicrous light characteristics which she could not but acknowledge were real excellences. Christie had an uncomfortable consciousness that there was something wrong in all this, even amid the interest and admiration which the young girl had awakened in her, but she was very far from realizing how wrong this spirit of criticism is, or how injurious the indulgence of it might prove to Miss Gertrude.

These things, as they came up, marred but little Christie's admiration of her bright and winning ways. The young lady's impatience and pride were never manifested where she or the boys were concerned; and the charm there was in constant intercourse with one of her own age was delightful. Notwithstanding the difference in station, the two young girls had many subjects of interest common to both, which they were never weary of discussing.

The enjoyment of their companionship was not all on Christie's side. Since her residence in her father's house, Miss Gertrude had had no companions of her own age for whose society she cared. She was constantly surprised and delighted to find how entirely her brother's little nurse could understand and sympathize with some of her moods and fancies. She brought out her favourite books and discussed her favourite subjects, and spoke to her of many things as she had never spoken to any one since she bade adieu to her young cousins at home.

It cannot be denied that Christie's evident admiration of her helped to bespeak Miss Gertrude's good-will. But the young lady was not very vain. She really liked Christie, and took pleasure in her society; and she admired the tact and patience with which she managed little Claude.

The first few days of their intercourse was to each like the reading of a pleasant book; nor did their interest in each other fail as they grew better acquainted.

CHAPTER XV.

'CHRISTIE,' said Gertrude, coming into the green room just as the little nurse had arranged the crib for Claude's mid-day nap, 'did you ever read " The Lady of the Lake " ? '

Christie was sitting down, with a basket of little socks and a bunch of darning-cotton in her hand, and she looked up eagerly as she entered.

' No, I never read it; but I have heard of it. It is a nice book, isn't it ? '

' Yes. Get your work ready, and I'll tell Martha to look after Clement for the next two hours, and I will read to you while Claude sleeps. I have read it once ; but I would like to read it again.'

And she did read it. Soon Christie's socks and darning-cotton were forgotten, and she sat listening intently. It was something entirely new to her, and she yielded herself to the charm of the book with an eagerness that delighted the reader. Miss Gertrude liked the book at the second reading even better than at the first. She enjoyed it this time for herself and Christie too.

'There seems so much more in a book when you have anybody to enjoy it with you,' she said, at the end of an hour. 'But I am tired of reading aloud. You must take it a while now.'

'But I have got out of the way of reading aloud,' said Christie; 'and besides, I do not read so well as you.'

'Oh, never mind; you'll read well enough. And give me the basket; I'll darn your socks in the meantime.'

'The socks? Oh, I had forgotten them! But there is very little to do. I'll read a while if you like; but I know I don't read so well as you.'

She took the book, however, and another hour passed rapidly away. She shut the book with a sigh when Claude moved.

This was the first of many such readings. During the hours when Claude was asleep and Clement under the immediate superintendence of Martha, Miss Gertrude brought her book into the green room and shared the pleasure it gave her with her little brother's nurse. And at other times, too, when the little boys were amusing themselves together in the garden, they read and discussed their books, sitting in the cedar walk, or under the shadow of the locust-tree. And a very pleasant month they had. Christie had great enjoyment in all this; and apparently Miss Gertrude had no less; for she refused several invitations, and broke more than one engagement with her aunt, rather than interfere with these new arrangements.

But one day Miss Gertrude came into the green room with a cloud upon her brow. It was plain that something was the matter

'It has been a great deal too pleasant to last long,' she said, throwing down a letter which she held in her hand. 'Here is papa coming home immediately. I wouldn't mind his coming,' she added, checked by the look of surprise on Christie's face. 'I shall be very glad to see him; and he won't make much difference— he is so seldom at home. Besides, he will let me please myself about things. He has no fancy for my going here and there at everybody's bidding. But Mr. Sherwood is coming with him—Mrs. Seaton's cousin— a very disagreeable person; at least, I think so. Mamma thinks him wonderfully good, and he is a great favourite with papa, too. I am sure I don't know why. I think he is conceited; and he is an Englishman, besides.'

Christie laughed.

'That's not a very good reason.'

'Perhaps not. But he has such a cool, indifferent way of asserting the superiority of the English over all other nations, as though the question need not be discussed. "It must be quite evident to everybody," his manner seems to say.'

After a pause, Miss Gertrude continued:

'And that is not all. He is very meddlesome. He is always telling mamma what ought to be expected from a young lady like me, and getting her to annoy me about lessons and other things; at least, I think so. I know he thinks me quite childish; and sometimes he interferes between Clement and me. What do you think he had the impertinence to say to me once? That no one was fit to govern who had not learned to obey. That it would be wiser for me to learn the

lesson of obedience myself, than to attempt to teach it
to my little brother.'

'And what answer did you make?' asked Christie,
after a little hesitation.

'I turned and walked out of the room; and I did not
see him again. I chose to be out of the way when he
came to say good-bye. I dare say that is one reason
why I don't like the thought of his coming just now.
I feel a little awkward, you know. I owe him one
good turn, however. If it had not been for him, I
think father would have listened to Aunt Barbara and
sent me to school. I ought to thank him for that.'

'And didn't you want to go to school?' asked
Christie, in some surprise.

'No, indeed! I never was at school, you know. We
had a governess and teachers at home. I am to have
private teachers for some things here, when the summer
is over, unless I should be sent to school, after all.'

When the gentleman made his appearance among
them the next day, he did not look like the formidable
person Christie imagined him to be. They were sitting
on the lawn, in the shadow of the locust-tree, when he
arrived; and before he went into the house he came and
shook hands with Miss Gertrude and the little boys.
Christie thought he must have quite forgotten his
falling-out with the young lady, he met her so pleasantly and frankly. The embarrassment was all on
her side.

As for the boys, they were beside themselves with
delight. It was easy to see they did not share their
sister's dislike. Poor little Claude clasped his arms
about his neck and kissed him eagerly. Clement, in

a way that showed he felt sure of his sympathy, began to tell him of the pony and the rabbits, insisting that he should come with him to the stable to see them at once.

The next day was Sunday. After a fortnight of lovely summer weather, a great change had taken place. The rain was falling in torrents, and the wind was whistling through the trees in the garden, when Christie looked out. A rainy day in the green room was by no means such a dreary matter as it used to be in Mrs. Lee's attic-nursery, with only a glimpse of driving clouds and dripping roofs to vary the dulness within. So Christie comforted little Claude for the want of his morning ride and ramble in the garden, telling him how glad the dusty leaves and thirsty little flowers would be for all the bright drops that were falling on them. She told him how the bees, that had been so busy all the week, must take a rest to-day, and how warm and dry the little birds would be in their nest in the pear-tree, for all the driving rain. Setting him in his favourite chair by the window, she amused him with talk like this, as she went about putting things in order in the room. While she comforted him she comforted herself; for the rain had brought a disappointment to her too. It had been arranged that Martha should take charge of Claude while Christie went to church in the morning, where she had not been for several Sabbaths. But remembering Mrs. Greenly's oft-repeated warnings against exposing herself to dampness, she did not like to venture in the rain. So she had to content herself at home.

This was an easier matter than it had sometimes been. As the morning wore away, and the time approached for the little boy to take his usual sleep, she was quite contented to be where she was.

'It is very pleasant, all this reading with Miss Gertrude,' she said. 'She is very kind, and I like her very much. But I shall be glad to be alone for a little while.'

Claude's eyes closed at last, and she was just taking her Bible from the table beside her, when the door opened and Miss Gertrude entered.

'I only heard this minute from Mattie that you did not go to church, after all,' she said. 'No wonder! What a rain! Papa thought it was too bad to take out the horses. He is tired, too, after his journey. Is it half-past eleven? Everybody is lazy on Sunday morning. But there will be an hour or two before lunch yet. I have brought our friend "Jeanie." There will be time for a chapter or two.'

Christie looked up with an expression of surprise and doubt on her face.

'Jeanie Deans, is it? But it is the Sabbath-day!'

Miss Gertrude laughed.

'Well, what if it is? I'm sure there is no harm in the book. You looked exactly like Aunt Barbara when you said that; I mean, all but her cap and spectacles. "The moral expression" of your face, as she would say, was exactly the same.'

Christie laughed, but said nothing.

'You don't mean to tell me that there is any harm in the book?' continued Miss Gertrude.

'It is not a right book for the Sabbath, though,' said Christie, gravely.

'Well, for my part, I don't see that a book that it is right to read every other day of the week can be so

very bad a book for Sunday,' said Miss Gertrude,
sharply.

Christie made no reply.

'I declare, I like Aunt Barbara's way best; to call all
tales wicked at once, and have nothing to do with them
—these vile novels, as she calls them. Come, now, you
are not in earnest?'

'I am quite in earnest,' said Christie, gently, but
firmly.

'And you have been reading or listening to this, or
something like it, all the week! Well, that is what
I should call straining at a gnat and swallowing a
camel.'

'Well, perhaps it is. I never thought about it in
that way before. But I am sure it is not right to read
such books on the Sabbath-day. And perhaps it is
wrong to read them at all—at least, so many of them as
we have been reading. I almost think it is.'

She spoke sorrowfully, but not in any degree offen
sively. Indeed, she seemed to be speaking rather to
herself than to Miss Gertrude. Yet the young lady was
offended. Assuming the tone and manner with which
she sometimes made herself disagreeable, she said:

'I should regret exceedingly to be the means of
leading you to do anything that you think wrong. I
must try and enjoy my book by myself.' And without
looking towards her, she walked out of the room.

For a little while Christie sat motionless, gazing at
the door through which she had disappeared, and thinking sorrowfully that this was a very sad ending to a very
pleasant time. But there was a sharper pain at her
heart than any that this thought awakened. All those
days that had been so bright in passing had a shadow

over them as she looked back upon them. To what end and purpose had all their intercourse tended? What was the cause of the feeling of uneasiness, almost of guilt, that had come on her now and then at quiet moments? It had clung to her all the morning. She was not very wise or far-sighted. She could not reason from cause to effect, or analyze her own feelings very closely. But even when she was congratulating herself on the prospect of a quiet time she was half conscious that she was not very glad to find herself alone. When she sat down with the Bible in her hand, there fell on her spirit no such blessed sense of rest and peace as used to transform the dim attic into something pleasanter than this pretty green room, and fairer than the summer garden.

'There is something wrong,' she said to herself, as she listened to Miss Gertrude's footsteps on the stair. 'I am afraid I am one of the folk that Mrs. Grey used to tell about, that an easy life is not good for. Better the weary days and nights than to fall back into my old ways again, just content with the pleasure the day brings, without looking beyond. Who would have thought that I could have forgotten so soon? It is just this foolish novel reading, I think. Aunt Elsie said it was a snare to me; and Effie said something like it once.

'Well, I'm not likely to have more of it,' she continued, with a sigh. 'I suppose I ought to be glad that Miss Gertrude went away vexed; for I dare say I should not have had courage to-morrow to tell her that so much of that kind of reading is not good for me, Sabbath or week-day. It couldn't have lasted long, at any rate. Of course, when Mrs. Seaton comes home it

will be quite different. Well, it will be better for me
—a great deal better. I must be watchful and humble
To think that I should grow careless and forget, just
when I ought to be so mindful and thankful!'

A few tears fell on the leaves of her little Bible; but
by and by the former peace came back again, as she felt
herself half resting indeed on the only sure foundation.
The foolish fancies that had haunted her imagination
all the week vanished before the influence of the blessed
words on those familiar pages. They were precious
still, though the strange charm of her new companionship had turned her thoughts from them for a time.
She forgot her idle dreams, the foolish fancies she had
indulged, the vain longing for this or that earthly good
for herself and for all at home that had at times for the
last few days taken possession of her. The peace which
flows from a sense of pardon and acceptance and a firm
trust was for the time enjoyed. To be and to do just
what God willed seemed infinitely desirable to her.

'"Great peace have they that love Thy law,"' she
murmured. 'I do love it; and I have the peace.'

Very humble and earnest were the prayers that rose
beside the bed of little Claude that day, and very grave,
yet happy, was the face that greeted his waking.
Christie needed all her patience, for this was one of
Claude's fretful days. He grew weary of being confined
to one room; he longed for the company of his sister
and Clement. His brother came in for a little while
after he had had his dinner; but he was in one of his
troublesome moods, and vexed and fretted Claude so
much that Christie was fain to give him over to Martha's
charge, bidding him not come into the green room till
he was ready to be good and kind.

In the meantime, Miss Gertrude was enjoying her book in her own room; or, rather, she was not enjoying it. It had lost much of its interest to her. She was not in a humour to enjoy anything just then. She wandered into the parlour at last, thinking a chat with her father, or even with Mr. Sherwood, would be better than her book. But her father was in the library, with the door shut, and Mr. Sherwood had gone out, notwithstanding the rain. The deserted room looked dreary, and she went to her own again.

At six she went down to dinner. They were not a very lively party. Mr. Seaton looked sleepy, and yawned several times before they went to the dining-room. Mr. Sherwood was very grave, and, indeed, 'stupid,' as Gertrude thought.

'What a misfortune a rainy Sunday is!' she said at last. 'One scarcely knows what to do with one's self. This has seemed twice as long as other days.'

'Pray don't let any one hear you say that, my dear,' said her father, laughing. 'If one rainy Sunday exhausts the resources of a well-educated young lady, I am afraid her prospects are not the brightest.'

Miss Gertrude laughed.

'Oh, father, I haven't quite got to that state of exhaustion! But I have been dull and stupid—not able to settle myself to the enjoyment of anything—all day.'

'Where are the boys?' asked her father.

'Claude is in the green room, with his nurse. Indeed, I suppose both boys are there just now. After dinner I shall send for them. Claude really seems better; he runs about again.'

'Stay,' said Mr. Sherwood. This reminds me that I brought a letter last night for the new nursemaid; at least, I suppose so;' and he took a letter from his pocket, and laid it on the table.

'You don't mean that you brought that home last night, and have kept it till this time?' said Miss Gertrude, with much surprise.

'Tut, tut, my child!' said her father, touching the hand outstretched to take the letter. She withdrew her hand without a word.

'You could not have been more indignant had the letter been for yourself. It is not such a terrible oversight,' said Mrs. Lane, or Aunt Barbara, as she was commonly called, who had looked in on her way from church. 'If it is like most of the letters of that sort of people, it would be little loss though she never got it. Such extraordinary epistles as I sometimes read for my servants!'

'This seems quite a respectable affair, however,' said Mr. Seaton, reading the direction in Effie's fair, clear handwriting:

Christina Redfern,

Care of J. R. Seaton, Esq.

'That is a very pretty direction—*very.*'

'I am very sorry, and very much ashamed of my carelessness,' said Mr. Sherwood. 'I hope, Miss Gertrude, you will forgive me, and I will never do so again, as little boys say.'

But he did not look either very sorry or very much ashamed, Miss Gertrude thought, and she made no reply. The rather uncomfortable silence that followed was broken by a low voice at the door:

'Am I to take the children, Miss Gertrude?'

Master Clement answered :

'No, I shan't go to bed yet.   It's only seven o'clock'

'Come in,' said Mr. Seaton, kindly.   'I want to know how these little fellows have behaved since their mother went away.'

Christie came forward shyly, curtseying, in some confusion, to Mrs. Lane, whom her short-sighted eyes did not discern till she was close upon her.

'I hope they have been good and obedient, and have not given you much trouble?' said Mr. Seaton again.

A little smile passed over Christie's mouth. 'Master Clement is Miss Gertrude's boy, sir,' she said, as she stooped to buckle the belt of that active young gentleman.

'And I'm very good.   She punishes me when I ain't good.'

'I'm afraid she has enough to do, then.   And the doctor thinks Claude is better, does he?' he asked, caressing the pale little face that lay on his shoulder.

'Yes,' said Christie, doubtfully.   'He says he is better.'

There was no mistaking the look of wistful interest that overspread her face as she looked at the child.

'He is very good and patient, almost always,' she added, as she met the little boy's smile.

'I'm a great deal better,' said Claude.   'The doctor says I may ride on the pony some day.'

'Have you had much to do with children?' asked Aunt Barbara.

'I lived with Mrs. Lee eight months.'

'And she parted with you because she needed a person of more experience?'

'Yes, I suppose so. I wasn't strong enough Mr. Lee thought. I was very sorry.'

It was a sore subject with Christie yet, and the colour went and came as she spoke.

'And where were you before?' asked Mr. Seaton, wishing to relieve her embarrassment.

'I was with our own children, at home. I was one of the children then myself. I never was away from home before my father died.'

'Look, here is something for you. Cousin Charles says it is for you. It is a letter,' said Clement, holding it up.

If there had been ten Aunt Barbaras in the room, Christie could not have restrained the expression of surprise and pleasure that rose to her lips at the sight of Effie's familiar handwriting, and her hands quite trembled as she took it from the little boy.

'Now, Claudie,' said the young lady, coming forward, 'it is time for you to go with Christie. Say "good-night" to father and Aunt Barbara.'

For a single moment the look of peevish resistance that used to come so often to the child's face passed over it, but it changed as Christie stooped down, saying softly:

'Will you walk? or shall I carry you, as they carried the little boy home from the field?'

'And will you tell me more?' he asked, holding out his hand.

'Oh, yes; and how glad his mother was when he grew better again. Now walk a little bit, and I will carry you up-stairs. The doctor says he ought to be encouraged to walk,' she said to his father, as she set him down.

The child bade them 'good-night' quite willingly, and went.

'Clement, stay with me,' said his sister. 'Christie will not get much good of her letter for the next two hours, if you are with her.'

Clement was very willing to stay. But for all that Christie did not get much good of her letter for an hour and more, except the good it did her to hold it in her hand, and feeling the delight that was in store for her. Miss Gertrude came to the green room some time after, to find her still rocking and singing to the wakeful Claude.

'You don't mean you haven't read your letter yet?' she said, in astonishment.

'I have opened it. They are all well. I like to be sure of a quiet time to read a letter.'

'Well, take the lamp and go over there. I will take care of him for the present.'

'He is just asleep now,' said Christie, hesitating. She was thinking that she would like to have the room to herself before she read her letter, but as Miss Gertrude seated herself in the low rocking-chair, she had only to take the lamp and go to the other side.

She soon forgot Miss Gertrude, Claude, and all besides, except Effie and the bairns at home. Effie had the faculty, which many people of greater pretensions do not possess, of putting a great deal into a letter. They were always written journalwise—a little now, and a little then; and her small, clear handwriting had come to be like print to Christie's accustomed eyes. So she read on, with a smile on her lip, quite unconscious that the eyes that seemed to be seeing nothing but the bright embers were all the time furtively watching her. Miss Gertrude longed for a peep into the unseen world in which her humble friend was at that moment revelling. She felt positively envious of the supreme content that was expressed on Christie's plain, pale face.

She would not have understood it had the peep been granted. She never could have understood the interest which in Christie's mind was connected with the various little items of news with which Effie's letter was nearly filled. There was the coming and going of the neighbours, a visit from blind Alice, and her delight in her canary. There was an account of Jennie's unprecedented success in chicken-raising, and of little Will's triumphant conquest of compound division; and many more items of the same kind. There were a few words —a very few—about the day Christie had spent in the cemetery with John Nesbitt, which brought the happy tears into her eyes; and that was all.

No, the best came last. The letter had been opened again, and a slip of paper had been added, to tell how Effie had got a letter from Mrs. Lee. It was a very short letter, scarcely more than a line or two; but Effie was to keep it safe to show to Christie when she came home. In the meantime she must tell her that she had never in all her life been so proud and happy as she had been when she read to Aunt Elsie what a help and comfort her dear little sister had been to the writer in the midst of sickness and sorrow; and more than that, how, by means of her little Bible and her earnest, humble words, she had opened to her a way to a higher hope and a better consolation than earth could give, and how the lady could not go away without doing what she knew would give her friend more pleasure

than anything else she could do. She must tell
Christie's sister how good and patient and useful she
had been.

'And so, Christie, when you are weary or desponding,
as I am afraid you sometimes are, I think you may take
a little rest and pleasure from the thought that you
have been favoured to be made the giver of a "cup of
cold water to one of *His* little ones."'

Oh, it was too much! Such words from her dearest
sister Effie! And to think that Mrs. Lee should have
written them that last night, when she must have been
so weary! And had she really done her good? Oh, it
was too much happiness! The letter fell from her
hands, and her face, as she burst into happy tears, was
hidden by them. It was only for a moment, however.
She fancied herself quite unobserved as she took up
her precious letter.

'Are they all well at home?' asked Miss Gertrude,
as Christie, having stealthily wiped away all traces of
her tears, came and sat down on the other side of the
cot, where Claude was now sleeping soundly.

'They are all quite well. My aunt is better.
Everything is just as usual.'

'Your sister is a very pretty writer, is she not?' she
asked.

'Yes, she writes very plain and even. Her writing
is easily read.' But Christie did not offer to show her
the letter, as Miss Gertrude half hoped she would. It
was not altogether for the gratification of her curiosity,
nor chiefly for that, she wanted to see it. Though her
companion was sitting there, with her cheek leaning on
her hand, so gravely and so quietly, she knew that her
heart was by no means so quiet as her outward appear-

ance seemed to indicate. She saw that it was ready to overflow with emotion of some kind—happiness, Miss Gertrude thought, but was not sure.

But it could not be all happiness. Christie must be longing for the sight of the sister whose written words could call forth such tears as she had seen falling even now. And she wished to be able to sympathize with her, to say some word that would establish confidence between them. Besides, she had a feeling that she ought to atone for her petulance in the morning. At any rate, she wanted to be sure that Christie did not resent it.

But Christie said nothing. She sat quite still, and her thoughts were far away. When she roused herself, it was not to speak, but to take up her little Bible, that lay within reach of her hand.

'How fond you seem to be of that book!' said Miss Gertrude, as she watched her turning over the leaves.

'Yes,' said Christie, quietly. 'Effie gave it to me.'

'Are you going to read now?'

'I was looking for something that Effie wrote about. I can't mind the exact words, and I am not sure where to find them.' And she still turned over the leaves.

'Have you found it?' said Miss Gertrude, when she paused.

'Yes; I have found it. Here it is. "And whosoever shall give to drink unto one of these little ones a cup of cold water only, in the name of a disciple, shall in no wise lose his reward."'

She read it slowly and gravely, but Miss Gertrude could by no means understand the look of mingled doubt and pleasure that she saw on her face when she had done.

'Well?' she said, inquiringly.

But Christie had nothing to say. Her face was bowed down on her hands, and she did not raise it till she heard the door open and shut; and when she looked up, Miss Gertrude was gone

CHAPTER XVI.

A TALK IN THE GARDEN.

THE next day was rainy, and the next, and the next. There was not a glimpse of sunshine till Friday, and then it was only a glimpse. There was no such thing as going into the garden, or even into the wide gallery that ran along the ends of the house. The only change that little Claude enjoyed all that time was being daily taken into the drawing-room while the green room was aired, or into the dining-room when his father was at home, a little while before he went to bed. He did not grow worse, however. He seemed quite contented with Christie, and fretted less when Clement left him than he used to do.

He was growing very fond of his nurse. She was gentle and patient with him, never sparing herself when he needed to be amused. But her firmness was equal to her gentleness. She never suffered herself to be persuaded to indulge him in anything that had been forbidden by the doctor; and she was faithful to the letter in obeying all his directions. The little boy soon learned to yield to her in all things, and the fretful violence that used to excite fever and exhaust his strength seldom appeared now. The green room was Christie's acknowledged domain. The 'masterful' Clement was taught that he was only admitted there on condition of good behaviour; and really, considering all things, he was very good. He was encouraged to be much in the green room during those rainy days, for his merry ways and pleasant childish talk did his little brother a great deal of good.

As for Miss Gertrude, I am sorry to say she did not recover her good-humour so soon as she ought to have done. She did not resent what she called Christie's reproof about the book half so much as she did her slowness in responding to her offered sympathy about the letter. She fancied that the little nurse ought to have been very much flattered by the interest she had tried to show in her affairs, and was displeased at the silence with which her advances had been received.

Poor Christie had offended very unconsciously. With her mind full of her letter and all the associations it had awakened, she had been quite unmindful of Miss Gertrude and her attempts to make up the little falling-out of the morning. She only began to realize that the young lady must have been offended, when the days passed over with only a brief visit to Claude. Even then she believed that her vexation rose from what had passed about the book.

But Miss Gertrude was very much out of sorts with herself too. If it had not been a rainy day, she would have availed herself of her Aunt Barbara's invitation to spend the day with her. But a rainy day at Aunt Barbara's was not to be thought of. She took a long time to write a short letter to Mrs. Seaton, in Scotland

Then she took a fit of practising her music, which, she said to herself, she had sadly neglected of late. Then she read a little. Then she went into the kitchen and superintended the making of a pudding after a new recipe which some one had given to her.

Then she dressed for dinner. But the time is very long from nine in the morning till six at night, when it is rainy without and gloomy within. It wanted full an hour of the usual time for her father's return when she was quite ready to receive him. She wandered into the dining-room. There were no signs of the dinner-table being laid. She wandered into the drawing-room, and passed her fingers over the keys of the piano once or twice. But she could not settle to steady playing, or, indeed, to anything else.

'I wonder what has become of Master Clement all this time? It is time Martha was in the dining-room. I will go and see.'

She went into the nursery; but it was deserted. She called, but received no answer. A sound of voices from the green room drew her there, and the door opened on as merry a game as one could wish to see. Claude sat in his usual place in the arm-chair, and scattered on the carpet before him were a number of pictured and lettered blocks which his father had brought home. These Master Clement was examining with much pretended gravity. He was looking for the letter C, which Christie had pointed out to him. Whenever he made a mistake and pointed out the wrong letter, he punished himself by creeping on his hands and knees under Claude's crib; and whenever Christie's nod and smile proclaimed that he was right, he vaulted over the crib, with such laughter and grimaces, and such a shaking of his tangled curls over his face, that Claude laughed and clapped his hands from sympathy.

Miss Gertrude leaned over the chair and watched the play.

'How noisy you are, Clement!' she said, at last.

'Yes; but it is nice noise. I'm very good to-day, Tudie.'

'Are you? I am very glad to hear it, and very much surprised too.'

'Are you cross to-day?'

'Why? What makes you ask?'

'Oh, because you haven't been here.'

'I have been busy writing a letter to your mother.'

'Did you tell her that I am a good boy? I am a very good boy; and so is Claudie.'

A leap and a grimace more astonishing than any he had yet accomplished sent Claude into fits of laughter.

'I declare,' said Miss Gertrude, looking down upon him, 'I don't believe your mother would know you if she were to see you now! Why, there is quite a colour in his lips. He really seems better, doesn't he?'

'Yes, and he has been very good and easily amused all day, though he has not been able to go out.'

There was silence for a time. Both girls stood watching the game that was going on. But soon Christie said:

'If you please, Miss Gertrude, will you show me that stitch again? I have quite lost it.'

'Yes,' said Miss Gertrude; 'I will show you. It is quite easy.'

'Yes, I dare say it is. I am afraid I am very dull at learning it.'

She was watching the expert fingers of Miss Gertrude admiringly. It was a piece of work she had commenced long before, but getting tired of it, she had offered to teach Christie, who was to finish it.

'It is very pretty,' said Christie, 'and quite easy, when one knows the way.'

'Yes, it is quite easy,' said Miss Gertrude. But her manner was quite different from what it had been at the last lesson.

'She is not going to be vexed with me, if I can help it,' said Christie to herself; and in a little while she said, again:

'Miss Gertrude, have you any objection to my copying this pattern out of your book, to send to Effie? I am going to write to her. She is very quick at such work.'

'Certainly not; no objection at all. You can copy it if you like—if you think your sister can make anything of it.' Then, a little ashamed of her ungracious manner, she added, 'I will copy it for you—and another, a much prettier one. When shall you send your letter away?'

'Oh, I am very much obliged! I write so slowly that there is no haste about it. I shall not have my letter ready till Friday.'

The next day Miss Gertrude made herself very busy with her practising, and with a magazine that Mr. Sherwood had brought home. The day following she spent with her aunt, who sent for her in the morning. Thursday, she was as tired of her dignity as she was of the rain, and came into the green room with a smiling face, and a nice book in her hand. Christie received her exactly as she would have done had there been no interruption of their intercourse. She did not for a moment think of resenting Miss Gertrude's coolness. She had been busy every moment of her spare time during these few days, writing to her sister, and she had missed her society far less than it would have pleased the young lady to know. But she was very glad to see her back again, and to hear her declare, as she seated herself in the arm-chair, that after all the green room was the very pleasantest in the house. So, with no more words about it, they fell into their old, pleasant ways again.

Mrs. Seaton's return made less difference in their manner of life than they supposed it would. She seemed to Christie a very different person from the pale, anxious invalid that went away so unwillingly; and indeed she was. Her health and spirits were quite restored. Instead of falling back into the retired mode of life that had become habitual to her since the illness of her little boy, she went into society, as she had done before; and as her circle of friends was large, she had very little time to devote to her children, and Christie continued to have almost as much care of Claude as she had had during his mother's absence.

There was one change which at first seemed anything but a pleasant one; they left the pretty green room for a smaller one in a higher story At first it seemed a dull, dismal place, but Christie learned to love it very much before she left it.

Miss Gertrude's lessons commenced again soon after the return of Mrs. Seaton, but there was nothing more said of her going to school, at least for the present. She was not old enough to go much into society, and she had plenty of time to devote to the readings in the upper nursery, as Christie's new room was called. Her interest in these readings was not uniform. Sometimes for several days at a time her visits were few and brief; but on the whole, she enjoyed them very much, and did not neglect them very long.

The balconied window of the green room was not the only one at which the locust-tree made pleasant music. It shaded also one of the library windows. The library had become so much the resort of Mr. Sherwood that it almost came to be considered as his room. He spent much of his time in it undisturbed. So it happened one day, when he was not at all busy, he heard the sound of voices beneath, and looking out, discovered that the nursery party had placed themselves on the rustic seat that always stood there. The September wind had scattered many of the long, slender leaves of the locust; but they had come there rather to enjoy the sunshine than the shade. He could see them quite plainly—Claude sitting on his cushion, Clement running here and there about the lawn, Miss Gertrude, as usual, with her book, and Christie with her work. He could not hear what they said, except a word now and then from the children's shrill voices. Miss Gertrude pretended to read, but evidently the reading did not prosper; and by and by the book was laid aside, and in the conversation that followed the girls seemed to take an equal part. Mr. Sherwood was quite astonished to find himself wishing that he could hear what they were saying; but he could not, except when Miss Gertrude's voice was raised in warning or in reproof, as Master Clement pursued his own pleasure in a distant part of the garden.

By and by the sound of wheels was heard in the garden, and Miss Gertrude rose quickly.

'Oh, here come visitors!' she exclaimed. Her face was turned towards the window, and he heard every word plainly. 'Let us go to the cedar walk. I don't want to go in; and if they don't see me they will never think of me. Come, Christie.'

She lifted Claude from his cushion and ran away with him, leaving Christie to follow with the shawls and other things. The book was left behind on the bench, and when the visitors were safe in the house, Mr. Sherwood could not resist the desire he felt to go down to see what it was. As he passed the drawing-room door, Mrs. Seaton looked out.

'If you are going into the garden, Charles, and should see Miss Gertrude, tell her Mrs. Jordan is here, and has asked for her.'

'I dare say she won't thank me for the message,' he said to himself, as he picked up the book and took his way to the cedar walk. He smiled to himself as he turned over the leaves.

'You are inquired for,' he said. 'Mrs. Seaton bade me tell you that Mrs. Jordan is in the drawing-room with her daughters, and they have asked for you.'

'Oh, dear me! And I thought I was safe for this time! But I don't think I will go. They'll forget all about me in a few minutes.'

'Mrs. Seaton wishes you to go, however,' said Mr. Sherwood, gravely.

Miss Gertrude shrugged her shoulders. They had more than once differed as to the nature and extent of duty she owed to her step-mother. She said nothing, however, but rose.

'I'm going too,' said Clement. 'Tudie, you must take me.'

'Cousin Charles, carry me!' entreated Claude.

'No, Clement; you are not to come unless you are sent for. And I'll come back directly.'

Mr. Sherwood took one turn in the garden, and came back to the cedar walk in time to hear the end of Christie's story:

'And so, when the blind man heard the noise of so many people passing by, he wondered. And they told him that Jesus was passing by, and that all the people were following Him. And he asked, "Is it Jesus, who healed the ruler's little daughter?" Then he began to call out, as loud as he was able, "Jesus, Jesus, Thou Son of David, have mercy on me!" And all the people told him to be still, and not make such a noise. But he thought, "Perhaps Jesus will never come this way again!" so he cried out all the more.

'Well, Jesus heard him, and He stood still and waited till the blind man came up to Him. And then He said, "What wilt thou that I should do unto you?" And the man said, "Lord, that mine eyes might be opened."

'And with a single word that Jesus spoke, his eyes were opened; and he saw the earth, and the sky, and the wondering crowd, and Jesus. Just think how glad he must have been to come out of darkness to see so many beautiful things! And how good and kind Jesus was!'

'Will Jesus ever come again? And could He make me well and strong like Clement? Oh, I wish He would come!'

It was a very entreating little face that was turned towards her as he spoke. She did not answer him at once, but kissed him, and stroked his hair with loving hands.

'Will He ever come again?' he repeated, eagerly.

'My child, He is near us now. He does not forget little children, and the sick and the blind and the sorrowful. And He hears us, just as He heard the blind Bartimeus, and He cares for us and helps us all the same, though He has gone to heaven.'

'And will He make me well again?'

'I don't know. If it is best He will. And if He does not make you well, He will make you good and patient, and willing to be sick. And you will be happy—more happy than when you were quite strong and well. Don't you remember how He took the little children up in His arms and blessed them?'

'Yes; and He said, "Suffer the little children to come unto Me."' But the little boy looked very sad as he said it.

Mr. Sherwood took another turn in the garden and approached them from the other side. Christie was wrapping Claude in a plaid, and preparing to wheel him round the garden—as quiet and uninteresting a person, to all appearance, as one could fancy a child's nurse to be.

'Carry me, Cousin Charles,' entreated little Claude. 'It is so much nicer than to be drawn in the carriage. Do take me for a little while.'

'We'll play horses,' said Clement, making his appearance at the moment, 'and I'll drive. Now, up and away!'

Christie sat down to her work again, while they carried on a merry game up and down the cedar walk, with much shouting and laughter from all.

'And now that must do,' said Mr. Sherwood, seating himself on the bench that always stood there. 'Your horse is very tired, and he must rest before he goes farther. Sit still, Claude. I am not too tired to hold you—only too tired to run any more.'

'He is very warm,' said Christie, laying down her
work to come and pin the plaid more closely about
him. She did it very gently, and there was no mistaking the loving looks the little boy gave her.

'I found this book as I came out,' said Mr. Sherwood.
'Was it you or Miss Gertrude who was making it your
study?'

'Did I leave it behind me? It was very careless,'
said Christie, in some confusion. 'We were both reading it; that is, Miss Gertrude read, and I listened.'

'"Evidences of the Truth of Revealed Religion,"'
he read, turning to the title-page. 'Which of you is
troubled with doubts on that subject?'

'Neither of us, I hope,' said Christie, quietly. She
did not quite like the tone in which he spoke.

'But what is the use of reading the book, if you are
quite sure already of what it professes to teach?'

'The book was Miss Gertrude's choice,' said Christie,
scarcely knowing what to say.

'Oh, then it is Miss Gertrude whose faith is waver-
ing?'

Christie shook her head.

'One day Miss Gertrude asked me something about
which I was quite sure, but I couldn't tell her why I
was so sure; and she found this book, and we thought
we would read it.'

'To make you more sure?' said Mr. Sherwood,
smiling.

'No, sir, not that. Nothing could make me more
sure than I am that the Bible and all it teaches is true.
But it is well to be able to tell why I am sure.'

'And so you are sure of these things without knowing
why you are sure?'

Christie sent a grave, questioning look into his face, and said :

'I think the true knowledge of these things is not learned in books, unless it is in the Bible—and not in that, unless God teaches one.'

After a pause, she added :

'It must be true, you know. What can one trust to, if not to the Word of God ? What else is there that does not fail us in the time of need, in some way or other ?'

'Not much, indeed,' said Mr. Sherwood, gravely.

'Nothing,' repeated Christie, 'except the word and promise of God. They never fail—never change— never !'

'Do they never change ? What were you telling that boy just now about the blind man that was healed for the asking ? But you could not tell Claude that the same power could make him strong and well again, though I am sure you wish it were so.'

'But I am quite sure He could ; and He would, if it were best.'

'But why is it not best for him as well as it was for the blind man ? He wishes it, and all who love him wish it. And our poor little Claude is not the only one. Think how much suffering there is in the world that might be relieved.'

Christie looked puzzled and anxious for a moment.

'But it is not that He has changed, or that He breaks His promise. I cannot say just what I would, but I don't think it is quite the same. You know when Christ came into the world it was not merely to do that kind of good to men ; it was to save them. And it was necessary that He should prove to them that He was the Son of God, by doing what none but God could do. So He opened blind eyes, and healed their diseases, and raised the dead. And besides, they were to know another way: "Surely He hath borne our griefs and carried our sorrows!" They might have known He was the Messiah by that too.' She stopped suddenly, and then added: 'It is different now.'

'And so, having done enough to prove all that, He forgets the troubles people in the world have now. Does He?'

'It is not that He forgets, or breaks His promise,' said Christie, hesitatingly, yet earnestly. 'He has not promised that His people should never have trouble in the world; quite the contrary. But He promises always to be with them, to support and comfort them through all. And that is as good as though they were to have none—and, indeed, far better.'

She spoke very earnestly. Her face was flushed, and the tears filled her eyes, but she spoke very modestly and humbly too.

'Well, it does not seem that *you* are troubled with doubts, anyway,' said Mr. Sherwood, rising, and placing Claude on the seat she had prepared for him.

'No; I do not doubt. It must be a great unhappiness to think at all about these things and not be sure and quite at rest about them.'

'And what would you say to any one who suffered this great unhappiness?'

The question was gravely, even sadly, asked. There was not the echo of mockery in his tone that had made Christie shrink during the first moments of his being there. She looked up wistfully into the face that was still bending over the child.

'I don't know,' she said. 'I cannot tell—except to

bid him ask, as the blind man asked, "Lord, that mine eyes might be opened !" '

He went slowly down the cedar walk, and Christie watched him with wistful eyes. Whether he asked the gift of sight or not, there was one who, after that day, did ask it for him.

CHAPTER XVII.

THE SECRET OF PEACE.

GERTRUDE could not find her book. All that Christie could tell her about it was that she had seen it in Mr. Sherwood's hand in the cedar walk, and that he did not leave it when he went away. She looked for it in the library and in the drawing-room, but it was nowhere to be seen. She had a great objection to asking him for it. Mr. Sherwood sometimes condescended to jest with the young lady on some subjects about which they did not agree; and she did not like his jests. So time passed on, till the third day.

'I'll ask him for it at dinner,' she said to herself. 'He is never so provoking when father is there.'

But a good opportunity occurred before dinner. Mr. Sherwood was standing in the hall, waiting for Mrs. Seaton, whom he was to take into town, when Miss Gertrude passed him on her way up-stairs.

'Mr. Sherwood,' she said, 'you picked up a book in the garden the other day. It was very careless in me to leave it there. Will you give it to me now?'

'I ought to apologize to you for having kept it so long,' he answered, gravely. 'I will get it for you this moment.'

Miss Gertrude looked up to see whether there was not a smile upon his face. She had no idea that her new 'whim' for serious reading was to be allowed to pass without remark. But his look was quite grave as he turned into the library.

'Do you like this?' he asked, when he came out with the book in his hand.

'I don't know. I have not read much of it,' she answered, quickly, moving towards him to take the book. He gave it to her without speaking.

A glance at his face induced her to say, 'Are you not well to-day, Cousin Charles?'

It was one of Miss Gertrude's 'whims' always to address him formally as 'Mr. Sherwood'; and in his agreeable surprise at her familiarity, he smiled brightly But his face grew grave again as he said:

'Yes; I am quite well—only, perhaps, a little more indolent and self-indulgent than usual.'

About this time there came a letter from Effie, in which there was one sentence that cost Christie many a wondering and anxious thought.

'My dear little sister, let your light shine, and who knows but you may be the means of blessing to this household also?'

'Effie doesn't know,' said Christie to herself. 'She thinks I have grown good and wise, but she is much mistaken. I am sure if I did any good to Mrs. Lee I don't know how it happened. And besides, she was ill and in trouble, and had need of the little help and comfort I could give her. But Miss Gertrude! She is the only one I come very near to here; and she is so quick and beautiful and strong—so much above me in every way. Oh, if Effie were to see her, she

would never think of my being able to influence her.
Everybody admires Miss Gertrude; and I am but a
nursemaid, and hardly that.'

And yet the humble little maid did influence Gertrude as the days and months passed on; but Mrs.
Seaton and her gay friends in the drawing-room were
not more unconscious of the influence for good she was
exerting over the wayward young lady than was the
little maid herself.

Gertrude only vaguely realized that she was beginning
to see and estimate things differently from what she
used to do—half thinking, as her mother did, that it
was because she was growing older and more sensible.
She found herself thinking, now and then, that her
standard of right was not exactly what it used to be
before she had compared opinions with Christie. In
her intercourse with her own family and with others
also, she often found herself measuring their opinions
and actions by Christie's rule. But she by no means
realized that her own opinions and actions were
gradually adjusting themselves to the same rule. Yet
so it was.

She liked to watch Christie. She was never weary
of admiring the patience with which she bore the
changing moods of her little charge, when illness made
him fretful or exacting. Gertrude saw that she was
learning to love the little boy dearly; but she also saw
that it was not merely her love for him that made her
so faithful in doing her duty to him, nor was it to
please the mother and sister or win their confidence,
for she was equally faithful in matters that could never
come to Mrs. Seaton's knowledge, and Gertrude knew
by experience that *her* pleasure was never suffered

to interfere where Claude's interest or comfort was concerned.

No; Christie lived that useful, patient life from higher motives than these. 'She does what is right because it is right,' said Gertrude to herself. She saw her quite cheerful and contented from day to day, doing the same things over and over again, with few pleasures—with none, indeed, unless the hour or two of reading which they managed almost daily to get could be called such.

And yet, by a thousand tokens, Gertrude knew that she would have enjoyed keenly many pleasures that were quite beyond her hopes—leisure, and books, and going to school, and the power to give gifts and confer favours. To be able to live at home, with no heavy cares pressing on the family, would be real happiness for her. All this Gertrude gathered from the conversations they sometimes had, from occasional remarks, and from her intense delight when letters from home came.

And yet she did not repine in the absence of these things. She was happy in the performance of her duties, whether they were easy or not, and enjoyed the few simple pleasures that came in her way.

'It is not because she is stupid, or that she does not know anything else,' said Gertrude to herself. 'She enjoys reading and learning as well as I do, and makes a far better use of the chance she has: and yet she lives on from day to day, wearying herself with little Claude, and stitching away, as though she cared for nothing beyond. Wouldn't she enjoy being rich, and sending things to her family! Why, the delight she had over that common gray plaid that she sent to her aunt was

quite absurd—and quite touching too. It cost her two
months' wages at the very least, but she did not seem
to think of that. The only thing that marred her
happiness at all that day was the want of a few pence
that would have enabled her to buy a warm pair of
slippers to go with the shawl. She doesn't seem to
think of herself. I wonder why?'

And Gertrude watched her still, thinking her often
needlessly particular in the performance of small duties,
and losing patience now and then, when these things
interfered with her wishes. But the more she watched
her daily life the more sure she felt that Christie had
some secret of sweet peace which she had not yet found.
She knew that her strength and cheerfulness daily
renewed came from none of the helps to which one in
her circumstances might naturally look. It was not
the knowledge that she was valued, nor the feeling that
little Claude was beginning to love her dearly, that
sustained her; though Gertrude could see that these
were pleasant and precious to the little maid. It was
not even the thought of home, or Effie's letters, or the
pleasant word they brought of how she was missed and
how they wished her with them. It was not the hope
of the time when they should all be together again.
To these ardent young people this re-union seemed by
no means impossible, or even distant. With Gertrude's
help, Christie often built castles in the air, about a farm
which was to be the wonder of the country-side, where
they were all to live together, and where Gertrude
herself was to pass many a pleasant day.

But it was not this, nor all of these, that brought
the look of sweet contentment to that pale face, when
she thought herself quite unobserved. It was there

sometimes when she was wearied. She was not naturally hopeful or cheerful. She had none of that happy
self-confidence which makes burdens light and causes
difficulties to disappear. The source of her courage
and patience was out of herself. Her gentle cheerfulness, flowing evenly through long days and weeks,
sprang from some unseen fountain, pure and free and
never-failing.

Sometimes it came into the young lady's mind that
Christie's constant study of her little Bible had something to do with her being so different from any one
she had ever known before. But both of them were a
little shy about speaking of these things. They talked
about the histories, and even about the doctrines, of the
Bible. The stories that little Claude so delighted in
all came from the Bible; and Christie had no shyness
in speaking to him. To these stories, and the simple
comments made on them, Gertrude sometimes listened
when she seemed to be occupied with far other matters,
and she would have liked very much to have heard
more on some of the themes of which these conversations gave her only a hint. But Christie seldom talked
about herself. It was only by slow degrees that she
came to understand the secret of her content.

Coming one night later than usual into the upper
nursery, she found Christie sitting with her little Bible
in her hand. She shut it as Gertrude sat down beside
her, but she did not put it away.

'I suppose it is too late to begin to read anything
now?' said Gertrude. 'I have been helping Miss
Atherton to dress. You should have seen her! Her
dress was splendid—too splendid for so small a party,
mother thought. I wish I had called you to see her.'

'I wish you had, indeed,' said Christie, with real interest, for she was a great admirer of anything pretty. 'I should like to have seen her. She is beautiful always.'

'Yes, but dress makes a difference even in beautiful people. I have seen ladies who looked quite plain at home by daylight, who were thought great beauties by those who only saw them at parties. But Miss Atherton is always beautiful. She will shine to-night.'

Gertrude sat for a little while gazing into the fire.

'Would you like to have gone with her?' asked Christie.

'No, I think not; I am sure not. I was asked, you know, and I dare say mother would not have objected to my going. But I find these parties very stupid.'

'Miss Atherton does not find them stupid, I should think.'

'Miss Atherton! Oh, no! But she is quite different. I dare say I should like them well enough too, if I were quite grown up, and a belle like her. But one like me is only in the way in such a place, unless she sits quiet in a corner. That is all very well for a little time, but it soon becomes stupid enough.'

'But you are not a little girl. You are fifteen,' said Christie.

'Yes, I am too old to be contented with a seat in a corner, so I don't like parties yet. And I do believe father thinks it is because I am so sensible.'

Christie could not help laughing at the half-grave, half-comic way in which this was spoken.

'It must be very pleasant to be a belle, however,' continued Gertrude, meditatively, 'to have all eyes fixed on you in admiration, and to eclipse all the rest of the stars.'

'But that doesn't often happen, except in books, I fancy,' said Christie.

'Well, I suppose not. It couldn't happen very often. But it must be delightful when it *does* happen. Don't you think so?' she added, as Christie's face grew grave. 'Wouldn't you like to shine, as Miss Atherton will, at the Youngs' to-night?'

'You forget I don't know about these things,' said Christie.

'Nonsense! You can imagine how it would seem. I can imagine how it would seem to be drawn over the snow by reindeer, or to be carried away in a balloon. Now, tell me—wouldn't you like to be beautiful and rich, and admired by everybody?'

'I can imagine something I would like far better.'

What, the model farm, and to live at home? Oh, but if you are to wish, you know, you may as well wish for riches and beauty and all the rest at once! You would never stop short at your farm and contentment, if you had your wish.'

Christie shook her head. 'I think I would not wish at all.'

'Do you mean that you are so satisfied with your lot that you would not have it different if your wish could change it?' asked Miss Gertrude, in some surprise.

Christie hesitated a moment.

'I mean that I don't know what is best for me or for those I love, and He who has appointed our lot does; and so all things are best as they are.'

'Do you mean that you would rather be as you are, living away from home, among strangers, poor and not very strong, than to have all that we sometimes talk about, and to be able to be benevolent and live at home with your sisters ? '

'Ah, that would be very pleasant ; at least, it seems so now. But still it might not be best for us. If it would be best, we should have it so, I am quite sure.'

Gertrude opened her eyes in amazement.

'But I don't know what you mean by *best*,' she said, presently.

'Don't you ?' said Christie, smiling a little. 'Well, I am not good at explaining things. I don't mean what is pleasantest just now, but what is really best for us all, now, and—and afterwards.'

'Do you mean to say that you are better off here as Claude's nurse than you would be if you were to live at home, or go to school, as you were wishing you could the other day ? If you had your choice, is that what you would choose ?'

'Oh, I don't speak about a choice. I am content not to choose ; at least, almost always I am content. I know it is best for me to be here, or I shouldn't be here.'

'But, do you know, that seems to me quite absurd. Why, according to that, everybody is just in the right place. No one ought to have any wish to change, even to be better. All the world is just as it ought to be.'

'I can't tell what is best for all the world and everybody,' said Christie, gravely. 'I was only speaking of myself and Effie, and the rest at home.'

'But I suppose what is true for you is true for other people also—for me, for instance ! Don't you think I have anything left to wish for ? Do you think I am in

the very best place I could be in for my happiness now
and always?'

'I don't know,' said Christie, looking wistfully into
her face. 'I hope so. I cannot tell.'

'But what makes you so sure in your own case, then,
if you can't tell in mine? I think few people would
hesitate as to which of us is most happily placed.
What makes you so sure of yourself?'

Christie did not reply for a moment. She was slowly
turning over the leaves of her Bible. When at last she
stopped, it was to read softly:

'"For a man's life consisteth not in the abundance of
the things which he possesseth."'

And, farther on:

'"Consider the ravens: for they neither sow nor
reap; which neither have storehouse nor barn; and God
feedeth them: how much are ye better than the fowls?

'"Consider the lilies how they grow: they toil not,
they spin not; and yet I say unto you, that Solomon in
all his glory was not arrayed like one of these.

'"If then God so clothe the grass, which to-day is,
and to-morrow is cast into the oven, how much more
will He clothe you, O ye of little faith!"'

Gertrude had half expected some such answers. She
did not speak, but watched her as she continued to turn
the leaves. She read again:

'"And we know that all things work together for
good to them that love God."'

'That is all very well,' she said; 'but that is for one
as well as another, for me as well as you. And besides,
people don't take all things just as they stand. I am
sure all the people I know live as though their life *did*
consist in the abundance of the things they possess.'

'Well, I suppose the promise is not good to them,' said Christie; 'but that does not hinder its being good to others.'

Then one need not trouble one's self about what is to happen, according to that? One may just rest content and let things take their course?' said Gertrude, incredulously.

'Yes, that is just what one may do, when one is sure of a right to claim the promise.'

'But what do you mean by having a right? And why should one have a right more than another?' asked Gertrude, impatiently. But all the time she was saying to herself that the quiet little maid before her was one of those who might be content.

'I don't mean that any one has a right to claim the fulfilment of any promise, except the right that God gives. You know the verse says it is to them that love God for whose good all things work together. God's people, it means—those who love Him, and those whom He loves.'

Looking into her earnest face, it was not easy for Gertrude to answer lightly, but in a little while she said :

'Well, Christians ought to be very happy people according to that.'

'Surely,' said Christie, earnestly, 'and so they are.'

'Well, I know some of them who don't seem very happy. And they strive for riches and greatness, and all that, just as though their happiness depended upon it.'

'But no real child of God does that,' said Christie, eagerly.

'Oh! as to that I can't say. They call themselves Christians.'

'Well, we can't always judge people by just seeing them,' said Christie. 'There's many a one who seems to be living just as other folk live, and going the round that other folk go, and all the time he may be really very different. I am not good at speaking about these things, but I know that to a child of God His simple promise is worth more than houses or lands, or anything that this world can give. No; we have nothing to fear. Only we forget and grow desponding.'

The last words were spoken rather to herself than to Miss Gertrude. She sighed; but her face was quite untroubled as she rose, and laying down her Bible, began to arrange the things in the room.

'You always say, "child of God,"' said Gertrude, wishing still to prolong the conversation. 'Does that mean just a Christian, or does it mean something more?'

'Yes. "As many as received Him, to them gave He power to become the sons of God, even to them that believe on His name." Yes, it means just the same. You see, it seems to bring us very near to Him, speaking of Him as a Father, and of Christ as an Elder Brother. You know a child will never want for anything that a loving father has to give, if it is for his good; and so surely the children of God may well rest content with what He appoints for them. The only wonder is that they are ever otherwise than content.'

Gertrude made no reply, and there was a long silence.

'"A child of God." "Content with what He sends them." There is something wonderful in it. She is one of them, I dare say; and that is what makes her so different from almost any one I know. I wish I could understand it. It must be worth a great deal to know that one is a child of God. I wish she could tell me more about it.'

But Christie did not seem inclined to say more on any subject that night. She moved here and there in silence, putting things to rights in the room. Gertrude rose at last.

'That is a hint that it is time for me to go,' she said. Christie laughed.

'Well, yes. You know Mrs. Seaton was displeased to find us sitting up the other night when she came home. It is nearly ten.'

'Oh, she won't be home to-night till the small hours have struck. Miss Atherton will take care of that. There is no fear of her finding us up to-night.'

There was an expression of surprise on Christie's countenance.

'Oh, I know very well what you mean. That makes no difference, you would say. Well, I suppose we must do what she would wish, the same as if she were here, though I don't feel the least sleepy. Good-night.'

CHAPTER XVIII.

THE CURE FOR A BAD TEMPER.

THE first days of winter passed away rapidly. Gertrude continued to watch Christie's daily life, and to draw her own conclusions from what she saw. Humble, patient, and self-denying she always saw her, and almost always she was peaceful and happy. Not quite always; for Christie was not very strong, and had her home-sick days, and was now and then despondent. But she was rarely irritable at these times. She was only very quiet, speaking seldom, even to little Claude, till the cloud passed away. And when it passed it left the sunshine brighter, the peace of her trusting heart greater than before.

It is not to be supposed that Gertrude watched all this with no thought beyond the little nurserymaid. When she had settled in her own mind that it was her religion which made Christie so different from most of the people with whom she had come in contact, she did not fail to bring into comparison with her life the lives and professions of many who wished to be considered Christians. This was not the wisest course she could have taken, but happily she went farther than

this. Comparing her own life and conduct with that
of Claude's nurse, she did not fail to see how far it fell
short.

There was nothing very difficult in Christie's daily
duties. She had no opportunities for doing great
things, or for bearing great trials. But seeing her
always as she saw her, Gertrude came to feel that the
earnestness, the patience, the self-forgetfulness, with
which all her little duties were done, and all her
little disappointments borne, would have made any life
beautiful. And seeing and feeling all this, there
gradually grew out of her admiration a desire to
imitate what seemed so beautiful in the little maid;
and many a time when she was disappointed or angry
did the remembrance of her humble friend help her
to self-restraint. With a vague idea that Christie's
power came from a source beyond herself, she groped
blindly and only half consciously for the same help.
She studied in secret the Bible that seemed to be so
precious to her, and she prayed earnestly—or she
believed she prayed—to be made wise and strong and
self-denying, and in short, did what might be done to
build up a righteousness for herself.

Of course she failed, and then came discouragement
and despondency; and while this mood lasted, all the
days in the upper nursery were not happy ones. For
Gertrude, vexed with herself and her failure, grew
impatient and exacting with all the world; and as all
the world was not at the young lady's command, a great
deal of her discomfort was visited on Christie.

As for Christie, she was very patient and forbearing
with her, waiting till her unkind moods were over, not

answering her at all, or waiting and watching for an opportunity to win her from an indulgence of her spleen. Sometimes she succeeded, sometimes her gentleness served to irritate the wayward girl to sharper words or greater coldness. But save by silence, or a look of grieved surprise, her unkindness was never resented.

A half perception of how it was with the young lady helped her greatly to endure her petulance. She longed to help her, but she did not know how to do so by words. So she prayed for her and had patience with her, saying to herself, if Miss Gertrude was in earnest to do right, God would guide her to Himself in time.

'Do you know you speak to me just as you speak to Claude when he is fretful and naughty,' said Gertrude one day, when she had been more than usually irritable and unhappy.

'Do I?' said Christie, looking up, gravely; but she smiled brightly enough when she saw by Gertrude's face that the cloud was passing away for this time.

'Yes. If you would pat me gently, and smooth my hair, and offer to tell me a story, the illusion would be complete. Why don't you tell me to take myself and my books down-stairs? I am sure you must be sick of the sight of me.'

Christie laughed, and shook her head.

'Come, now, confess that you were just saying to yourself, How cross and unreasonable she has been all day!'

'No; I was wondering what could be vexing you, and wishing I could help you in some way.'

There is nothing vexing me that you can help.   It is just my nature to be cross and disagreeable.   I don't suppose there's any help for that.'

Christie laughed quite merrily now.

'It's a wonder I never found out that was your nature before.'

'Oh, well, you are finding it out now.   I only found it out lately myself.   I never in all my life tried so hard to be good and patient and self-denying, and I was never so bad in all my life.   There are times when I quite hate myself; and I am sure I shouldn't wonder if you were to hate me too.'

She had been gazing moodily into the fire, but she turned as she said this, and met the wistful, almost tearful, eyes of Christie fixed upon her.

'I wish you could tell me something to do,' she added.   'You know so much more about these things than I do.'

Christie shook her head with a sigh.

'Oh, no; I know very little; and even what I know I can't speak about as other people can.   You must have patience with yourself,'—'and pray,' she would have added; but Miss Gertrude cut her short.

'Oh, yes! it is easily said, "have patience."   I would give a great deal to be naturally as gentle and patient and even-tempered as you are.'

'As I am!' said Christie, laughing; but she looked grave in a moment.   'That shows how little you know of me, if indeed you are not mocking me in saying that.'

'No; you know very well I am not mocking you now, though I was a little while ago.   I don't think I

have seen you angry since you came here—really angry,
I mean.'

'Well, no, perhaps not angry. Do you really think
I am gentle and even-tempered?' she asked, suddenly,
turning her face towards her. 'I am sure I used not
to be. But then I have so little to try me now.'

'Well, I think you have had enough just for to-day,
what with the boys and with me. But if you were not
always patient and good, what changed you? What
did you do to yourself? Tell me about it, as Claude
would say.'

.'Oh, I don't know what I could tell,' said Christie,
in some embarrassment. 'I only mind what a peevish,
good-for-nothing little creature I was. The others
could have had little pleasure with me, only they were
strong and good-tempered and didn't mind. Even to
Effie I must have been a vexation; but mother gave
me to her care when she died, and so she had patience
with me. I was never well, and my mother spoiled
me, they said. I'm sure it was a sad enough world to
me when she died. And then my aunt came to live
with us, and she was so different. And by and by we
came to Canada, and then everything was changed.
I mind, sometimes, if a body only looked at me I was
in a pet. I was not well, for one thing, and I used to
fancy that my aunt liked me less and had less patience
with me than with the rest; and no wonder, when I
think of it. Effie was good and kind to me always,
though I must have tried her many a time.'

'Well,' said Miss Gertrude, 'but you don't tell me
what changed you.'

'Well, I can't tell. I believe I was never quite so

bad after the time Effie gave me my Bible.' And she gave Miss Gertrude the history of the miserable day with which our story commenced—of her trying to pray under the birch-tree by the brook, of Effie's coming home with the book-man, and of their walk to the kirk and the long talk they had together.

'And it was soon after that that my father was hurt and my aunt grew ill again. We had a very sorrowful winter. But there is one good thing in having real trouble to bear; one doesn't fret so much about little things, or about nothing at all, as I used to do. I think that winter was really happier to me than any time I had had since my mother's death. I was with my father a great deal towards the end; and though he was so ill and suffered so much, he was very kind and patient with me.'

There was a long pause before Christie could go on again, and she rather hurried over the rest of her tale.

'After he died we left the farm. I came here with Annie. I was very home-sick at first. Nothing but that I couldn't bear to go home and depend on Aunt Elsie kept me here. I thought sometimes I must die of that heart-sickness, and besides, I made myself unhappy with wrong thoughts. In the spring Annie went away. I couldn't go, because Mrs. Lee and the children were ill; you mind I told you about that. I was unhappy at first; but afterwards I was not, and I never was again—in the same way, I mean.'

The work she had been busy upon dropped from her hands, and over her face stole the look of peace and sweet content that Gertrude had so often wondered at. For a little while she sat quite still, forgetting, it seemed, that she was not alone; and then Gertrude said, softly.

'Well, and what then?'

Christie drew a long breath as she took up her work.

'Well, after that, something happened. I'm afraid I can't tell it so that you will understand. It seems very little just to speak about, but it made a great difference to me. I went to the kirk one day when a stranger preached. I can't just mind the words he said, at least I can't repeat them. And even if I could I dare say they would seem just common words to you. I had heard them all before, many a time, but that day my heart was opened to understand them, I think. The way that God saves sinners seemed so plain and wise and sure, that I wondered I had never seen it so before. I seemed to see it in a new way, and that it is all His work from beginning to end. He pardons and justifies and sanctifies, and keeps us through all; and it seemed so natural and easy to trust myself in His hands. I have never been very unhappy since that day, and I don't believe I shall ever be very unhappy again.'

There was a long silence. Miss Gertrude was repeating to herself, over and over again:

'His work, from beginning to end! He pardons, justifies, sanctifies, and saves at last.'

So many new and strange thoughts crowded into the young girl's mind that for the moment she forgot Christie and her interest in all she had been saying. Word by word she repeated to herself, 'pardons,' 'justifies,' 'sanctifies,' 'saves.'

'I cannot understand it.' And in a little while,

bewildered with her own speculations, she turned from the subject with a sigh.

'Well, and what else?' she said to Christie.

'Oh, there is no more. What were we speaking about? Oh, yes; about having patience. Well, when one has a great good to fall back upon, something that cannot be changed or lost or taken from us, why, it is easy to have patience with common little things that cannot last long and that often change to good. Yes, I do think I am more patient than I used to be. Things don't seem the same.'

It filled Gertrude with a strange unhappiness to hear Christie talk in this way. The secret of the little maid's content appeared so infinitely desirable, yet so unattainable by her. She seemed at once to be set so far away from her—to be shut out from the light and pleasant place where Christie might always dwell.

'I don't understand it,' she repeated to herself. 'If it were anything that could be reasoned out or striven for, or even if we could get it by patient waiting. But we can do nothing. We are quite helpless, it seems.'

In her vexed moments Gertrude sometimes took pleasure in starting objections and asking questions which Christie found it difficult to answer.

'It is all real to her, though. One would think, to see her sitting there, that there is nothing in the world that has the power to trouble her long. And there really is nothing, if she is a child of God—as she says. What a strange thing it is!'

She sat watching the little absorbed face, thinking over her own vexed thoughts, till the old restless feeling would let her sit no longer. Rising, she went to the window and looked out.

'What a gloomy day it is!' she said. 'How low the clouds are, and how dim and gray the light is! And listen to the wind moaning and sighing among the trees! It is very dreary. Don't you think so, Christie?'

Christie looked up. 'Yes, now that you speak of it, it does seem dreary; at least, it seems dreary outside. And I dare say it seems dreary in the house to you. Have they all gone out?'

'Yes; and there is to be no six o'clock dinner. They are to dine in town and go to some lecture or other. I almost wish I had gone.'

'I promised Claude that if he was very good he should go down to the drawing-room, and you would sing to us,' said Christie. 'We must air the nursery, you know.'

'I have been very good, haven't I, Tudie?' said the little boy, looking up from the pictures with which he had been amusing himself.

'Very good and sweet, my darling,' said Gertrude, kneeling down by the low chair on which her little brother sat. She put her arms around him, and drawing his head down on her breast, kissed him many times, her heart filling full of tenderness for the fragile little creature. The child laughed softly, as he returned her caresses, stroking her cheeks and her hair with his little thin hand.

'You won't be cross any more, Tudie?' he said.

'I don't know, dear. I don't mean to be cross, but I dare say I shall be, for all that.'

'And will you sing to Christie and me?'

'Oh, yes; that I will—to your heart's content.'

She had taken him in her arms, and was sitting with

him on her lap, by this time; and they were silent, while
Christie moved about the room, putting things away
before they should go down-stairs.

'Christie,' said Gertrude, 'do you know I think
Claude must be changed as you say you are? He is so
different from what he used to be!'

Christie stood quite still, with the garment she had
been folding in her hands.

'He is much better,' she said. 'He does not suffer
as he used to do.'

'No. Well, perhaps that is it. Do you think he is
too young to be changed? But if the change is wrought
by God, as you say it is, how can he be too young?'

Christie came and knelt beside them.

'I don't know. I suppose not. You know it is said,
' Suffer the little children to come unto Me."'

The little boy looked from one to the other as they
spoke.

'It was Jesus who said that Jesus, who opened the
eyes of the blind man. And He loved us and died for
us. I love Him dearly, Tudie.'

The girls looked at each other for a moment. Then
Christie kissed his little white hands, and Gertrude
kissed his lips and his shining hair, but neither of them
spoke a word.

'Now, Tudie, come and sing to Christie and me,' said
the child, slipping from her lap, and taking her hand.

'Yes; I will sing till you are weary.' And as she
led him down stairs and through the hall, her voice rose
clear as a bird's, and her painful thoughts were banished
for that time.

But they came back again more frequently and pressed

more heavily as the winter passed away. She put a restraint on herself, as far as Christie and her little brothers were concerned. When she felt unhappy or irritable, she stayed away from the upper nursery. She would not trouble Christie any more with her naughtiness, she said to herself; so at such times she would shut herself in her room, or go out with her mother or Miss Atherton to drive or pay visits, so as to chase her vexing thoughts away. But they always came back again. She grew silent and grave, caring little for her studies or her music, or for any of the thousand employments that usually fill up the time of young people.

Even Clement was permitted to escape from the discipline of lessons to which he had been for some time condemned during at least one of Miss Gertrude's morning hours. She no longer manifested the pride in his progress and in his discipline and obedience which had for some time been a source of amusement and interest to the elder members of the family. Master Clement was left to lord it over Martha in the lower nursery as he had not been permitted to do since his mother's visit to the sea-side.

'What ails you, Gertrude?' said Mrs. Seaton, one Sabbath afternoon. 'Are you not well? What are you thinking about? I declare, you look as if you had not a friend in the world!'

Gertrude was sitting with her chin leaning on her hand and her eyes fixed on the gray clouds that seemed to press close down on the tops of the snow-laden trees above the lawn. It was already growing dark, and the dreariness of the scene without was reflected on the girl's face. She started at the sound of her mother's voice.

'I am quite well,' she said, coming towards the fire,

slightly shivering, 'but somehow I feel stupid ; I suppose just because it is Sunday.

'That is not a very good reason, I should think,' said Mrs. Seaton, gravely. 'What were you thinking about?'

'I don't know; I have forgotten. I was thinking about a great many things. For one thing, I was thinking how long the winter is here.'

'Why, it is hardly time to think about that yet,' said Miss Atherton, coming forward from the sofa where she had been sitting; 'the winter is hardly begun yet. For my part, I like winter. But,' she added, pretending to whisper very secretly to Miss Gertrude, 'I don't mind telling *you* that I get a little stupid on Sunday myself.'

'Frances, pray don't talk nonsense to the child,' said Mrs. Seaton.

'It is not half so much of a sin to talk nonsense as it is to look glum, as Gertrude does. What ails you, child?

Gertrude made no answer.

'Are you unwell, Gertrude?' asked Mrs. Seaton.

'No, mother; I am perfectly well. What an idea!' she said, pettishly.

'She looks exactly like her Aunt Barbara,' said Miss Atherton. 'I declare, I shouldn't be surprised if she were to turn round and propose that I should read that extraordinary book I saw in her hand this morning! She looks capable of doing anything in the solemn line at this moment.'

Gertrude laughed, but made no answer.

'You do not take exercise enough,' said Mrs. Seaton. 'You have not been like yourself for a week.'

'I dare say that is it, mamma.'

'Of course she is not like herself!' said Miss Atherton.

'She is exactly like her Aunt Barbara. Gertrude, my dear, you're not thinking of growing good, are you?'

'Don't you think it might be of some advantage to the world if I were to improve a little?' asked Gertrude, laughing, but not pleasantly.

'Well, I don't know. I am afraid it would put us all out sadly. Only fancy her "having a mission," and trying to reform me!'

'Pray, Frances, don't talk that way,' said Mrs. Seaton; but she could not help laughing at the look of consternation the young lady assumed.

'Ah, I know what is the matter with her!' exclaimed Miss Atherton, just as the gentlemen came in. 'It is your fault, Mr. Sherwood. You are making her as wise as you are yourself, and glum besides. It is quite time she were done with all those musty books. I think for the future we will consider her education finished.'

'What is the matter, young ladies? You are not quarrelling, I hope?' said Mr. Seaton, seating himself beside them.

'Oh, no! It is with Mr. Sherwood I am going to quarrel. He and his big books are giving Gertrude the blues. It must be stopped.'

'I am sorry Miss Gertrude is in such a melancholy state,' said Mr. Sherwood, laughing; 'but I am quite sure that neither I nor my big books have had anything to do with it. I have not had an opportunity to trouble her for a week, and I doubt whether she has troubled herself with any books of my selection for a longer time than that.'

'Oh, well, you need not tell tales out of school,' said Miss Atherton, hastily, noticing the look of vexation that passed over Gertrude's face. 'I am going to take the refractory young lady in hand. I think I can teach her.'

I don't doubt it,' said Mr. Sherwood, with a smile and a shrug; 'but if I were to be permitted to name a successor in my labours, it certainly would not be you.'

'Hear him!' exclaimed Miss Atherton, with indignation which was only partly feigned. 'As if I were not to be entrusted with the instruction of a chit like you! Gertrude, can't you think of something terribly severe to say to him? Tell him you are to have nothing more to do with him.'

Gertrude shook her head and laughed.

'I am very well content with my teacher,' she said.

'And as a general thing, I have been very well content with my pupil,' said Mr. Sherwood, looking grave. 'I should like nothing better than to teach her still.'

'Charles, is it decided? Are you going away?' asked Mrs. Seaton.

'Yes, I am going; and the sooner the better, I suppose.'

'If one could really be sure that it is best for you to go,' said Mrs. Seaton, with a sigh. 'But it is sad that you should go alone, perhaps to be ill among strangers.'

'By no means. I have no thought of being ill,' said Mr. Sherwood, cheerfully. 'My going is not altogether, nor chiefly, on account of my health. This is the best season for my long-talked-of Southern trip, and I dare say the milder climate will suit me better than the bitter Canadian winds.'

There was a great deal more said about his going

which need not be repeated. Gertrude listened to all, sadly enough.

'I know how it will end,' she said to herself; 'I shall have to go to school after all.'

She thought at first this was her only cause of regret. But it was not. Mr. Sherwood and she had become much better friends within the last few months than they used to be. As a general thing, the lessons had been a source of pleasure to both, and of great profit to Gertrude. In his capacity of teacher, Mr. Sherwood never teased and bantered her as he had been apt to do at other times. Indeed, he had almost given up that now ; and Gertrude thought it much more pleasant to be talked to rationally, or even to be overlooked altogether, than to be trifled with. Besides, though he put a cheerful face on the matter of leaving, he was ill, and sometimes despondent; and it seemed to her very sad indeed that he should go away among strangers alone.

'Will you answer my letters if I write to you ? Or will you care to hear from me ?' asked Mr. Sherwood, as he bade her good-bye.

'Oh, yes, indeed ! I should care very much. But I am afraid you would think my letters very uninteresting—such letters as I write to the girls at home. You would not care for them ?'

'I shall care very much for them. Promise me that you will tell me everything—about your reading, and your visits, and about your little brothers, and their nurse even. I think I shall wish to hear about everything here, when I am so far away.'

Gertrude promised, but not very eagerly. An impulse

seized her to ask him to forgive all her petulant speeches and waywardness, but when she tried to do it she could not find her voice. Perhaps he read her thought in her tearful eyes and changeful face, and grew a little remorseful as he remembered how often he had vexed her during the first months of their acquaintance. At any rate, he smiled very kindly as he stooped to kiss her, and said, earnestly:

'We shall always be good friends now, whatever happens. God bless you, my child! and good-bye.'

CHAPTER XIX.

MORE CHANGES.

But I must not linger with Miss Gertrude and her troubles. It is the story of Christie that I have to tell. They went the same way for a little while, but their paths were now to separate.

For that came to pass which Gertrude had dreaded when Mr. Sherwood went away. It was decided that she should go to school. She was too young to go into society. Her step-mother, encouraged by Miss Atherton, might have consented to her sharing all the gaieties of a rather gay season, and even her father might have yielded against his better judgment, had she herself been desirous of it. But she was not. She was more quiet and grave than ever, and spent more time over her books than was at all reasonable, as Miss Atherton thought, now that no lessons were expected from her.

She grew thin and pale, too, and was often moody, and sometimes irritable. She moped about the house, and grew stupid for want of something to do, as her father thought; and so, though it pained him to part

with her, and especially to send her away against her
will, he suffered himself to be persuaded that nothing
better could happen to her in her present state of mind
than to have earnest occupation under the direction of
a friend of the family, who took charge of the education
of a few young ladies in a pleasant village not far from
their home.

It grieved her much to go. She had come to love
her little brothers better than she knew till the time
for parting drew near. This, and the dread of going
among strangers, made her unhappy enough during the
last few days of her stay.

'I can't think how the house will seem without you,'
said Christie to her, one night, as they were sitting
together beside the nursery fire.

Gertrude turned so as to see her as she sat at work,
but did not answer her for a minute or two.

'Do you know, I was just thinking whether my
going away would make the least bit of difference in
the world to you?' she said, at last.

There was no reply to be made to this, for Christie
thought neither the words nor the manner quite kind,
after all the pleasant hours they had passed together.
She never could have guessed the thoughts that were
in Gertrude's mind in the silence that followed. She
was saying to herself, almost with tears, how gladly she
would change places with Christie, who was sitting
there as quietly as if no change of time or place could
make her unhappy. For her discontent with herself
had by no means passed away. It had rather deepened
as her study of the Bible became more earnest, and the
strong, pure, unselfish life of which she had now and

then caught glimpses seemed more than ever beyond her power to attain. When she tried most, it seemed to her that she failed most; and the disgust which she felt on account of her daily failures had been gradually deepening into a sense of sinfulness that would not be banished. She strove to banish it. She was indignant with herself because of her unhappiness, but she struggled vainly to cast it off. And when to this was added the sad prospect of leaving home, it was more than she could bear.

She had come up-stairs that night with a vague desire to speak to Christie about her troubles, and she had been trying to find suitable words, when Christie spoke. Her ungracious reply did not make a beginning any easier. It was a long time before either of them said another word, and it was Christie who spoke first.

'Maybe, after all, you will like school better than you expect,' she said. 'Things hardly ever turn out with us as we fear.'

'Well, perhaps so. I must just take things as they come, I suppose.'

The vexation had not all gone yet, Christie thought, by her tone; so she said no more. In a little while she was quite startled by Miss Gertrude's voice, it was so changed, as she said:

'All day long this has been running in my mind: "Whosoever drinketh of the water that I shall give him shall never thirst." What does it mean?'

'Jesus said it to the woman at the well,' said Christie. And she added: '"But the water that I shall give him shall be in him as a well of water springing up to everlasting life."'

'What does it mean, do you think—"shall never thirst"?'

Christie hesitated. Of late their talks had not always been pleasant. Gertrude's vexed spirit was not easy to deal with, and her questions and objections were not always easily answered.

'I don't know; but I think the "living water" spoken about in the other verses means all the blessings that Christ has promised to His people.'

She paused.

'His people—always His people!' said Miss Gertrude to herself.

'God's Spirit is often spoken of under the figure of water,' continued Christie. '"I will pour water on him that is thirsty!" and in another place Jesus Himself says, "If any man thirst, let him come unto Me and drink." Such an expression must have been very plain and appropriate to the people of that warm country, where water was necessary and not always easily got.'

Christie had heard all this said; and she repeated it, not because it answered Miss Gertrude's question, but because she did not know what else to say. And all the time she was trying to get a glimpse of the face which the young lady shaded with her hand. She wanted very much to say something to do her good, especially now that they were about to part. The feeling was strong in Christie's heart, at the moment, that though Miss Gertrude might return again, their intercourse could never be renewed—at least not on the same footing; and though it hurt her much to know it, her own pain was quite lost in the earnest

desire she felt in some way or other to do Miss
Gertrude good.   So, after a pause, she said, again—

'I suppose " to thirst " means to earnestly desire.
"Blessed are they who hunger and thirst after righteousness," you remember.   And David says, "As the
hart panteth after the water-brook, so panteth my soul
after Thee, O God !"   And in another place, " My soul
thirsteth for Thee." '

Gertrude neither moved nor spoke, and Christie went
on—

'And when it is said of them, " They shall never
thirst," I suppose it means they shall be satisfied out of
God's fulness.   Having His best gift, all the rest seems
of little account.   "Blessed is the man whom Thou
choosest, and causest to approach near unto Thee, that
he may dwell in Thy courts : he shall be satisfied with
the goodness of Thy house, and of Thy holy temple."
And in another place, "My soul shall be satisfied as
with marrow and fatness, and my mouth shall praise
Thee with joyful lips." '   And then, as she was rather
apt to do when deeply in earnest, breaking into the old
familiar Scottish version, she added—

'"They with the fatness of Thy house
    Shall be well satisfied ;
From rivers of Thy pleasures Thou
    Wilt drink to them provide.
Because of life the fountain pure
    Remains alone with Thee ;
And in that purest light of Thine
    We clearly light shall see." '

She stopped, partly because she thought she had said
enough, and partly because it would not have been easy

just then to have said more. Her face drooped over her
work, and there was silence again.

'Well,' said Miss Gertrude, with a long breath, 'it
must be a wonderful thing to be *satisfied*, as you
call it.'

'Yes,' said Christie, softly; 'and the most wonderful
thing of all is that all may enjoy this blessedness, and
freely, too.'

'I have heard you say that before,' said Miss
Gertrude; 'but it is all a mystery to me. You say all
who will may have this blessedness; but the Bible says
it is the man whom God chooses that is blessed.'

'Well,' said Christie, gravely, 'what would you have?
"By grace are ye saved through faith, and that not of
yourselves: it is the gift of God." "The gift of God is
eternal life through Jesus Christ our Lord." There is
nothing in all the Bible clearer than that. And surely
eternal life is a gift worthy of God to give.'

'But He does not give it to all,' said Miss Gertrude.

'To all who desire it—to all who seek for it in Jesus'
name,' said Christie, earnestly.

'But in another place it says, "No man can come
unto Me, except the Father, who hath sent Me, draw
him." '

Gertrude did not speak to-night, as she had sometimes done of late, in the flippant way which thoughtless young people often assume when they talk on such
subjects. Her voice and manner betrayed to Christie
that she was very much in earnest, and she hesitated
to answer her; not, as at other times, because she
thought silence was the best reply, but because she
longed so earnestly to say just what was right.

'This change which is so wonderful must be God's work from beginning to end, you once said,' continued Gertrude. 'And since we have no part in the work, I suppose we must sit and wait till the change comes, with what patience we may.'

'It is God's work from beginning to end,' repeated Christie, thoughtfully. 'We cannot work this change in ourselves. We cannot save ourselves, in whole or in part. Nothing can be clearer than that.'

'Well?' said Gertrude, as she paused.

'Why, it would be strange indeed if so great a work was left to creatures so weak and foolish as we are. None but God could do it. And if a child is hungry or thirsty or defiled, what needs he to know more than that there is enough and to spare for all his wants in the hands of a loving Father? There would be no hope for us if this great change were to be left to us to work. But the work being God's, all may hope. I suppose I know what you mean,' she added. 'I have heard my father, and Peter O'Neil, and others, speak about these things. Peter used to say, "If God means to save me He will save me; and I need give myself no trouble about it." That is true in one sense, but not in the sense that Peter meant. I wish I could mind what my father used to say to him, but I cannot. Somehow, I never looked at it in that way. It seemed to me such a wonderful and blessed thing that God should have provided a way in which we could be saved, and then that He should save us freely, that it never came into my mind to vex myself with thoughts like these. I was young, only a child, but I had a great many troubled unhappy thoughts about myself;

and to be able to put them all aside—to leave them all behind, as it were, and just trust in Jesus, and let Him do all for me—oh, I cannot tell you the blessed rest and peace it was to me! But I did not mean to speak about myself.'

'But I want you to tell me,' said Gertrude, softly.

'I cannot tell you much,' said Christie, gravely. 'I am not wise about such things. I know there are some who make this a stone to stumble over—that we can do nothing, and we must just wait. But don't you remember how it is said, "Seek ye the Lord while He may be found; call ye upon Him when He is near." "They that seek Me early shall find Me." And in the New Testament, "Ask, and ye shall receive; seek, and ye shall find." And Jesus Himself said, "If any man thirst, let him come unto Me and drink." And in another place it is said, "The Spirit and the bride say, Come. And let him that heareth say, Come. And let him that is athirst come. And whosoever will, let him take the water of life freely."

'Surely all this means something. God would never bid us come unless He was willing to receive us. Having given His Son to die for us, how can we doubt His willingness to receive us? Surely no one who is weary and heavy laden need stay away, when He bids them come. He says, "I will heal your backslidings; I will receive you graciously; I will love you freely. A new heart will I give to you, and a right spirit will I put within you." Ah, that is the best of all!'

There was a pause again, and then Christie added—

'I can't say all I wish to say. Though I see all this clearly myself, I haven't the way of making it clear to others. But there is one thing sure. It is just those who feel themselves to be helpless that have reason to hope. "For while we were yet without strength, in due time Christ died for the ungodly." Why need any one hesitate after that?'

Little more was said; but if ever Christie prayed earnestly she prayed for Gertrude at that hour. And afterwards, when they met again, in circumstances well calculated to dispel all foolish shyness in speaking about such things, Gertrude told her that she too was praying as she had never prayed before. And the happy tears that stood in their eyes as they spoke afforded good evidence that these petitions, though silent, had not ascended in vain.

The days that followed the departure of Gertrude were uneventful ones. Only one thing happened before spring came to break the quiet routine of Christie's life. The little boy Claude loved her better every day, but no better than she loved him. And as time passed on, and his health, notwithstanding the frequent recurrence of bad days and sudden turns of illness, continued steadily to improve, the influence for good which his little nurse and her simple teachings had over him became more apparent to all the household.

She was treated by Mrs. Seaton with a consideration which she had not been in the habit of showing her servants. Hitherto the daily drives of the little invalid had been shared by his mother or Gertrude, while Christie was expected during their absence to perform such duties in the nursery as could not well be attended to while the children were with her. But after Gertrude went away it was usually so arranged that Christie should go with him. She was growing tall, but she was very slender; and though she never complained of illness, it was easy to be seen that she had not much strength to fall back upon. Grateful for her loving care of her helpless little boy, Mrs. Seaton spared her all possible labour, while she trusted her implicitly in all that concerned both children.

'If she were only a little stronger, I should consider myself very fortunate in having a nurse in every way so suitable for my little boy,' said Mrs. Seaton many a time. And many a time, as the spring approached, Christie said to herself:

'If I were only a little stronger!'

The one event that broke the monotony of her life after Miss Gertrude went away was a visit from her sister Effie. The visit was quite unlooked for. Christie returned from a walk with Claude one day, to find her sister awaiting her in the upper nursery. To say that the surprise was a joyful one would be saying little, yet after the first tearful embrace, the joy of both sisters was manifested very quietly. The visit was to be a very brief one. Two days at most were all that Effie could spare from home and school. But a great deal may be said and enjoyed in two days.

'How tall you have grown, Christie!' was Effie's first exclamation, when she had let her sister go. 'But you are not very strong yet, I am afraid; you are very slender, and you have no colour, child.'

'I am very well, Effie. You know I was always a "white-faced thing," as Aunt Elsie used to say. But you—— John was right. You are bonnier than ever.'

Effie laughed a little, but she looked grave enough in a minute.

'Are you lame still, Christie? I thought you were better of that.'

'Oh, it is nothing, Effie. It is not the old lameness that used to trouble me. I fell on the stairs the other day, and hurt my knee a little, that is all. It is almost well now.'

I could never tell of all the happy talk that passed between the sisters during those two days, and if I could it would not interest my readers as it interested them. Indeed, I dare say some of it would seem foolish enough to them. But it was all very pleasant to Christie. Every incident in their home life, everything that had taken place in their neighbourhood since her departure, was fraught with interest to her. She listened with delight to the detailed account of circumstances at which Effie in her letters had only been able to hint; she asked questions innumerable, and praised or blamed with an eagerness that could not have been more intense had all these things been taking place under her eyes.

The sunny side of their home life was presented to Christie, you may be sure. The straits to which they had sometimes been reduced were passed lightly over, while the signs of brighter days, which seemed to be dawning upon them, were made the most of by Effie's hopeful spirit. The kindness of one friend, and the considerateness of another in the time of trouble, were dwelt on more earnestly than the straits that had proved them. 'God had been very good to them,' Effie said many times; and Christie echoed it with thankfulness. Nor is it to be supposed that Effie listened with less interest to all that Christie had to tell, or that she found less cause for gratitude.

At first she had much to say about Miss Gertrude and the little boys, and of her pleasant life since she had been with them. But by little and little Effie led her to speak of her first months in the city, and of her trials and pleasures with the little Lees. She did not need much questioning when she was fairly started. She told of her home-sickness at first, her longings for them all, her struggles with herself, and her vexing thoughts about being dependent upon Aunt Elsie. Of the last she spoke humbly, penitently, as though she expected her sister to chide her for her waywardness.

But Effie had no thought of chiding her. As she went on to tell of Mrs. Lee's illness and of her many cares with the children, she quite unconsciously revealed to her interested listener the history of her own energy and patience of all that she had done and borne during these long months.

Of Mrs. Lee's kindness she could not speak without tears. Even the story of little Harry's death did not take Christie's voice away as did the remembrance of her parting with his mother.

'I am sure she was very sorry to part with me,' she said. 'Oh, she had many cares; and sorrows too, I am afraid. And you may think how little she had to comfort her when she said to me that I had been her greatest comfort all the winter. She was very good and kind to me. I loved her dearly. Oh, how I wish I could see her again!'

'You *will* see her again, I do not doubt,' said

Effie, in a low voice. Christie gave her a quick look.

'Yes, I hope so—I believe so.'

After a little while, Effie said:

'If I had known how unhappy you were at first, I think I would have called you home. But I am not sorry that you stayed, now.'

'No; oh, no. I am very glad I came. I think after Annie went away I was worse than I was at first for a little while; but I was very glad afterwards that I did not go with her, very glad.'

'Yes,' said Effie, softly. 'You mind you told me something about it in a letter.'

So, shyly enough at first, but growing earnest as she went on, Christie told her about that rainy Sabbath morning when she went to the kirk, where Jesus, through the voice of a stranger, had spoken peace to her soul.

'I couldna see him with my blind eyes from where I sat. I shouldna ken him if I were to see him now. But what a difference he made to me! Yes, I know; it wasna he, it was God's Holy Spirit; and yet I would like to see him. I wonder will I ken him when we meet in heaven?'

Effie could not find her voice for a moment, and soon Christie went on:

'After that everything was changed. It seemed like coming out of the mist to the top of the hill Do you mind at home how even I could get a glimpse of the sea and the far-away mountains, on a fair summer morning? Nothing was so bad after that, and nothing will ever be so bad any more. I don't think if even

the old times were to come back I should ever be such
a vexation to you again, Effie.'

'Would you like to go home with me, Christie?' said
Effie. Christie looked up eagerly.

'Yes; for some things very much, if you thought
best. I am to go in the summer, at any rate. Would
you like me to go now, Effie?'

'It is not what I would like that we must think
about. If I had had my way, you would never have
left home. Not that I am sorry for it now, far from
it; and though I would like to take you with me—
indeed, I came with no other thought—yet, as there is
as good a reason for your staying as there ever was for
your coming, and far better, now that you are contented,
dear, I am not sure that I should be doing right to take
you away before summer. They would miss you here,
Christie.'

'Yes,' said Christie, with a sigh, 'I dare say they
would. But I must go home when summer comes,
Effie. Why, it is more than a year and a half
since I have seen any of them but Annie and
you.'

'Yes,' said Effie, thoughtfully. She was saying to
herself that for many reasons it was better for Christie
to stay where she was, for a time at least. She had
kept the sunny side of their home life in Christie's
view since she had been there. But it had another
side. She saw very plainly that Christie was more
comfortably situated in many ways than she could
possibly be at home, to say nothing of the loss of the
help she could give them, and the increase of expense
which another would make in their straitened household.

Yet there was something in Christie's voice that made her heart ache at the sad necessity.

'I don't believe it will grieve you more to stay than it will grieve me to go home without you,' she said, at last. 'I have been trying to persuade myself ever since I came here that I had better take you home with me. But I am afraid I ought to deny myself the happiness.'

It was not easy to say this, as was plain enough from the tears that fell on Christie's head as it sank down on her sister's breast. Christie had rarely seen Effie cry. Even at the sad time of their father's death, Effie's tears had fallen silently and unseen, and she was strangely affected by the sight of them now.

'Effie,' she said, eagerly, 'I am quite content to stay. And I must tell you now—though I didna mean to do so at first, for fear something might happen to hinder it—Mrs. Seaton said one day, if Claude still grew better, she might perhaps send him with me for a change of air, and then I should be at home and still have my wages to help. Wouldna that be nice? And I think it is worth a great deal that Mrs. Seaton should think of trusting him with me so far away. But he is better, and I have learned what to do for him; and he is such a little child we need make no difference for him at home. Would you like it, Effie?'

Yes, Effie would have liked anything that could bring such a glow to her sister's face; and she entered into a discussion of ways and means with as much earnestness as Christie herself, and they soon grew quite excited over their plans. Indeed, all the rest of the visit was passed cheerfully. Mrs. Seaton, after seeing and talking with Effie, confirmed the plan about sending Claude with Christie in the summer, provided it would be agreeable to them all.

'He has become so attached to her, I hardly know how he could do without her now,' said Mrs. Seaton. 'And I suppose nothing would make Christie willing to forego her visit at home when summer comes.'

To tell the truth, Mrs. Seaton was greatly surprised and pleased with the sister of her little nurse. She knew, of course, that Christie had been what her country-people called 'well brought up,' and she had gathered from some of Gertrude's sayings that the family must have seen better days. But she was not prepared to find in the elder sister that Christie had mentioned, sometimes even in her presence, a person at all like Effie.

'She had quite the appearance of a gentlewoman,' said Mrs. Seaton. 'She was perfectly self-possessed, yet simple and modest. I assure you I was quite struck with her.'

The brief visit came to an end all too quickly. The hope of a pleasant meeting in summer made the parting comparatively easy, and helped Christie to feel quite contented when she found herself alone. She was in danger sometimes of falling into her old despondent feelings, but she knew her weakness and watched against it, and made the most of the few pleasures that fell to her lot.

'I won't begin and count the weeks yet,' she said to herself. 'That would make the time seem longer. I will just wait, and be cheerful and hopeful, as Effie bade me; and surely I have good cause to be cheerful. I only wish I were a little stronger.'

The winter seemed to take its leave slowly and unwillingly that year, but it went at last. First the brown sides of the mountains showed themselves, and then the fields grew bare, and here and there the water began to make channels for itself down the slopes to the low places. By and by the gravel walks and borders of the garden appeared; and as the days grew long, the sunshine came pleasantly in through the bare boughs of the trees to chequer the nursery floor.

The month of March seemed long; there were many bleak days in it. But it passed, as did the first weeks of April. The fields grew warm and green, and over the numberless budding things in the fields and garden Christie watched with intense delight. The air became mild and balmy, and then they could pass hour after hour in the garden, as they used to do when she first came.

But Christie did not grow strong, though often during the last part of the winter she had said to herself that all she needed to make her well again was the fresh air and the spring sunshine. Her old lameness came, or else she suffered from a new cause, more hopeless and harder to bear. The time came when a journey to or from the upper nursery was a wearisome matter to her. Wakeful nights and languid days became frequent. It was with great difficulty sometimes that she dragged herself through the duties of the weary day.

She did not complain of illness. She hoped every day that the worst was over, and that she would be as well as usual again. Mrs. Seaton lightened her duties in various ways. Martha, the nurse in the lower nursery, was very kind and considerate too, and did what she could to save her from exertion. But no one thought her ill; she did not think herself so. It was the pain in her knee, making her nights so sleepless and wearisome, that was taking her strength away, she thought; if she could only rest as she used to do, she would soon be well. So for a few days she struggled on.

But the time came when she felt that it would be vain to struggle longer. After a night of pain and sleeplessness she rose, resolved to tell Mrs. Seaton that she feared she must go home. She was weak and worn out, and she could not manage to say what she had to say without a flood of tears, which greatly surprised her mistress. She soothed her very kindly, however, and when she was quiet again, she said—

'Are you so ill, Christie ? Are you quite sure that you are not a little home-sick with it, too ? I do not wonder that you want to see that kind, good sister of yours, but if you will have patience for a week or two, I will send Claude with you.'

But Christie shook her head. 'I am not at all home sick,' she said. 'And I don't think I am very ill either ; but the pain in my knee is sometimes very bad. It grows worse when I walk about, and then I cannot sleep. I am afraid I must go home and rest awhile.'

'Is it so very bad ?' said Mrs. Seaton, gravely. 'Well, the doctor must see it. You shall go to him this very afternoon—or we may as well have him here. If he thinks there is anything serious the matter, something must be done for it, whether you go home or not.

Don't be anxious about it. I dare say you will be as well as ever in a day or two.'

But the doctor looked grave when he examined it, and asked some questions about it, and the fall on the stairs, which seemed to have brought on the trouble. To Christie he said nothing, but his grave looks did not pass away when she left the room.

'She must go home, then, I am afraid,' said Mrs. Seaton. 'I am very sorry to lose her. I don't know what Claude will do without her.'

The doctor looked grave.

'Where is her home? Far away in the country, is it not? It will never do to let her go away there. She must go to the hospital.'

'The hospital!' exclaimed Mrs. Seaton. 'Is it so very serious?'

'It may become very serious unless it is attended to. No time ought to be lost. Could she go to-day, or to-morrow morning?'

Mrs. Seaton looked very troubled.

'Must she go? She was brought up in the country. It seems necessary she should have fresh air. I am afraid her health would suffer from confinement. Could she not remain here? Of course, if she needs advice she must not think of going home. But could she not stay here?'

'It is very kind in you to think of such a thing, but I am afraid she will need more attention than she could possibly get at this distance from town. She will be very comfortable there. Indeed, it seems to me to be her only chance of a speedy recovery.'

'But it seems unkind to send her out of the house,

now that she is ill. I can't bear to do it,' said Mrs. Seaton.

'Not at all, my dear madam. It is done every day; and very well it is that there is a place where such people can be received when they are ill.'

'But Christie is very unlike a common servant. She is such a gentle, faithful little thing; the children are so fond of her too.'

'No one knows her good qualities better than I do, after what I saw of her last winter. But really it is the very best thing that could happen to her in the circumstances. Shall I tell her? Perhaps it would be as well.'

Christie was greatly startled when they told her she must go to the hospital. Her first thought was that she could not go—that she must get home to Effie and the rest before she should grow worse. But a few words from the doctor put an end to any such plan. A little care and attention now would make her quite well again; whereas if she were to go home out of the reach of surgical skill, she might have a long and tedious season of suffering—if, indeed, she ever fully recovered. She must never think of going home now. She must not even think of waiting till she heard from her sister. That could do no possible good, and every day's delay would only make matters worse.

He spoke very kindly to her.

'You must not let the idea of the hospital frighten you, as though one ought to be very ill indeed before they go there. It is a very comfortable place, I can tell you. I only wish I could get some of my other patients there. They would stand a far better chance of recovery than they can do with the self-indulgence and indifferent nursing that is permitted at home. You will be very well there; and if you have to look forward to some suffering, I am quite sure you have patience and courage to bear it well.'

Courage and patience! Poor little Christie! The words seemed to mock her as she went about the preparations for her departure. Her heart lay as heavy as lead in her bosom. She seemed like one stunned by a heavy blow. It destroyed the pain of parting with the little boys, however. She left them quietly, without a tear, even though poor little Claude clung to her, weeping and struggling to the very last. But her face was very pale, and her hands trembled as she unclasped his arms from her neck, and hurried away, saying to herself 'Shall I ever see his face any more?'

CHAPTER XX.

HER first night in the hospital was very dreary. No one can be surprised to hear that she shed some sorrowful tears. She was not taken into a public ward, the kindness of Mrs. Seaton procured for her a private room while she should be there. There were two beds in it, but the other was unoccupied, and after the first arrangements had been made for her comfort, she was left alone.

How solitary she felt as she sat listening to the street noises, and to the voices and footsteps that came from other parts of the house. The street was so narrow and so far beneath that she could see nothing that was passing in it. The weather-beaten roofs and glimpses of dusty tree-tops that formed the view reminded her of the sorrowful days she had passed in Mrs. Lee's attic nursery, and a feeling very like the old miserable homesickness of that time made her close her eyes and drop her face upon her hands.

Poor Christie! She had never prayed half so earnestly that she might be strong and well again as she now prayed that she might not be left to fall into

an impatient, murmuring spirit. She shrank from the
thought of a renewal of these heart-sick longings as she
had never shrunk from the thought of enduring bodily
pain. She prayed with all her heart that, whatever
suffering lay before her, God would give her strength
and patience to bear it—that she might be made willing
to abide His time, with no impatient longings as to
what the end might be.

God has many ways in which He comforts His children.
Leaning her tired head on the low window-sill, Christie
slept and dreamed, and in her dream, peace came to
her spirit. A strange, soft light spread around her, like
the gleam she had once seen fall on the sea in the early
morning. Only the sea seemed near now, and there
were strange, bright forms flitting over it, and on the
other side, far away yet near, her mother beckoned to
her. She knew it was her mother. Her smile was
the very same, and the loving look in her eyes. But,
oh, she had grown so beautiful! Gazing and stretching
her arms towards her, she seemed conscious of a sweet
and awful Presence, before which the shining sea and
the bright forms, and even her mother's glorified face,
vanished.

I have called thee by thy name. Thou art Mine.
I go to prepare a place for you.

Whether the words were spoken, or whether she read
them as in a book, or whether it was only a remembrance
of what she knew to be true, she could not tell, but it
brought peace ineffable.

She woke at the touch of the nurse, with a start and
a sigh of disappointment. But there was more than
patience in the smile with which she answered her kind
chiding; and the woman, looking in her face, kept

silent, feeling vaguely that words of encouragement, such as she spoke often, as mere words of course, to patients under her care, were not needed here.

So when Christie rose to a new day in this strange, sad place of suffering, it was with an earnest desire to be contented and hopeful during the few weeks she expected to spend in it. It was by no means so difficult a matter as she at first supposed. She was not confined to her room, but was permitted at stated times to go with the nurse into the public wards; and though the sights she saw there saddened her many a time, she was happy in having an opportunity of now and then doing a kindness to some poor sufferer among them. Sometimes it was to read a chapter in the Bible, or a page or two in some book left by a visitor; sometimes she had the courage to speak a word in season to the weary; once or twice she wrote a letter for some patient who could not write for herself. All this did her good; and the sight she had of the sufferings of others did much to make her patient in bearing her own.

Then, too, she could work; and Mrs. Seaton had kindly supplied her with some of the pretty materials for fancy work which Effie and Gertrude had taught her. In this way many an hour, which would otherwise have been very tedious, passed away pleasantly and even quickly. She had books too; and once, during the first month of her stay, Mrs. Seaton visited her, and several times proved her kind remembrance of her by sending her some little gift—as a bunch of flowers, a book, or some little delicacy to tempt her variable appetite. Martha came almost every Sabbath, and from her she heard of the little lads and sometimes of Miss Gertrude. So the first few weeks passed far more pleasantly and rapidly than she had thought possible.

When the doctor decided that she must not wait to hear from her sister before placing herself under surgical care in the hospital, Christie intended to write immediately to tell her of her changed prospects, but when she thought about it again she hesitated.

'It will only be for a little while,' she said. 'I will wait for a week or two at least A month, or even six weeks, will soon pass; and if I can write and tell them I am almost well again, it will not be half the vexation to Effie and the others to know that I am here. I will wait a little while at least.'

She waited a month and then wrote—not that she was nearly well again, but hopefully, more hopefully than she felt, for she could not bear that Effie and the rest at home should be made unhappy about her. So she did not tell them that she had been there a whole month, and that she was no better, but rather worse. She told them how kind everybody was to her, and how the doctor gave her good hopes of soon being as well as ever and able to get home again.

'Oh, how glad I shall be when that time comes!' wrote poor Christie. 'But you must not think, Effie, that I am fretful or discontented. There are many things to make it pleasant for me here that I cannot write to you about, and the doctors tell me that when I get over this I shall very likely be better and healthier than ever I was; and whatever happens, we are quite sure that this trouble was sent to us by One who cares for us. He has not forsaken me and never will, I am very sure of that.'

If Effie could have known of all the tears that fell

before that letter was fairly folded and sent away, she would hardly have taken all the comfort from it that Christie intended she should; for notwithstanding the doctor's frequent and kind assurances that her knee was doing well, and that she soon would be as well as ever again, her heart sometimes began to fail her. She did not think that she was in danger, she did not doubt but that she should see the green leaves and the wheat-fields at home. It never came into her mind that month after month, each growing longer and more painful, might pass before a change should come. And she never, even in the dreariest days, doubted that all would be well in the end.

But six weeks, two months passed, and she grew no better, but rather worse. The active measures thought necessary to check the progress of the disease in her limb caused her often great suffering. Her rest was uncertain, and broken by troubled dreams. It was only now and then that she was at all able to interest herself in the work that at first gave her so much pleasure. Even her books wearied her. She was quite confined to her room now, and, of course, left the greater part of the time alone. She was not often obliged to keep her bed all day, but being moved to her chair near the window, she could not leave it again but with the help of the nurse. Hour after hour she used to sit, leaning back wearily, listening to the distant sounds in the house or the street, watching the clouds or the rain-drops on the window if the day was overcast, or the motes dancing in the sunshine if it were fair.

Oh, how long these days seemed to her ! The leaves were not fully out when she came in, and now summer was nearly over. She used to think how the harvest-fields were growing yellow, and how busy all the people at home would be at work gathering in the grain. The roses had come and gone. The numberless blossoms of the locust-tree had nodded and breathed their fragrance in at the nursery window, and faded, and it was almost time for the few late blossoms whose coming had so surprised her last year.

Was it any wonder that many a time her pillow was wet with tears? She tried not to murmur. The nurse and the doctors, too, thought her very patient and quiet, and praised and encouraged her, telling her their hopes that her suffering would not last much longer. But still she grew weaker every day, far weaker than she knew, for she could not try her strength now by walking in the hall or climbing the broad stairs that led to the wards. Yes, she grew weaker. Her appetite quite failed, and except when the doctor gave her something to ease the pain and soothe her restlessness, she slept little at night, but dozed in her chair through the day, starting many a time from a dream of home, or of the days when she was so happy with Gertrude and little Claude, with a pang which was always new and hard to bear.

Thus awaking one day, she opened her eyes to see a grave, kind face bending over her. She did not recognize it immediately, but raised herself up to look again, as it was withdrawn. She knew the voice, though, which said so kindly:

' My poor child, I fear you have suffered much.'

With a flow of tears such as no one had seen her shed since she came, she grasped the kind hand that was held out to her. It was only for a moment, however.

'I beg your pardon, sir,' she said; 'I couldn't help it. I am so glad to see you.'

It was of no use to try to check her tears. They must flow for a minute or two.

'You remind me so much of Miss Gertrude and my little lads,' she said at last, with a smile, which was sadder to see than her tears, her much-moved visitor thought. 'I don't often cry, but I couldn't help it,' and her voice broke again.

'I have just seen them all,' said Mr. Sherwood. 'They are all at the sea-side, as you know. They are all well; at least little Claude is no worse than usual. Miss Gertrude made me promise to come to see you. She never knew, till she joined Mrs. Seaton at the sea-side, how it was with you. And see, she sent you this.'

'I thought she had forgotten me,' said Christie, faintly, as she took, with trembling fingers, a little note he held out to her. She did not read it, however, but lay quite still with her eyes closed, exhausted with her tears and her surprise.

'Mrs. Seaton thought you might have gone home by this time,' said Mr. Sherwood. 'I suppose she did not know you had been so ill. I hope I may tell Miss Gertrude, when I write, that you will soon be well again.'

'I don't know,' said Christie, slowly. 'I hope I am not any worse. I must have patience, I suppose.'

'I have no doubt you are very patient,' said Mr. Sherwood, hardly knowing what else to say.

'I try to be patient, but I am restless with the pain sometimes, and the time seems so long. It is not really very long. I came in May, and now it is August; but it seems a long time—longer than all my life before, it sometimes seems.'

Mr. Sherwood did not often find himself at a loss for something to say, but he sat silent now. There came into his mind what Christie had said to little Claude in the cedar-walk that day, about all things happening for good, and how Jesus, if He saw that it would be best for him, could make the little boy strong and well with a word, as He did the blind man. But it would have seemed to him like mockery to remind her of that now.

For in truth the first sight of the girl had startled him greatly. He had come to the hospital more than half believing that he should find that she had gone home to her friends well. She was greatly changed; he would not have known her if he had met her elsewhere. Her face was perfectly colourless, after the flush which her surprise at seeing him had excited, had passed away; her eyes seemed unnaturally large, and her brow far higher and broader than it used to be; and her hand, lying on the coverlid, seemed almost as white as the little note she held in it. What could he say to her? Not, surely, that she would soon be well again, for it seemed to him that she was past any hope of that.

'You have not read your letter,' he said.

'No; I shall have that afterwards; and it is so long since I saw any one that I ever saw before. Did Miss Gertrude like her school?'

'Yes; I think she liked it. She has grown, I think, and she is greatly improved in many ways.'

'She was always good to me,' said Christie, softly.

'Well, I don't know. She told me she was often very

cross and unreasonable with you,' said Mr. Sherwood, smiling.

'Well, sometimes, perhaps. But I loved her. I sometimes wonder if I shall ever see her again.'

'As soon as she comes home you may be sure of seeing her, and that will not be long now—unless, indeed, you are better, and should go home before she comes,' he forced himself to add.

Christie made no reply to that, but in a little while she asked about the children; and though Mr. Sherwood was surprised, he was not sorry that she did not speak any more about herself till he rose to go away.

'Must you go?' she asked, wistfully. 'When you hear from Miss Gertrude again, perhaps you will come and tell me about her?'

'That I will,' said Mr. Sherwood, heartily; 'and I would come before that if I could do you any good I am sure I wish I could.'

'Oh, you have done me good already. I shall have something to think about all day—and my letter, besides. I thank you very much.'

Just then her eyes fell on a flower in his button-hole. He took it out and offered it to her.

'Oh, I thank you! I didn't mean to ask for it. It will be company for me all day.'

'Are you quite alone from morning till night? Poor child! No wonder that the time seems long!'

'The nurse comes in as often as I need anything. But she thinks, they all think, it would be better if I were to go into one of the wards. I can work or read very little now, and the time would not seem so long with faces to see, even if they are sad faces.'

Mr. Sherwood still lingered.

'Do your friends know that you are here ? Do they know how ill you are ?' he asked.

'Oh, yes; they know I am in the hospital. I have been waiting till I should be a little better, to write again to Effie. I must write soon. She will be anxious about me, I'm afraid.'

Her face looked very grave in the silence that followed. Mr. Sherwood would fain have spoken some hopeful words, but somehow they did not come readily into his mind; and when the nurse at the moment came into the room, he withdrew.

But he did not forget the wan face of that suffering child. It followed him into the sunny street and into the quiet library. Alone and in company, all day long, he was haunted by the wistful eyes of that patient girl as no sorrowful sight had ever haunted him before.

Mr. Sherwood was not what could be called a benevolent man, a lover of his kind. He enjoyed doing a kind act when it came in his way—as who does not ? But that he should go out of his way to do kind things for people in whom he had no special interest, only that they were in trouble and needed help, he had not thought his duty. He had had troubles of his own to bear, but they had not been of a kind that other people could help much. At any rate, people had not helped him; he had not sought help. Possibly he would have resented the idea of any one's bearing his burdens for him, and no doubt he thought that in this sad, disappointing world, each one must bear his own. He had called at the hospital because Miss Gertrude had asked him to call, and hoping that he should find the little nurse already safe at home with her friends; but however this might be, he had no thought of anything but pleasing his little cousin in the matter.

Yet he had borne great and sore troubles in his life-time—sickness and sorrow and disappointment. He carried the marks of those troubles still, perhaps because he had never learned that the way to heal one's own sorrows is to do what may be done for the healing of the sorrows of others. Certainly no such thought had ever come into his mind, and he was quite surprised to find that the pale face and wistful eyes of Christie still followed him. He did not try to banish the thought of her as he sometimes tried to banish painful thoughts. He felt deeply for her. There were few days after that in which Christie did not have some token of his remembrance. Sometimes it was a bunch of flowers or a little fruit, sometimes a book or a message from Gertrude. Sometimes he sent, sometimes he went himself, for the sake of seeing the little pale face brighten at his entrance.

After a little time he found her no longer in her solitary room, but in one of the wards. It was not very large or very full. Many of the white beds, that stood in rows against the walls, were unoccupied; and most of the patients seemed not very ill, or on a fair way to recover. But it seemed to Mr. Sherwood a very sad thing indeed that the eyes which shone with such eager longing when he spoke of the fields and gardens, or of the hills and valleys that he had seen in his wanderings, should open day after day upon a scene so dreary.

What a strange, sad picture of life it seemed to him. There were old faces and young—faces on which years of sin and sorrow had set their seal, young faces that looked old, and faces old and worn and weary, yet

Y

growing slowly back into the look they must have had as little children, as the end drew near.

There were a few bright faces even there. A young servant-girl occupied the bed next to Christie on one side. She had been burned severely, but not dangerously, in saving a child committed to her care from a serious accident. She suffered much at first, but quite patiently, and in a day or two was cheerful, even merry, at the thought of getting away to the country, where her home was. She went away soon, and so did others —some joyfully, with recovered health and hope, others to be seen no more among the living.

'Do you like this better than to be quite alone?' asked Mr. Sherwood one day, as he sat by Christie's bed, watching the strange, painful scenes around him. She did not answer for a moment, and her face saddened as her eye went down the long ward, thinking of the peculiar sorrow of each of the suffering inmates.

'For some things I like it better. It is less trouble to the nurse, and the time does not seem so long. It is very sad, though,' she added. 'Even when I am free from pain myself, there is sure to be some one suffering near me. But I am getting used to it. Folk get used to anything in time, you know.'

Almost always he left her cheerful, and though her recovery seemed day by day no nearer, she never seemed to doubt that she would soon be well, at least she never expressed any doubt to her kind friend till one day after he had been many times to see her.

September had come in more sultry and warm than August had been; even out in the open streets, towards the mountain, the motionless air was hot and stifling. It was a trying day in the narrow alleys and in the low parts of the city, where many an invalid lay moaning and wishing for the night to come.

In the ward where Christie lay the windows were darkened, and coming out of the glare of the sun, for a moment Mr. Sherwood thought it cool and pleasant there. It was close and unwholesome, however, as it was everywhere, and Christie was more restless and feverish than he had ever seen her. She was now very often that way in the afternoon, she told him; but when his eyes were accustomed to the dim light, he saw that there were traces of tears on her flushed cheek, and he noticed that even now it was all that she could do to keep her voice steady as she spoke.

He did not ask her what troubled her; he had an instinctive feeling that the question would bring back her tears, but he said, cheerfully:

'You look as if you needed a good sleep. Suppose I read to you a little?'

Her Bible lay on the pillow, and he took it up. She laid herself down wearily, and rested her cheek on her hand. The book opened most readily at the Psalms, and he read what first met his eye.

'"They that wait on the Lord shall be as Mount Zion, that cannot be removed. As the mountains are round about Jerusalem, so the Lord is round about His people, from henceforth even for ever."'

Christie's countenance lighted up with pleasure as he read, and the tears that had been close at hand flowed freely. It was only a summer shower, however, and they were soon dried, but the smile remained. Mr. Sherwood looked at her a little surprised.

'"They that wait on the Lord shall be as Mount Zion,

that cannot be removed,"' she repeated. 'Surely that ought to be enough to make me content.'

'And was it because you had forgotten it that I found you with such a sad face to-day?' he asked, gravely.

He read on, while Christie lay quite still, her eyes closed, and Mr. Sherwood thought she slept; but when he stopped reading she opened her eyes, and thanked him gratefully. She was evidently soothed and comforted, and Mr. Sherwood could not help wondering at the change.

'I had a letter from my sister Effie, since you were here,' said she.

'I trust you had no bad news? Are all well at home?'

'They are all well now, but little Will had the scarlet fever, and Effie couldn't leave him; and now her holidays are over, and she cannot come to see me.'

'Did you expect her?'

'I did not expect her; but now her holidays are over, she cannot possibly come, I know.'

'I fear you must be greatly disappointed!' said Mr. Sherwood, kindly.

'Yes, at first. For a little while I felt as though no one cared for me, but that was foolish and wrong. If Effie had known how ill I am, she would have come, though it is such a long way. I am afraid I have not done right in not telling her.'

'But you cannot mean that your sister does not know that you are here, and that you are very ill?' said Mr. Sherwood, in some surprise.

'She knows I am here, but she does not know all. I had just written to her when the doctor told me I must come here for a while, so I waited till I should be able to tell her I was better. When I wrote I did not tell her how long I had been here; there was no use in troubling them all at home, for it would make them very sorry to know I was suffering all alone, and they cannot spare either time or money to undertake the journey here. I kept hoping 1 should soon be better. She thinks, I suppose, that I am quite well and at my work in the nursery again. But I am afraid she ought to know just how I am. I am not better, and if anything were to happen——'

If any one had asked Mr. Sherwood if he thought Christie was likely to recover, he would hardly have said that her case was a very hopeful one. But when he heard Christie speaking in this way, his impulse was (as it too often is in such circumstances) by cheerful and hopeful words to put the too probable event out of her thoughts, and he said:

'But you are not to think anything is to happen. Why, we shall have you ready for a race with Master Claude in the cedar walk before the winter sets in. At the same time, I do not wonder you are anxious to see your sister. I wish for your sake she were here.'

Christie shook her head.

'I am not better, and I don't know what to do. Effie couldn't very well come, even if I were to ask her; and it would only trouble them all to know that I am no better after all this time. Still, they would think—if anything were to happen——' but she could not finish her sentence.

Mr. Sherwood was much moved. It seemed only natural to him that the poor young girl should shrink from the thought of a fatal termination of her sufferings, though he felt sure that, as far as any one could be prepared for the mysterious change, Christie was prepared for it. He longed to say something to soothe and comfort her, but no words came to his mind. Taking up the Bible, he read the very same portion again:

' " They that wait on the Lord shall be as Mount Zion, that cannot be removed; " ' and then he added, softly:

' You are in good hands.'

Christie's face brightened as she turned her bright, tearful eyes upon him.

' I know it, I am quite sure of it; and Effie too. I don't know why I should be anxious and troubled when I have so sure a promise. I am not strong. I suppose that makes a difference. But I *know* all will come out right.'

CHAPTER XXI.

THE NIGHT GROWS DARKER.

BUT the thing which 'might happen,' and at the thought of which Christie shuddered and turned pale, was not what Mr. Sherwood supposed it to be. It was not the natural shrinking from death which all must feel when it is first impressed upon the mind not only that it is inevitable, but that it is near. Christie knew that she was very ill. She knew that she was not growing better, but rather worse. Yet it had never entered into her mind that possibly she was to die soon. The dread that was upon her was not the dread of death. I think if she had suddenly been told that she was going to die, the tidings might have startled her, because not anticipated; but believing, as she did, that death could not separate her from her chief treasure, she would not have been afraid. It was of something else that she was thinking, when she said to her kind friend that Effie would be shocked if it came to pass.

She had awakened one day from a momentary slumber into which she had fallen to hear some very terrible words spoken beside her. She thought she had been dreaming till she heard them repeated, and then she opened her eyes to see the kind faces of the attending physician and another looking at her.

'You have been asleep,' said one of them, kindly; and Christie thought again she must have been dreaming, for they spoke to her just as usual, praising her patience and bidding her take courage, for she would soon be well again. She must have been dreaming, she said to herself, twenty times that day. Nothing so terrible as the dread that was upon her could possibly be true; and yet the thought came back again and again.

'I am afraid she must lose it,' she thought she heard one of them say.

'Yes; it looks like that now,' as it seemed to her was the reply.

She could not forget the expression; and during the days and nights that followed, the remembrance of the words came back, sometimes as a dream, sometimes as a certainty. Had she been asleep, or was it true that she must be a cripple all her life? Must she henceforth be helpless and dependent, when her help was so much and in so many ways needed? Had her terrible sufferings been all in vain? Were all these restless days and nights only to have this sorrowful ending? How could she ever bear it? How could she ever tell Effie and the rest at home?

Many times in the day, when there was no one near, she determined to ask the doctor, that she might know the worst or have her fears set at rest, but she could not find the courage to do so. She did speak to the nurse, but she knew nothing about the matter, or said she did not, and quite laughed at her fancies, as she called

them. But the fancies still lingered, and for a week or
two the face she turned to meet her friend was grave
and anxious enough.

He came almost every day now, he hardly knew why.
Whatever the cause might be, he could not but see that
his coming was always hailed with delight. Wherever
the charm might be, whether in his voice or in the
words he read, he could not tell; but he saw that his
visits soothed her restlessness, and helped to banish
the look of doubt and pain that too often saddened
her face.

Sometimes he read the Bible, and stranger as he had
for many years been to its sacred pages, he could not
help yielding himself to the charm which the wonderful
words he read there must ever have to a thoughtful
mind. But the charm which the words had for his
patient listener was something quite different from this.
It was not the grandeur or sublimity of the style, or
even the loftiness of the thought, that made her listen
with such interest. She liked the simplest passages
best. The simple narratives of the evangelists never
lost their power to please her. Some word or promise,
in which he saw little beauty, had often power to excite
her deepest emotion, and he could not but wonder as he
saw it.

He read other books too—little books left by visitors;
very foolish little books he thought them often, and he
could not but smile as he marked the interest with
which she listened; but he never by smile or word
intimated to her that he thought them trifling, at least
he was never conscious of doing so. But he sometimes
read in the grave, questioning eyes which Christie
turned on him, a doubt whether that which was so

real and so comforting to her was of any value to him.

He could not but confess to himself that, seen from Christie's point of view, the subjects discussed in them must seem of grave importance; and he never lost the feeling, as he sat by her bed, that they had a meaning to her that was hidden from him.

Very few words were spoken between them at such times. When Christie asked a question or made a remark, there was a clearness and simplicity in her way of speaking, a strength and freshness in what she said, that often surprised as well as interested him. He did not always understand her, and yet he could not believe that she was speaking of things too high for her.

The thought flashed upon his mind one day, as he sat by her bed, What if among these things which were revealed to her but hidden from him, lay the secret of the happiness he had been so long and so vainly pursuing? There are things hidden from the wise and prudent, and revealed only to babes—even to such little ones as this suffering child.

Looking up as the thought passed through his mind, he met her eyes fixed wistfully upon him. She withdrew the gaze quickly, in some confusion, but in a moment looked up again.

'What is it, Christie? You looked as though you were afraid I would read your thoughts. What grave question are you meditating now?'

Christie smiled.

'No, I was not afraid. I was wondering what could make you so kind to me. I need not have wondered, though. I know quite well why it is.'

Do you? Well, suppose you tell me what you

mean by "so kind," and then why it is that I am "so kind" to you. I should really like to know,' said Mr. Sherwood, laughing.

'I need not tell you the first,' she said, with a smile. 'You know that very well, and it would take me too long to tell all. I think the reason of your kindness is because God has put it into your heart to be so. It is one of the ways He takes to help me to bear my troubles.'

The last words were spoken very gravely.

'Then it seems you don't think I am one of the good people who take delight in kind offices.'

'I am sure no one could be kinder than you have been to me,' she said, eagerly.

'But you don't think it is my way to be kind to people generally; I am not a philanthropist. Is that it?'

Christie looked puzzled and a little anxious.

Nay, you are not to look disconsolate about it,' said Mr. Sherwood, laughing. 'It is quite true. I am not at all like a benevolent person in a book. I was kind to you, as you call it, first to please my little cousin Gertrude, and then to please myself. So now you have the secret of it all.'

'Oh, but it is true for all that that God put it into your heart to come so often,' said Christie, with glisten-ing eyes. 'Your kindness gives me double pleasure when I think of it in that way.'

'Well, it may be so,' said Mr. Sherwood, gravely; 'but I don't think it is generally supposed that God chooses to comfort His little ones by means of such a person as I am.'

Christie's eyes were fixed wistfully upon him again.

Such as you !' she exclaimed, quite unconsciously, as Mr. Sherwood thought, for she said no more just then.

'I was writing to Effie to-day, and I tried to tell her how good you have been to me. But I could not. I could never make her understand it, I know. She would need to see it for herself.'

'My poor child,' said Mr. Sherwood, smiling, 'do you know you are talking foolishly? and that is a thing you seldom do. You are making a great deal out of a very little matter. The chances are that you do quite as much good to me as I shall ever do to you.'

'Oh, I wish I could think so! If I could get my wish for you——' She paused suddenly.

'Well, what would you wish for me?' asked Mr. Sherwood, still smiling at her eagerness. 'I dare say I should have no more trouble in this world if you could have your wish.'

Christie shook her head.

'I don't think I ever wished that for you, and yet I have, too, in a way; for if that which I ask for you every day were to come to pass, you *might* have trouble, but it would never seem like trouble to you any more.'

'Well, I suppose that would answer every purpose of not having any more trouble, and you are very kind to wish it. But you say "*ask*"; so I suppose it is something which is in the giving of your Friend above?'

'Yes,' said Christie, softly; and then there was a pause.

'And what is it? Is it the "new heart and the right spirit" we were reading about the other day? That seems to be the very best blessing that one can have, in your opinion. And do you really think I shall ever get it?'

'I hope you will,' she answered, eagerly. 'I believe you will, if you only ask for it.'

'Ah, well, I don't know. I have a fancy that your asking will be more to the purpose than mine.'

'I shall never forget to ask it for you. I have never forgotten it since——' she hesitated.

'Since when?' asked Mr. Sherwood.

'Do you remember the day you came into the cedar walk, when I was telling little Claude the story of the blind man, and what you said to me that day? I don't think I have ever forgotten since to pray the blind man's prayer for you.'

Mr. Sherwood was greatly surprised and touched. That was long ago. He had been far away since then. Once or twice, perhaps, in connection with the remembrance of his little cousins, the thought of their kind, quiet nurse had come back to him. And yet she had never in all that time forgotten to ask for him what seemed to her to be the best of all blessings.

'And do you do that for all your friends?' he said. 'How came you to think of doing this for me?'

'You did not seem very happy, I thought. You seemed like one searching for something that you could not find; and so I asked that your eyes might be opened.'

'Well, some day you must tell me how your eyes were opened, and perhaps that may help me.'

'Oh, no. I have nothing to tell, only I was very miserable often and discontented and troublesome. Afterwards it was all changed, and I was at peace.'

She lay quite still, as if she were weary, and when

Mr. Sherwood spoke again it was only to say good-bye.

But afterwards, at different times, she told him of the great happiness that had come to her through the grace of God, and he listened with an interest which sometimes increased to wonder. He mused on the simple recitals of the young girl with an earnestness which he could not explain to himself, and read the chapters which she pointed out as having done her good, partly for the pleasure of talking them over with her, and partly, too, because he began to see in God's Word what he had never seen in it before.

But I had no thought of saying all this about Mr. Sherwood. It was of the sad, yet happy days that Christie passed in the hospital that I wished to write, and they were drawing to a close now. But let me say just one word more about her friend. It all came to pass as Christie had been sure it would. The day came when, earnestly as blind Bartimeus, he prayed, 'Lord, that mine eyes may be opened!' And He who had compassion on the wayside beggar had compassion on him, and called him out of darkness into His marvellous light. I dare say she knows the glad tidings now. If she does not, she will know them soon, on the happy day when the friends shall meet 'on the other side of the river.'

One day when Mr. Sherwood came, he brought Gertrude with him. She had been prepared to find Christie very ill, but she had no thought of finding her so greatly changed. She was scarcely able to restrain her emotion at the sight of the pale, suffering face that told so sad a tale, and she was so much excited that Mr. Sherwood did not like to go away and leave them together, as he had at first meant to do. She tried to say how grieved she was to see Christie so ill, but when she began to count how many months she had been lying there, her voice suddenly failed her.

'Yes; it is a long time,' Christie faintly said. But she thought herself no worse for a few days past. She had suffered much less with her knee of late, and she was beginning to hope that the worst was passed. She did not say much more about herself, except in telling how kind Mr. Sherwood had been to her; but she had a great many questions to ask about the little boys, especially Claude, and about Gertrude herself, and all that she had been doing since they parted.

What a contrast they presented, these two young girls. There stood the one, bright and strong, possessing all that we are wont to covet for those we love—health and beauty, home and friends, and a fair prospect of a long and happy life. Sick and sorrowful and alone lay the other, her life silently ebbing away, her hold on the world and all it has to give slowly but surely loosening. Yet, in the new light which was beginning to dawn upon him, Mr. Sherwood caught a glimpse of a contrast more striking still. On the couch before him lay a little suffering form, wasted and weary, soon to be hidden from the light, little to be mourned, quickly to be forgotten. But it soon vanished as from that lowly cot there rose before his gaze a spirit crowned and radiant and immortal.

Which was to be pitied? which to be envied? Before one lay life and its struggles, its trials and its temptations. With the other, these were past. A step more and the river is passed, and beyond lies a world of endless glory and bliss.

They did not linger very long. Promising to bring her back soon, Mr. Sherwood hurried Gertrude away.

'Cousin Charles,' said she, eagerly, as they went down the long passage together, 'we must take her away from this place. Nay, don't shake your head. Mother will listen to what you say, and she will be willing to do much for one who did so much for her little boy. Only think of her lying all these months in that dreary room! Did you not hear her say she had not seen a flower growing all the summer? Oh, Cousin Charles, you will surely help me to persuade mother?'

'My dear,' said Mr. Sherwood, gravely, 'I fear she is not well enough to be moved. I do not think the physicians would consent to let her be taken away.'

'But are they making her better? I am sure the fresh air of the country would do her more good than all their medicines. Oh, such a suffering face! And her hands, Cousin Charles—did you notice her hands? I am afraid I have come too late. But she will surely grow better again when she is taken away from this place. It would kill any one to lie there long in that great room among all those poor suffering creatures. If I could only get her away! It would not cost much to take her, with a nurse, to some quiet place, if we could not have her at the house. I shall have money of my own some time. Cousin Charles, will not you speak to mother for me?' She was growing very eager and excited.

'Hush!' he said, gently. 'Nothing but the impracticability of it could have prevented me from removing her to her own home, for which she has been pining so sadly. Have patience, and we will try what can be done. We will speak to the doctor about it.'

The physician was, fortunately, disengaged, and the subject of Christie's removal suggested to him. But he objected to it more decidedly now than he had when Mr. Sherwood had spoken of it some time before. It was doubtful whether in her present weak state she could bear removal, even if she could be as well cared for elsewhere. It was becoming doubtful whether her constitution could hold out much longer. Indeed, it could hardly be said to be doubtful. There was just one chance for her, he said; and then he spoke low, as though he did not wish Miss Gertrude to hear—but she did.

'You do not mean that her knee is never to be well again?' she asked, with a shudder.

'We have for some time feared so,' said the doctor. 'Within a day or two symptoms have appeared which seem to indicate an absolute and speedy necessity for amputation. Poor little thing! It is very sad for her, of course.'

'Does she know it?' asked Miss Gertrude, steadying her voice with a great effort.

'I think she is not altogether unprepared for it. She must know that she is not getting better, and I fancy she must suspect the necessity from something she once said to the nurse. Poor girl! she seems to grieve quite as much on account of her friends as on her own.'

'Have they been informed of this—of the possible result of her illness?' asked Mr. Sherwood.

'She has written to them several times during the summer, I believe. They seem to be very poor people, living at a distance—quite unable to do anything for her.'

They were soon on their way to meet Mrs. Seaton, who had made an appointment with them, but Miss Gertrude was quite overcome by what she had seen and heard.

'Poor Christie! To think that all these weary months of waiting must end thus! I cannot help thinking we have been to blame.'

'My child, why should you say so?'

'To think of it coming to this with her, and her friends not knowing it! Her sister never would have left her here all this time, if she had thought her in danger. She ought to know at once.'

'Yes; they must be told at once,' said Mr. Sherwood. 'But I fancy, from what the doctor said, they can't do much for her; and from the poor little thing herself I have gathered that the only one who could come to her is her elder sister, on whom the rest seem to be quite dependent.'

'But she must come, too,' said Gertrude, eagerly. 'That is Effie. There is no one in all the world like Effie, Christie thinks. Oh, Cousin Charles, they have not always been poor. And they have suffered so much and they love each other so dearly!'

'Gertrude, my child, there is a bright side even to this sad picture. Do you think that the suffering little creature, lying there all these months, has been altogether unhappy?'

Gertrude struggled with her tears, and said:

'She has the true secret of happiness.'

'Yes, I am sure of it. Seeing her, as I have, lying on that bed of pain, I have felt inclined rather to envy than to pity her. She has that for her own that a kingdom could not purchase—a peace that cannot be taken from her. I do not believe that even the sad necessity that awaits her will move her much now.'

His first words had stilled Miss Gertrude quite, and soon she found voice to say:

' Not for herself, but for her sisters. I am afraid they will think we have been very cruel. But it will be well with Christie, whatever happens.'

' Yes; it will be well with her, I do believe,' said Mr. Sherwood, gravely; and neither spoke again till they reached home.

CHAPTER XXII.

A CLOUD WITH A SILVER LINING.

THE shadows were lengthening one September afternoon, when Effie Redfern closed behind her the door of
her school-room, and took her way along the shady road
that led to the cottage which for more than two years
had been her home. The air was mild and pleasant.
The leaves on some of the trees were changing. Here
a yellow birch and beech, and there a crimson maple
betrayed the silent approach of winter. But the saddest
of the autumn days had not come. Here and there lay
bare, gray fields and stubble land, with a dreary wintry
look; but the low pastures were green yet, and the
gaudy autumn flowers lingered untouched along the
fences and waysides.

It was a very lovely afternoon, and sending on the
children, who were inclined to lag, Effie lingered behind
to enjoy it. Her life was a very busy one. Except an
occasional hour stolen from sleep, she had very little
time she could call her own. Even now, her enjoyment
of the fresh air and the fair scene was marred by a vague
feeling that she ought to hasten home to the numberless
duties awaiting her.

These years had told on Effie. She was hopeful and trustful still, but it was not quite so easy as it used to be to throw off her burden, and forget, in the enjoyment of present pleasure, past weariness and fears for the future. No burden she had yet been called to bear had bowed her down; and though she looked into the future with the certainty that these would grow heavier rather than lighter, the knowledge had no power to appal her. She was strong and cheerful, and contented with her lot.

But burdens borne cheerfully may still press heavily; and quite unconsciously to herself, Effie wore on her fair face some tokens of her labours and her cares. The gravity that used to settle on it during the anxious consideration of ways and means was habitual now. It passed away when she spoke or smiled, but when her face settled to repose again, the grave look was on it still, and lay there like a shadow, as she passed along the solitary road that afternoon. Her thoughts were not sad—at least, they were not at first sad. She had been considering various possibilities as to winter garments, and did not see her way quite clear to the end of her labours. But she had often been in that predicament before. There was nothing in it then to make her look particularly grave. She had become accustomed to more perplexing straits than little Will's jacket could possibly bring to her, and she soon put all thoughts of such cares away from her, saying to herself that she would not let the pleasure of her walk be spoiled by them.

So she sent her glance over the bare fields and changing woods and up into the clear sky, with a sense of release and enjoyment which only they can feel who have been kept close all day and for many days at a task which, though not uncongenial, is yet exhausting to strength and patience; but the shadow rested on her still. It deepened even as her eye came back from its wanderings, and fell on the dusty path she was treading.

Amid all the cares and anxieties of the summer—and what with the illness of the children and their narrow means they had not been few nor light—there had come and gone and come again a vague fear as to the welfare of her sister, Christie. Christie's first letter— the only one she had as yet received from her—did not alarm her much. She, poor child, had said so little that was discouraging about her own situation, and had spoken so hopefully of being out of the hospital soon, that they had never dreamed that anything very serious was the matter with her. Of course, the fact of her having to go to the hospital at all gave them pain, but still it seemed the best thing she could have done in her circumstances, and they never doubted but all would soon be well.

As the weeks passed on with no further tidings, Effie grew anxious at times, and wondered much that her sister did not write, but it never came into her mind that she was silent because that by writing she could only give them pain. They all thought she must be better—that possibly she had gone to the sea-side with the family, and that, in the bustle of departure, either she had not written, or her letter had been mislaid and never been sent.

But somehow, as Effie walked along that afternoon, the vague fear that had so often haunted her came back with a freshness that startled her. She could not put it from her, as she might have tried to do had she been speaking to any one of it. The remembrance that it was the night of the mail, and that, if no letter came, she must endure another week of waiting, made her heart sicken with impatient longing. And yet, what could she do but wait and hope?

'And I must wait cheerfully too,' she said to herself, as she drew near home and heard the voices of the children. 'And after all, I need not fear for Christie. I do believe it will be well with her, whatever happens. Surely I can trust her in a Father's hands.'

'How long you have been, Effie!' cried her little sister, Kate, as she made her appearance. 'Mrs. Nesbitt is here, and Nellie and I have made tea ready, and you'll need to hasten, for Mrs. Nesbitt canna bide long; it is dark so soon now.'

Effie's face brightened, as it always did at the sight of a friend, and she greeted Mrs. Nesbitt very cheerfully.

'Mrs. Nesbitt has a letter for you, Effie,' said Aunt Elsie; 'but you must make tea first. The bairns have it ready, and Mrs. Nesbitt needs it after her walk.'

Effie fancied that the letter Mrs. Nesbitt had brought came from some one else than Christie, or she might not have assented with such seeming readiness to the proposal to have tea first. As it was, she hastened Nellie's nearly-completed arrangements, and seated herself behind the tray. Mrs. Nesbitt looked graver than usual, she thought; and as she handed her her cup of tea, she said, quietly:

You have had no bad news, I hope?'

'I have had no news,' said Mrs. Nesbitt. 'Alexander

told me there were two letters for you in the post, so I sent him for them, and I have come to you for the news.'

As she spoke she laid the two letters on the table. One was from Christie, but she broke the seal of the other one first. It was very short, but before she had finished it her face was as colourless as the paper in her hand.

'Well, what is it?' said her aunt and Mrs. Nesbitt, in the same breath. She turned the page and read from the beginning:

'MY DEAR MISS REDFERN,—I have just returned from visiting your sister at the hospital. I do not think you can have gathered from her letters how ill she is, and I think you ought to know. I do not mean that she is dangerously ill, but she has been lying there a long time; and if you can possibly come to her, I am sure the sight of you would do her more good than anything else in the world. Christie does not know that I am writing. I think she has not told you how ill she is, for fear of making you unhappy; and now she is troubled lest anything should happen, and her friends be quite unprepared for it. Not that you must think anything is going to happen, but come if you can.

'My dear Miss Redfern, I hope you will not think me impertinent, but father wishes me to say to you that we all beg you will let no consideration of expense prevent your coming. It will be such a comfort to Christie to have you here.'

There was a postscript, saying that the poor girl had been in the hospital since the end of April.

'The end of April!' echoed Aunt Elsie and Mrs. Nesbitt at once. Effie said nothing, but her hands trembled very much as she opened the other letter. I need not copy Christie's letter, we already know all she had to tell. Effie's voice failed her more than once as she read it.

Fearing to make them unhappy at home, yet desiring

to have them prepared for whatever might happen to her, the letter had cost Christie a great deal of anxious thought. One thing was plain enough to all; she was very ill and a little despondent, and longed above all things to see Effie and get home again. The elder sister having read it all, laid it down without speaking.

'Effie, my dear,' said Aunt Elsie, 'you will need to go.'

'Yes; I must go. How I could have contented myself all this time, knowing she might be ill, I am sure I cannot tell. My poor child!'

Mrs. Nesbitt looked at her anxiously, as she said : ' My dear bairn, you have nothing to reproach yourself with. You have had a very anxious summer, what with one care and another.'

Effie rose with a gesture of impatience, but sat down again without speaking. She blamed herself severely; but what was the use of speaking about it now? She took up Christie's letter and read again the last sentence.

' It grieves me to add to your burdens, Effie. I hoped to be able to lighten them, rather. But such is not God's will, and He sees what is best for us all. I do so long to see you again—to get home. But I must have patience.'

'Have patience!' she repeated aloud. 'Oh, poor child! To think of her lying there all these weary months! How can I ever forgive myself!'

She rose from the table hastily. Oh, how glad she would have been to go to her that very moment. But she could not, nor the next day either. There were many things to be considered. They were too dependent

on her school to permit her to give it up at once.
Some one must be found to take her place during her
absence.   Sarah must be sent for at the neighbouring
village, where she had been staying for the last month.
The children and Aunt Elsie must not be left alone.
There were other arrangements to be made, too, and
two days passed before Effie was ready to go.

She saw Mrs. Nesbitt again before she went, and her
kind old friend said to her some of the things she had
meant to say that night when the letters were read.
She was able to hear them now.   They would have
done no good in the first moments of her sorrow, as
Mrs. Nesbitt very well knew.

'Effie, my bairn,' said she, gravely, 'you have trouble
enough to bear without needlessly adding to it by
blaming yourself when you ought not.   Even if you
had known all, you could not have gone to your sister,
except in the sorest need.   Has there been a single
day when you could have been easily spared?   And
you could have done little for her, I dare say, poor
lassie.   And you may be sure the Lord has been caring
for her all this time.   He has not forgotten her.'

'She says that in her letter many times,' said Effie.

'My dear, there is a bright side to this dark cloud,
you may be sure.   Whichever way this trouble ends,
it will end well for this precious lamb of Christ's fold.
And you are not to go to her in a repining spirit, as
though, if you had but known, you could have done
other and better for her than the Lord has been doing.
We cannot see the end from the beginning, and we
must trust the Lord both in the light and in the
darkness.'

Effie made no answer for a moment. She then said, in a low voice:

'But I never felt sure that it was right for her to go from home. She never was strong.'

'But you were not sorry, when you saw her in the winter, that she had gone. You mind you told me how much she had improved?'

'Yes; if I had only brought her home with me then. She must have been worse than I thought. And it must seem to her so neglectful in us to leave her so all the summer.'

'My dear lassie,' said Mrs. Nesbitt, gravely, 'it is in vain to go back to that now. It has been all ordered, and it has been ordered for good, too. The Lord has many ways of doing things; and if He has taken this way of quickly ripening your little sister for heaven, why should it grieve us?'

'But,' said Effie, eagerly, 'you did not gather from the letter that she was so very ill? Miss Gertrude said not dangerously, and oh, I cannot but think she will be better when we get her home again.'

'That will be just as God wills. But what I want to say is this. You must go cheerfully to her. If, by all this, God has been preparing her for His presence, you must not let a shadow fall on her last days. It is a wonderful thing to be permitted to walk to the river's brink with one whom God has called to go over —an honour and blessing greatly to be coveted; and you must not lose the blessing it may be to you, by giving way to a murmuring spirit. Not that I am afraid for you,' she added, laying her hand on Effie's arm. 'All will be well; for I do believe you, and your

sister too, are among those whom God will keep from
all that can really harm. Don't vex yourself with
trying to make plain things which He has hidden.
Trust all to Him, and nothing can go far wrong with
you then.'

But it was with an inexpressible sinking of the heart
that Effie, when her hurried journey was over, found
herself standing at the door of the hospital. It was
the usual hour when the patients are visited by their
friends; and the servant, thinking she was some one
sent by the Seatons, sent her up to the ward at once,
without reference to the doctor or the matron of the
institution. Thus it was that with no preparation she
came upon the changed face of her sister.

If Effie should live to be a hundred years old, she
would never forget the first glimpse she had of that
long room, with its rows of white beds against the
wall. Every one of the suffering faces that she passed
stamped itself upon her memory in characters that can
never fade; and then she saw her sister.

But was it her sister? Could that face, white as
the pillow on which it lay, be Christie's? One thin,
transparent hand supported her cheek; the other—
the very shadow of a hand—lay on the coverlet. Was
she sleeping? Did she breathe? Effie stooped low
to listen, and raising herself up again, saw what
almost made her heart cease to beat.

That which Christie had dreaded all these weary
weeks, that which she could find no words to tell her
sister, had come upon her. 'I shall be a cripple all
my life,' she had written; that was all. Now the
thin coverlet betrayed with terrible distinctness her

mutilated form. Effie saw it, and the sight of it made the row of white beds and the suffering faces on them turn round. She took one step forward, putting forth her hands like one who is blind, and then fell to the floor.

The shock to Effie was a terrible one. For a while she struggled in vain with the deadly faintness that returned with every remembrance of that first terrible discovery. She was weary with her journey, and exhausted for want of nourishment, having eaten nothing all day. Her very heart seemed to die within her, and the earth seemed to be gliding from beneath her feet. She was brought back to full consciousness with a start, as she heard some one say:

'She ought not to have seen her. She must not see her again to-night. She must go away and come again in the morning.'

With a great effort she rose.

'No,' she said, quietly and solemnly; 'I cannot go away. I shall never leave her again, so help me God!'

She rose up, and with trembling fingers began to arrange her hair, which had fallen over her face. Some one gently forced her into a chair.

'You are not able to stand. It is in vain for you to make the effort,' said the doctor. Effie turned and saw him.

'I am tired with my journey' she said, 'and I have eaten nothing all day; but I am perfectly well and strong. I cannot go away. I must see my sister to-night. It was the surprise that overcame me, but I shall not be so again.'

There is not more than one woman in a thousand whose words the doctor would have heeded at such a time. Effie was that one. Instead of answering her, he spoke to the nurse, who left the room and soon returned with a biscuit and a cup of warm tea. Effie forced herself to take the food, and was refreshed. In a little while she was able to follow the nurse to the ward, and to seat herself calmly by her sister's bed.

Christie was still asleep, but happily for Effie she soon awoke. She could not have endured many minutes of that silent waiting. There was pleasure, but scarcely surprise, in the eyes that opened to fix themselves on her face.

'Have you come, Effie? I was dreaming about you. I am very glad.'

Effie kneeled down and kissed her over and over again, but she could not speak a word. Soon she laid her head down on the pillow, and Christie put her arms round her neck. There was a long silence, so long that Effie moved gently at last, and removing her sister's arms from her neck, found her fast asleep. The daylight faded, and the night-lamps were lighted in the room. There was moving to and fro among the beds, as the preparations for the night were made. But Effie did not stir till the nurse spoke to her.

'Your sister is still under the influence of the draught the doctor gave her. But we must waken her to give her some nourishment before she settles down for the night.'

The eyes, which Effie thought had grown strangely large, opened with a smile.

'Will they let you stay, Effie?' said she.

'Nothing shall ever make me leave you again.'

That was all that passed between them. Christie slept nearly all night, but to Effie the hours passed slowly and sorrowfully away. There was never entire quiet in the ward. There was moaning now and then, and feverish tossing to and fro on one or another of those white beds. The night-nurse moved about among them, smoothing the pillow of one, holding a cup to the lips of another, soothing or chiding, as the case of each required. To Effie the scene was as painful as it was strange. She had many unhappy and some rebellious thoughts that night. But God did not forsake her. The same place of refuge that had sheltered her in former times of trouble was open to her still, and when Christie awoke in the morning it was to meet a smile as calm and bright as that she had often seen in her dreams. For a little while it seemed to her she was dreaming now.

'If I shut my eyes, will you be here when I open them again?' she asked. 'Oh, Effie, I have so longed for you! You will never leave me again?'

'Never again,' was all that she had the power to answer.

That day they removed her from the public ward to the room she had at first occupied, and Effie became her nurse. They were very quiet that day. Christie was still under the influence of the strong opiate that had been given her, and worn out with anxiety and watching, Effie slumbered beside her.

On the second day they had a visit from Gertrude, and Christie quite roused herself to rejoice with her over Effie's coming. When the young lady declared, with delighted energy, that all Christie wanted to make her quite well again was the face of her sister smiling upon her, all three for a moment believed it. She was to have a week, or perhaps two, in which to grow a little stronger, and then she was to go home with Gertrude till she should be strong enough to go to Glengarry with Effie. No wonder she had been ill and discouraged, so long alone, or worse than alone, surrounded by so much suffering. Now she would soon be well again, Gertrude was quite sure.

And she did seem better. Relieved from the terrible pain which her diseased limb had so long caused, for a time she seemed to revive. She thought herself better. She said many times a day that she felt like a different person, and Effie began to take courage.

But she did not grow stronger. If she could only be taken out of town, where she could have better air, Effie thought she might soon be well. But to remove her in her present state of weakness was impossible. And every day that followed, the doubt forced itself with more and more strength on Effie that she would never be removed alive. The daily paroxysms of fever returned. At such times she grew restless, and sometimes, when she would wake with a start from troubled and uneasy slumbers, her mind seemed to wander. A word was enough to recall her to herself, and when she recognized her sister's voice and opened her eyes to see her bending over her, her look of glad surprise, changing slowly into one of sweet content, was beautiful to see.

She could not talk much, or even listen for a long time to reading, but she was always quite content and

at rest with Effie sitting beside her. A visit from
Gertrude or Mr. Sherwood was all that happened to
break the monotony of those days to them. Once little
Claude and his brother were brought to see her. They
had not forgotten her. Claude lay down beside her, and
put his little hand on her cheek, as he used to do, and
told her about the sea and the broad sands where they
used to play, and prattled away happily enough of the
time when Christie should come home quite well again.
Clement was shy, and a little afraid of her altered face,
and gave all his attention to Effie. But the visit
exhausted Christie, and it never was repeated. Indeed,
a very little thing exhausted her now.

One day Christie awoke to find her sister watching
the clouds and the autumn rain with a dark shadow
resting on her face. Her first movement sent it away,
but the remembrance of it lingered with Christie.
After a little time, when she had been made comfortable, and Effie had seated herself with her work beside
her, she said :

‘ Are you longing to get home, Effie ? ’

‘ No, indeed,’ said Effie, cheerfully, ‘ except for your
sake.’

‘ But I am sure they will miss you sadly.’

‘ Yes, I dare say they will ; but they don’t really
need me. Sarah is at home, and Katie and Nellie
are quite to be trusted even should she be called away.
I am not in the least troubled about them. Still, I
hope we shall soon get home, for your sake.’

‘ But without your wages, how can they manage ? I
am afraid——’

‘ I am not afraid,’ said Effie. ‘ I left all that in safe

A A

hands before I came here.   Our garden did wonderfully
well last year; and besides, we managed to lay by
something——and God is good.   I am not afraid.'

'And they have all grown very much, you say.   And
little Will!   Oh, how I should like to have seen them
all!   They will soon forget me, Effie.'

Effie started.   It was the first time she had ever said
anything that seemed to imply a doubt of her recovery.
Even now she was not quite sure that she meant that,
and she hastened to say:

'Oh, there is no fear of their forgetting you.   You
cannot think how delighted they all were when your
letters came.'

'They could not give you half the pleasure that yours
gave me.'

'Oh, yes, they did.   We always liked to hear all
about what you were doing, and about the children
and Miss Gertrude.   Why, I felt quite as though I had
known Miss Gertrude for a long time when I first met
her here the other day.   I almost think I should have
known her if I had met her anywhere.   She looks older
and more mature than I should have supposed from
your letters, and then I used to fancy that she might
be at times a little overbearing and exacting.'

'Effie, I never could have said that about Miss
Gertrude.'

'No, you never said it, but I gathered it—less
from what you said than from what you didn't say,
however.   Has Miss Gertrude changed, do you
think?'

'No, oh no! she is just the very same.   And yet I
am not sure.   I remember thinking when I first saw

her that she was changed. She looks older, I think. I wonder if she will come to-day? She promised.'

'But it rains so heavily,' said Effie. 'No, I don't think she will come to-day. It would not be wise.'

But Effie was mistaken. She had hardly spoken when the door opened, and Gertrude entered.

'Through all the rain!' exclaimed Effie and Christie, in a breath.

'Yes, I thought you would be glad to see me this dull day,' said Miss Gertrude, laughing. 'I am none the worse for the rain, but I can't say as much for the horses, however. But Mr. Sherwood was obliged to leave in the train this afternoon, and I begged to come in the carriage with him. Peter is to come for me again when he has taken him to the station. See what I have brought you,' she added, opening the basket she carried in her hand. There were several things for Christie in the basket, but the *something* which Miss Gertrude meant was a bunch of buttercups placed against a spray of fragrant cedar and a few brown birch leaves.

'We gathered them in the orchard yesterday. They are the very last of the season. We gathered them because Claude said you once told him that they reminded you of home; and then you told him of a shady place where they used to grow, and of the birch-tree by the burn. I had heard about the burn myself, but not about the buttercups.'

Coming as they did, the little tuft of wild flowers pleased Christie better than the fairest bouquet of hot-house exotics could have done.

Effie laughed.

'Buttercups are not great favourites with us at home,'

she said. 'They generally grow best on poor, worn-out land.'

'They are the very first I have seen this summer,' said Christie, with moist eyes.

They were all silent a little while.

'We were just speaking about you when you came in,' said she to Miss Gertrude.

'Were you? Well, I hope you dealt gently with my faults?' she said, blushing a little as she noticed the glance which passed between the sisters.

'We had not got to your faults,' said Christie.

'Well, you must be merciful when you do. See, Christie, I have got something else for you,' she added, as she drew out a little book bound in blue and gold. 'I thought of you when I read this. There is a good deal in the book you would not care about, but you will like this.' And she read :

> 'Of all the thoughts of God that are
> Borne inward unto souls afar
>   Along the Psalmist's music deep,
> Now, tell me if that any is,
> For gift or grace, surpassing this?—
>   He giveth His beloved sleep.'

And so on to the end. 'Do you like it?' she asked.

'Yes,' said Christie. But her eyes said much more than that.

'It reminded me of the time I found you sleeping among all the noises that were going on in the ward. There was talking and groaning and moving about, and you were quite unconscious of it all.

> '"God makes a silence through them all,"

she repeated :

'"And never doleful dream again
  Shall break his blessed slumbers, when
  He giveth His beloved sleep."'

There was a silence of several minutes, and then Christie said:

'Miss Gertrude, when you came in I was telling Effie that I thought you had changed since I first knew you.'

'And were you telling her that there was much need of a change?' said Miss Gertrude, with a playfulness assumed to hide the quick rush of feeling which the words called forth.

'Do you mind how we used to speak of the great change that all must meet before we can be happy or safe? You don't think about these things as you used to do. Miss Gertrude, has this change come to you?'

'I don't know, Christie. Sometimes I almost hope it has,' said she. But she could not restrain the tears. Effie saw them; Christie did not. Her eyes were closed, and her hands were clasped as if in prayer.

'I was sure it would come,' she said, softly. 'I am very glad.'

She did not speak again during Miss Gertrude's stay, and I need not repeat all that passed between the young lady and Effie. There were some words spoken that neither will forget till their dying day.

Before she went away, Gertrude came and kissed Christie; and when she was gone Effie came and kissed her too, saying:

'You ought to be very happy, Christie, with all your trouble. God has been very good to you, in giving you a message to Miss Gertrude.'

'I am very happy, Effie,' answered she, softly. 'I almost think I am beyond being troubled any more. It is coming very near now.'

She lay still, with a smile on her face, till she fell into a quiet slumber; and as she sat watching her, Effie, amid all her sorrow, could not but rejoice at the thought of the blessed rest and peace that seemed coming so near now to her little sister.

CHAPTER XXIII.

HOME AT LAST.

YES, the time was drawing very near. Effie could no longer hide from herself that Christie was no stronger, but rather weaker every day. She did not suffer much pain, but now and then was feverish, and at such times she could get no rest. Then Effie moved and soothed and sang to her with patience inexhaustible. She would have given half her youthful strength to have revived that wasted form; and one day, as she was bathing her hands, she told her so.

Christie smiled, and shook her head.

'You will have better use for your strength than that, Effie. I am sure the water in the burn at home would cool my hands, if I could dip them in it. Oh, if I could just get out to the fields for one long summer day, I think I should be content to lie down here again for another six months! In the summer-time, when I used to think of the Nesbitts and the McIntyres in the sweet-smelling hay-fields, and of the bairns gathering berries in the woods, my heart was like to die within me. It is not so bad now since you came. No, Effie, I am quite content now.'

Later in the day, she said, after a long silence :

'Effie, little Will will hardly mind that he had a sister Christie, when he grows up to be a man. I should like to have been at home once more, because of that. They will all forget me, I am afraid.'

'Christie,' said her sister, 'why do you say they will forget you ? Do you not think you will live to see them again ?'

'Do you think so, Effie ?' asked Christie, gravely.

Instead of answering her, Effie burst into tears, and laid her head down on her sister's pillow. Christie laid her arm over her neck, and said, softly :

'There is nothing to grieve so for, Effie. I am not afraid.'

Effie's tears had been kept back so long, they must have free course now. It was in vain to try to stay them. But soon she raised herself up, and said :

'I didna mean to trouble you, Christie. I know I have no need to grieve for you. But, oh ! I cannot help thinking you might have been spared longer if I had been more watchful—more faithful to my trust !'

'Effie,' said Christie, 'move me a little, and lie down beside me. I have something to say to you, and there can be no better time than now. You are weary with your long watching. Rest beside me.'

Her sister arranged the pillow and lay down beside her. Clasping her wasted arms about her neck, Christie said :

'Effie, you don't often say wrong or foolish things, but what you said just now was both wrong and foolish. You must never say it or think it any more. Have I not been in safe keeping, think you ? Nay ! do not grieve me by saying that again,' she added, laying her hand upon her sister's lips, as she would have spoken. 'It all seems so right and safe to me, I would not have anything changed now, except that I should like to see them all at home. And I dare say that will pass away as the end draws near. It will not be long now, Effie.'

She paused from exhaustion, only adding:

'I am not afraid.'

The much she had to say was not said that night. The sisters lay silently in each other's arms, and while Christie slumbered, Effie prayed as she had never prayed before, that she might be made submissive to the will of God in this great sorrow that was drawing nearer day by day.

After this they spoke much of the anticipated parting, but never sadly any more. Effie's prayers were answered. God's grace did for her what, unaided, she never could have done for herself. It gave her power to watch the shadow of death drawing nearer and nearer, without shrinking from the sight. I do not mean that she felt no pain at the thought of going back to her home alone, or that she had quite ceased to blame herself for what she called her neglect of her suffering sister. Many a long struggle did she pass through during the hours when Christie slumbered. But she never again suffered a regretful word to pass her lips; she never for a moment let a cloud rest on her face when Christie's eyes were watching her. She had soothing words for the poor child's restless moments. If a doubt or fear came to disturb her quiet trust, she had words of cheer to whisper; and when—as oftenest happened—her peace was like a river, full and calm and deep, no murmurs, no repining, fell from the loving sister's lips to disturb its gentle flow.

And little by little, as the uneventful days glided by peace, and more than peace—gratitude and loving praise —filled the heart of Christie's sister. What could she wish more for the child so loved than such quiet and happy waiting for the end of all trouble? A little while sooner or later, what did it matter? What could she wish more or better for any one she loved? It would ill become her to repine at her loss, so infinitely her sister's gain.

The discipline of these weeks in her sister's sick-room did very much for Effie. Ever since their mother's death, and more especially since their coming to Canada, a great deal had depended on her. Wise to plan and strong to execute, she had done what few young girls in her sphere could have done. Her energy had never flagged. She delighted to encounter and overcome difficulties; she was strong, prudent, and far-seeing, and she was fast acquiring the reputation, among her friends and neighbours, of a rare business woman.

It is just possible that, as the years passed, she might have acquired some of the unpleasing qualities so apt to become the characteristic of the woman who has no one to come between her and the cares of business or the shifts and difficulties incident to the providing for a family whose means are limited. Coming in contact, as she had to do, with a world not always mindful of the claims of others, she found it necessary to stand her ground and hold her own with a firmness that might seem hardly compatible with gentleness. Her position, too, as the teacher of a school—the queen of a little realm where her word was law—tended to cultivate in her strength and firmness of character rather than the more womanly qualities. It is doubtful whether, without the sweet and solemn break in the routine of her life which these months in her sister's sick-room made, she would ever have grown into the woman she afterwards became. This long and patient waiting for God's messenger gave her the time for thought which her busy life denied her.

Now and then, during the quiet talks in which, during her more comfortable hours, they could still indulge, there was revealed to Effie all the way by which God had led her sister; at the same time there was revealed all that He had permitted her to do for His glory, and at this she was greatly moved. She had only been a little servant-maid, plain and humble and obscure. There was nothing to distinguish her in the eyes of those who saw her from day to day. Yet God had greatly honoured her. He had made her a messenger of grace to one, to two perhaps to more. When that little, worn-out frame was laid aside, it might be, thought Effie, that the immortal spirit, crowned and radiant, should stand nearer to the throne than some who were held in honour by the wise and the good of this world.

Sitting there, listening and musing, Effie saw, more clearly than she ever could have seen in the bustle of her busy life, how infinitely desirable it is to be permitted to do God's work in the world. Those were days never to be forgotten by her. She grew thin and wan with confinement and watching, but as the time drew near when her present care should cease and she should go home again, her face wore a look of peace beautiful to see.

'Effie, said Christie one day, after she had been silently watching her a little while, 'you are more willing that I should go now, I think?'

Effie started.

'I shall be willing when the time comes, my dear sister, I do not doubt,' she said, with lips that smiled, though they quivered too. 'I cannot help being willing, and glad, for your sake.'

'And you ought to be glad for your sake too,' said Christie. 'You will have one less to care for, to be anxious about, Effie, and I shall be safe with our dear father and mother in the better world. I never could have helped you much, dear, though I would have liked to do so. I never should have been very strong, I dare say, and—I might have been a burden.'

'But if you had been running about in the fields with the bairns all this time, who knows but you would have been as strong as any of them?' said Effie, sadly.

But Christie shook her head.

'No; I have had nothing to harm me. And sometimes I used to think if I had stayed at home I might have fallen back into my old fretful ways, and so have been a vexation to myself and to Aunt Elsie; and to you even, Effie, though you never used to be vexed with me.'

'No, Christie, that could never have happened. God is faithful, and with His grace, all would have been well with you. There would have been no more such sad days for you.'

'No such day as that when you came home with the book-man and gave me my Bible,' said Christie, smiling. 'I wonder why I always mind that day so well? I suppose because it was the beginning of it all.'

Effie did not ask, 'The beginning of what?' She

knew well that she meant the beginning of the new life which God, by His Word and Spirit, had wrought in her heart. Soon Christie added:

'I wouldn't have anything changed now. It has all happened just in the best way; and this quiet time will do you good too, dear.'

'I pray God it may!' said Effie, letting both tears and kisses fall upon her sister's face.

'And you must tell Annie and Sarah and the bairns that they must be sure to come to us—our father and mother and me, and to JESUS—the Mediator—of the new covenant,' she slowly said; and overcome with weariness, she sank into a quiet sleep.

Christie grew weaker every day. She did not suffer much, and slept most of the time. Sometimes she was feverish and restless, and then Effie used to fancy that her mind wandered. At such times she would tell of things that happened long ago, and speak to Effie as she might have spoken to her mother during her childish illnesses, begging to be taken into her arms and rocked to sleep.

But almost always she knew her sister, even when she had forgotten where she was. Once she said there was just one place in the world where she could rest, and begged to be laid on the sofa in Mrs. Nesbitt's parlour at home. Often she begged her to let her dip her hands in the burn to cool them, or to take her where it was pleasant and cool, under the shadow of the birch-tree in the pasture at home. But a single word from Effie was always enough to soothe her, and to call up the loving smile.

Christmas came and went, and the last day of the old year found her still waiting, but with many a token that the close was drawing near. Gertrude came that day, and lingered long beside her, awed by the strange mysterious change that was beginning to show itself on her face. Christie did not notice her as she came in, and even Effie only silently held out her hand to her as she drew near.

'She will never speak again,' said the nurse, who had been watching her for several minutes.

All pain, all restlessness, seemed past. Effie, bending over her, could only now and then moisten her parched lips and wipe the damp from her forehead. Poor Effie! she saw the hour was at hand, but she was very calm. 'She has not spoken since daybreak,' she said, softly. 'I am afraid she will never speak again.' But she did.

After a brief but quiet sleep she opened her eyes. Gertrude knew that she was recognized. Stooping down to catch the broken words that came from her parched lips, she distinctly heard :

'I was sure always—from the very first—that God would bless you. And now—though I am going to die —you will do all for Christ—that I would like to have done.'

Effie was refreshed and strengthened by two or three hours of quiet sleep. The day passed, the evening came and went, and Christie gave no sign of pain or restlessness.

'It will be about the turn of the night,' said the nurse, raising the night-lamp to look on her face. But it was not. At the turn of the night she awoke, and called her sister by name. Effie's face was on the pillow beside her, and she kissed her softly, without speaking. Christie fondly returned her caress. She seemed strangely revived.

'Effie,' she said, 'do you remember something that our mother used to sing to us?—

'"No dimming clouds o'ershadow thee,
 No dull and darksome night,
 But every soul shines as the sun,
 And God Himself is light."'

Yes, Effie remembered it well, and she went on, with no break in her voice, as Christie ceased:

"No pain, no pang, no bitter grief,
 No woeful night is there;
 No sob, no sigh, no cry is heard;
 No will-awa', no care!"'

And many a verse more of that quaint, touching old canticle did she sing, all the time watching the smile of wonderful content that was beautifying the dying face.

'You are quite willing now, Effie?' she said, softly.

'Quite willing,' said Effie, softly.

'And it is coming very near now!'

'Very near, love. Very near now!'

'Very near!' She never spoke again. She lingered till the dawn of the new year's morning, all the time lying like a child slumbering in the nurse's arms, and then she died.

They did not lay her to rest among the many nameless graves which had seemed so sad and dreary to her in the beautiful burial-place one summer day. The spotless snow near her father's grave was disturbed on a winter's morning, and Christie was laid to rest beside him.

There she has lain through many a summer and winter, but her remembrance has not perished from the earth. There are loving hearts on both sides of the sea who still cherish her memory. Gertrude—no longer Miss Gertrude, however—in the new home she has found, tells the little children at her knee of her little brother Claude and his nurse, who loved each other so dearly on earth, and who now are doubtless loving each other in heaven ; and in a fair Canadian manse a grave and beautiful woman often tells, with softened voice, the sad yet happy tale of the sister who went away and who never came home again, but who found a better home in her Father's house above.

THE END.

PRINTED IN GREAT BRITAIN BY RICHARD CLAY & SONS, LIMITED, BRUNSWICK ST., STAMFORD ST , S.E., AND BUNGAY, SUFFOLK.

www.ingramcontent.com/pod-product-compliance
Lightning Source LLC
Chambersburg PA
CBHW030902270326
41929CB00008B/541